Literature, Music and Cosmopolitanism

Robert Fraser

Literature, Music and Cosmopolitanism

Culture as Migration

Robert Fraser
Open University
London, UK

ISBN 978-3-319-88610-7   ISBN 978-3-319-68480-2 (eBook)
https://doi.org/10.1007/978-3-319-68480-2

© The Editor(s) (if applicable) and The Author(s) 2018
Softcover re-print of the Hardcover 1st edition 2018
This work is subject to copyright. All rights are solely and exclusively licensed by the Publisher, whether the whole or part of the material is concerned, specifically the rights of translation, reprinting, reuse of illustrations, recitation, broadcasting, reproduction on microfilms or in any other physical way, and transmission or information storage and retrieval, electronic adaptation, computer software, or by similar or dissimilar methodology now known or hereafter developed.
The use of general descriptive names, registered names, trademarks, service marks, etc. in this publication does not imply, even in the absence of a specific statement, that such names are exempt from the relevant protective laws and regulations and therefore free for general use.
The publisher, the authors and the editors are safe to assume that the advice and information in this book are believed to be true and accurate at the date of publication. Neither the publisher nor the authors or the editors give a warranty, express or implied, with respect to the material contained herein or for any errors or omissions that may have been made. The publisher remains neutral with regard to jurisdictional claims in published maps and institutional affiliations.

Cover illustration: Fotosearch / Getty Images

Printed on acid-free paper

This Palgrave Macmillan imprint is published by Springer Nature
The registered company is Springer International Publishing AG
The registered company address is: Gewerbestrasse 11, 6330 Cham, Switzerland

IN EUROPE, AND FOR EUROPE

Contents

1 Culture as Migration — 1

2 Is There a Gibbon in the House? Migration, Post-nationality and the Fall and Rise of Europe — 17

3 Roma and Roaming: Borders, Nomads and Myth — 31

4 Of Sirens, Science and Oyster Shells: Hypatia the Philosopher from Gibbon to *Black Athena* — 51

5 Cultural Migration as Protestant Nostalgia: (1) British Listeners in Italy — 65

6 Cultural Migration as Protestant Nostalgia: (2) Milton, Ruskin and Religious Longing — 79

7 Cultural Migration as Protestant Nostalgia: (3) Purcell, the Popish Plot and the Politics of Latin — 85

8 Migrant Consciences in the Age of Empire: Charles Kingsley, Governor Eyre and the Morant Bay Rising — 97

9	Beyond the National Stereotype: Benedict Anderson and the Bengal Emergency of 1905–06 125
10	Migrating Stories: How Textbooks Fired a Canon 161
11	Towards a New World Order: Literacy, Democracy and Literature in India and Africa, 1930–1965 173
12	World Music: Listening to Steve Reich Listening to Africa; Listening to György Ligeti Listening to Reich 185
13	A Cultural Cosmopolis 195

Acknowledgements   205

Index   207

...alas, alas, say now the King...
Should so much come too short of your great trespass
As but to banish you, whither would you go?
What country, by the nature of your error,
Should give you harbour? go you to France or Flanders,
To any German province, to Spain or Portugal,
Nay, any where that not adheres to England,
Why, you must needs be strangers: would you be pleas'd
To find a nation of such barbarous temper,
That, breaking out in hideous violence,
Would not afford you an abode on earth,
Whet their detested knives against your throats,
Spurn you like dogs, and like as if that God
Owed not nor made not you, nor that the claimants
Were not all appropriate to your comforts,
But chartered unto them, what would you think
To be thus us'd? This is the strangers case;
And this your mountainish inhumanity.

From the play *The Book of Sir Thomas More*, Act II, Scene iv, believed to be by William Shakespeare, and in his own handwriting

British Library Harley Manuscript 7368

List of Figures

Fig. 3.1	"Queen Europa" from Sebastian Münster's *Cosmographia* (2nd ed., Basel, 1588), B.L.Ac.3838/45	34
Fig. 7.1	"Jehova, Quam Multi Sunt Hostes Mei". Henry Purcell's fair copy holograph from B.L.Add.Ms, 30930, *The Works of Henry Purcell* (Dom, 1680)	90
Fig. 10.1	John Constable, "Salisbury Cathedral from the Bishop's Grounds", 1823 (Victoria and Albert Museum, London)	162
Fig. 12.1	Ewe Nyayito Dance. Robert Fraser, *West African Poetry: A Critical History* (Cambridge University Press, 1986), 11, reproducing Jones (1959), Volume Two, 32–33	188
Fig. 12.2	Ewe Agbaza Dance, Steve Reich, *Writings on Music 1965–2000*. Edited with an introduction by Paul Hillier (Oxford University Press, 2002), 62	189

CHAPTER 1

Culture as Migration

The theme of this book is a response to that of a far more famous one, published in 1869 by the English poet, educator and visionary, Matthew Arnold. Until comparatively recently Arnold's *Culture and Anarchy* was read by students of British society as among the most trenchant—certainly the most influential—of those high-minded works of exhortation and prophecy to which mid-to-late Victorian authors liked to treat their readers. For much of the twentieth century it also fed into current social and educational debate, influencing at a subliminal level generations of critics, social commentators and teachers. Subtitled "An Essay in Political and Social Criticism", it portrays culture as a homogeneous and desirable quality. Culture for Arnold is "*a study of perfection*. It moves by the force, not merely or primarily of the scientific passion for pure knowledge, but also of the moral and social passion for doing good."[1] More straightforwardly, in a later book, *Literature and Dogma* (1876), Arnold defined culture as "the acquainting ourselves with the best that has been known and said in the world".[2]

"Mass culture", "popular culture", let alone "pop culture", would have been incomprehensible to Arnold. Indeed, though admirable in the abstract, culture was not, he reluctantly conceded, very popular in England. In reality the British people distrusted culture, since they associated it with intellectuality, which they hated in principle, and with what Arnold called "curiosity". Not merely did curiosity kill the cat; according to Arnold it offended the average Briton's sense of decency and moderation.

© The Author(s) 2018
R. Fraser, *Literature, Music and Cosmopolitanism*,
https://doi.org/10.1007/978-3-319-68480-2_1

"I have before now", he wearily remarked in the first chapter of *Culture and Anarchy*, "pointed out that we English do not, like the foreigners, use the word [curiosity] in a good sense as well as a bad sense. With us the word is always used in a somewhat disapproving sense. A liberal and intelligent eagerness about the things of the mind may be meant by a foreigner when he speaks of curiosity, but with us the word always conveys a certain notion of frivolous and unedifying activity."

So culture had its enemies in Victorian England, typified for Arnold by materialism, provinciality and middle-class self-satisfaction: everything, in other words that in 1869 went along with British commercial and imperial success. Forces such as these Arnold associated, paradoxically for his time, with culture's adversary and opposite: anarchy. Culture as such had little to do with such homebred virtues or vices. The work ethic—or Hebraism—owed little to the thought impulse or Hellenism. Despite this, with some and intellectual effort, culture in Arnold's sense of the word could be acquired by an educated English person—by the whole country, did they but try. The English of all classes, Arnold thought, could do with a lot more of it.

Despite—or more probably because of—its improving zeal, the twenty-first-century reader is apt to find Arnold's celebrated book stuffy and smug. Anachronisms scream from every page. There is, for example, the question of his self-identification with a group called "we", denoting the British alone. There is also his talk of "foreigners", enviously though suspiciously viewed. What is more, Arnold seems to see "culture" as a quality that can be detached from other aspects of a community. Schooled by sociology, we are nowadays apprehensive of using the word in this strange, if uplifting, sense. Arnold's scenario, moreover, seems to us impossibly value-laden. There is in him too much talk of moral improvement and of "things in the mind". Bodies, material artefacts, even money, seem to enjoy no place in his picture at all.

Most glaringly, for citizens of the so-called multicultural society, there is the fact that Arnold invariably uses "culture" as a singular noun. This is all the odder because the Romans, from whom we derive the word, tended to use it in the plural: *culturae*. It is tempting to think that Arnold saw culture as a singular quality because he was only aware of one: that of the British or English (in his book he uses the terms synonymously). Yet, as we have already seen, this was very far from being his view. If anything, "culture" for Arnold stemmed from overseas, though it might find a resting place in Britain. One might perhaps broaden the accusation by claiming that the "culture" he advocated was an exclusively European affair, that he saw

Europe as a homogeneous unit with local variations that included "us" and the "foreigners" (that is, other Europeans), whilst sidelining other continents. Yet Arnold, like his headmaster father Thomas Arnold of Rugby, was steeped in the literature and history of the Near East; so he would have had a hard job fitting in even to this expanded stereotype. Arnold's "culture" is universal, cosmopolitan, elitist. Are there bridges from his ideas to our own?

THE MEANINGS OF CULTURE

So habituated have twenty-first-century people become to travel and comparative generalisations about different "cultures" that it is difficult to register how recent the word is as used in our sense. In Roman times Cicero talks of two kinds of *culturae*: "agri culturae", cultivations of the fields, and "animi culturae", cultivations of the spirit or mind. Accordingly, until the 1860s its use in most European languages was confined to agriculture, religion and by extension to education. The first English use as applied to crops in the general sense of "cultivating the soil" is 1420. As applied to religious worship it is 1483, though the derivation is not from Latin *culturae* but from *cultus*, a cult or sect. Its extension to scholarship and training is a feature of the Renaissance. In 1510 Sir Thomas More talks of the need to apply ourselves "to the culture and profit" of our minds, a sense not a thousand miles from Arnold's. By 1550 the word appears with this meaning in French. By 1626 the agricultural application has been extended to imply the cultivation of particular crops, from which we get the specialised uses "arboriculture", "floriculture", "horticulture" and in France "viniculture". Two years later the word embraced the athletic improvement of the human body. By 1796, at the height of Britain's Agricultural Revolution, it is connected with the rearing of livestock.

Unsurprisingly, the shift to our modern analytical sense occurs in German. In 1860, with a little-known Zurich publisher, the Swiss historian Jacob Burckhardt issued his *Kultur der Renaissance in Italien*; it had little impact at first, though it was later to transform scholarly thinking about the Quattrocento. That Renaissance Italy possessed a culture unique to itself, however, was a fresh insight. With it we approach the relativistic notion of one social, political and social organisation as distinct from others; for Burckhardt the Renaissance Italian state had been an unrepeatable "work of art". To speak of a "culture" in this sense is close to talking of a "civilisation"; accordingly, when Burckhardt's book was finally translated into English in 1878, it was as *The Civilisation of the Renaissance in Italy*.

By 1867, two years before Arnold's diatribe, the term "culture" was first used in a related sense in English. Significantly, the context is a description of that particular kind of cross-channel migration known as an "invasion". After the Battle of Hastings, wrote Freeman in his history of *The Norman Conquest*, the Anglo-Saxons were confronted by "a language and a culture which was wholly alien to them".

From there it is but a short step to using the word in a scientific, quasi-objective sense, first attributed to that grandad of modern anthropology, Edward Burnett Tylor. Tylor was a wealthy Quaker denied a university education because of his religious affiliation. Afflicted with tuberculosis, he instead travelled to Mexico, where he became fascinated by the parallels he could perceive between the customs, myths and rituals of the ordinary people he encountered in his progress and those of the European peasantry. Gradually the notion of culture as something multiform and spread out began to take shape in his mind. The result was a series of works tracing the deep affinities between people and times, the most famous of which, *Primitive Culture* of 1871, bore a title that seemingly engages with, and challenges, the exclusivity implied by Arnold's book, published a mere two years before.

On the first page Tylor hazards a new definition. "Culture or civilisation taken in its wide ethnographic sense", he opines, "is that complex whole which includes knowledge, belief, art, morals, law, custom, and other capabilities and habits acquired by man as a member of society." Like Arnold, Tylor always used "culture" as a—frequently capitalised—singular noun, synonymous with its sister substantive "civilization". For Tylor, unlike Arnold, however, both culture and civilisation were diffused across the world, and across history. Each different society in different ages possessed a character of its own; yet beneath these apparent differences, certain constants were apparent. There was thus both a variety and a certain uniformity. Tylor goes on to dilate about this seeming paradox:

> The condition of culture among the various societies of mankind, so far as it is capable of being investigated on general principles, is a subject apt for the study of laws of human thought and action. On the one hand, the uniformity which so largely pervades civilization may be ascribed, in great measure, to the uniform action of uniform causes: while on the other hand its various grades may be regarded as stages of development or evolution, each the outcome of previous history, and about to do its proper part in shaping the history of the future.[3]

The "laws of human thought" that Tylor identifies in this passage are those of social evolution cross-pollinated from Darwin's biological theories with the study of society by later Victorians such as Herbert Spencer. For Tylor all societies had evolved, and were continually evolving, from stage to stage. Because all societies were on the same evolutionary journey, which they covered at different speeds, it was possible to compare them. The result was a method of analysis called the "comparative method", and a science that came to be known as Social Anthropology, the first chair of which in the University of Oxford Tylor came eventually to hold.

Yet Tylor says nothing about migration, for two very good reasons. The first is that, like most of the first few generations of anthropologists, he was interested in studying individual societies *in situ* so that he could observe the interplay in each case between social arrangements and their environment. It was therefore in his interests that each society appeared to stay still, just as a zoological specimen beneath the microscope ideally stays still. The second was that he was anxious to argue that the similarities he discerned between various societies in various places were the products of separate but parallel development, rather than of influence. If it could be proved that they had borrowed from one another, his argument was compromised, if not ruined.

By the mid-1870s, therefore, two contrasting senses of the term "culture" were available, both of which we have inherited: Arnold's, which stressed culture as an ideal that we might or might not attain; and Tylor's, according to which all people possess a culture, albeit of different kinds. From Tylor's comparative use of the singular noun, it was a fairly short step to pluralising it. By the turn of the century, the practice was commonplace. The modern cosmopolitan man, declared *The Spectator* on 27 June 1891, is one who prides himself on "speaking all languages, knowing all cultures, living amongst all races".

The Crux of Cosmopolitanism

The notion of cosmopolitanism features prominently in our title and is clearly going to be central to our discussion; again, it is a term whose application has shifted across time. Quite recently it has featured in the title of a stimulating book by the Ghanaian and British-born philosopher (currently resident in New York), Kwame Anthony Appiah. Appiah is the son of a marriage between an Ashanti noble, onetime Ghana nationalist politician, with a British author and artist, daughter of a former Socialist

Chancellor of the Exchequer. I will be taking a closer look at his background in the conclusion to the present book, but wish to start by citing what he has to say in his work *Cosmopolitism* (2010) on the complex question of the meaning of culture. One of his chapters is headed "Whose culture is it anyway?" and it begins by addressing the fraught issues of "cultural patrimony" and "intellectual copyright", both of which take their cue from conceptions of local, or else personal, belonging. In 1874, at the conclusion of the second British-Ashanti war, the state capital Kumasi was burned to the ground on the orders of the British commander, Garnet Wolseley, and the palace looted of its contents. A century later, in Mali, thousands of intricate terracotta figures depicting humans and animals were unearthed about three kilometres from the modern city of Djenné by an international team of archaeologists: in contravention of a UNESCO resolution, they were sold to collectors and museums around the world, which are reluctant to return them. Cultural nationalists have urged that they be sent back. It does not need the better-known example of the Elgin Marbles removed from the Parthenon in Athens between 1801 and 1805, and still in the British Museum in London, to underline the issues raised by these episodes. In all such instances, the campaign of retrieval is based on a feasible, if to Appiah questionable, proposition, which he summarises thus: "It is that, in simplest terms, cultural property be regarded as the property of its culture. If you belong to that culture, such work is, in the suggestive shorthand, your cultural patrimony. If not, not."[4]

The case is comparatively straightforward when it comes to physical objects, the fact of whose removal is simply ascertained, even if the rights and wrongs of the matter, and the question of ownership, are more difficult to resolve. When it comes to the less tangible products of culture—poems and pieces of music, for example—the relevant questions are far harder to sort out. Most nineteenth- and some twentieth-century commentators have assumed that English poetry and English music are the expression of the English nation and its people: they breathe its soul, as it were. In 1937 the composer Ralph Vaughan Williams published a book of essays entitled *National Music* dedicated to this proposition. Yet nobody for that reason would claim that the works of Edward Elgar should not be performed in Germany (where, indeed, his early reputation was made). And nobody in their right mind would assert that the symphonies of Joseph Haydn should not be performed in England where, in old age, he spent a couple of happy and productive years. To which nation does the music of George Frideric Handel belong: to Germany, in whose principality of Hanover he was born; to Italy, where he learned his trade as an opera composer between 1706 and 1712, and in whose language the libretti of all his operas (but not his oratorios) are couched; or to Britain, where he settled for the remaining forty-seven years of his life? Put like this, the question reduces itself to absurdity. Few would dare raise the question as to whether the mathematical discoveries of Srinivasa Ramanujan—born in 1887 in Tamil Nadu, whence in 1914 he moved to Cambridge where some of his best work was achieved—constitute a legacy of India or of England. At one level they belong to Ramanujan alone, and are part of his legitimate intellectual property. At the highest and most realistic level, they belong to humanity. Most fundamentally and triumphantly, they are ground-breaking mathematics.

It is Appiah's contention that all cultural masterpieces, be they sculptural, architectural, scientific, literary or musical, belong to humanity in this way. We owe it to one another to be curious about our various traditions, and such curiosity entails rights over them. This is part of what he means by cosmopolitanism. Besides, people move constantly, and culture and its outputs move with them. In support of this view Appiah quotes the verdict of Salman Rushdie, whose instinct in writing fiction has always been to stir the cultural melting pot. In 1988, the year in which his novel *The Satanic Verses* was subjected to an Iranian *fatwa*, Rushdie declared that this work "rejoices in mongrelisation and fears the absolutism of the Pure. Mélange, hotchpotch, a bit of this and a bit of that is how newness enters the world. It is the great possibility that mass migration gives the world, and I am determined to embrace it."[5] All of that is true though, *pace* Rushdie, perhaps it is not so new.

"The Strangers' Case"

Whatever way you look at it, notions of culture and cosmopolitanism are ineluctably tied in with the fact of widespread international migration. It for this very reason that the emergence over the last few decades of an academic discourse stressing the centrality of migration to human cultural formation has proved such a refreshing and revealing change. Increasingly, culture has come to be viewed less as an expression of place than a product of interaction and demographic shift. A recurrent difficulty, however, has been to classify, and to distinguish between, various kinds of human mass movement. If culture is notoriously difficult to pin down, migration and its analogues are just as elusive. Fifty years ago, the travel writer Bruce Chatwin proposed to his London publisher a grand work to be entitled *The Nomadic Alternative*, universalising his own temperamental condition of itchy feet. His proposal landed on the desk of the publisher's reader, Desmond Morris, author of the ethnographic-cum-zoological classic *The Naked Ape*, who reported back in some puzzlement: "What is a nomad? It gets a little confusing sometimes when I read his chapter headings." For Morris there was a fundamental difference between wandering away from and back to a fixed base, on the one hand, and wandering from place to place without a fixed base, on the other. He concluded, "As I said in *The Naked Ape*, the moment man became a hunter he had to have somewhere *to come back to* after the hunt was over. So a fixed base became natural for the species and we lost our old ape-like nomadism."[6]

In the half-century since then, the literature concerning human movement has grown exponentially, but the task of classification has proved no easier. Nomadism, exploration, asylum, adventure, tourism, crusading, all constitute varieties of human movement between territories and, as several recent commentators have observed, very often the motivations have been— and remain—mixed. The United Nations reductively defines a migrant as one who has stayed outside his or her country of origin for more than twelve months,[7] but such a description encompasses long-term overseas military personnel, diplomats, students on extended gap years, expatriates on long contracts, some international consultants and, historically, practically everyone (notably the *pieds noirs* of Algeria, or the *sahibs* and *memsahibs* of the erstwhile British Raj) who once staffed the various European empires. Useful as it is as a yardstick, the definition also begs the very question of personal and social identity, since it assumes that all of us possess a point of origin and ultimate belonging, which is far from universally true, even in the meanest bureaucratic or legal sense.

One matter is certain: the phenomenon is both exceedingly old and pressingly new. The first humans were certainly nomads. In terms of our history, in fact, it is movement that has constituted the rule, and settlement and belonging that have been the exceptions. In his influential book *Migration: A World History*, Michael H. Fisher traces the ramifying itineraries of our ancestral wanderings from East Africa outwards towards Eurasia, then by branching lines across to Australasia and the Americas, aided by land bridges exposed during the last ice age and subsequently engulfed. He further recounts tides of movement within the documented past resulting from Alexander the Great's predations, the Emperor

Constantine's expansion of the Roman Empire and the proselytising spread of Islam. The picture is then complicated by the slave trade, the growth of European empires in Asia and Africa, and economic migration since.[8] In their strongly argued *Exceptional People: How Migrants Shaped Our World and Will Define Our Future*, Ian Goldin, Geoffrey Cameron and Meera Balarajan have charted the impact of these historical perambulations on the sending and receiving countries, on families, communities and individuals. They conclude with a plea for migration to be viewed as a normative aspect of human history, and the principal hope for an integrated and prosperous global future: "So long as nationalism can legitimately trump the more universal claims of international co-operation, world development will be stalled. However, our national myths are gradually deconstructed as historical revision lays bare the truth about the central role of cross-cultural contact in the creation of new societies. When we ask ourselves the perennial question 'Who are we?' answering exclusively with nationalism is less and less convincing in the twenty-first century."[9]

The controversies surrounding this topic over the last few years have had a tendency to encourage writers on both sides of the debate to frame their arguments in terms of undiluted absolutes. Opponents of migration habitually and drastically exaggerate its detrimental effects, and underplay its considerable benefits. Correspondingly, in the face of such bald opposition, those committed to defending and promoting migration have sometimes portrayed it as an uncomplicated good that has invariably benefitted everybody everywhere. A further effect has been to cause historians to project this panacea both backwards and forwards, portraying the whole of human history in the process as one seething and ebullient panorama of restless motion and interchange. In Fisher's words, "We are all the descendants of migrants and we virtually all migrate during the course of our lives. From the origin of our Homo sapiens species about 200,000 BC until today, we have expanded our range over the entire planet. We have emigrated to seek new opportunities, often driven out by deteriorating social or physical environments. As the earth's climate has changed and our societies have developed, migration has enabled us to better our lives and those of our children."[10]

This is both richly true, and richly untrue. What we observe in reality in the human past is a rhythmic alternation. On the one hand, there have been periods of vigorous population shift, such as the *Völkerwanderung* or *migratio gentium* of which German historians of late antiquity used to speak when referring to alien incursions into the crumbling Roman Empire.[11] For historians such as Fisher, we are living through a second such age, in which an equivalent scenario is being played out on a global scale. On the other hand, there have always been comparatively static times during which the cultural demography of individual territories has tended to settle down. Were this not so, it would be impossible for any of us meaningfully to speak of national or regional characteristics. Nor would anybody ever experience homesickness, or indeed its opposite, wanderlust.

The rhythm is productive. There is a directive towards movement and penetration; there is also a directive towards, and a need for, retention. In order properly to convey and to share customs, attitudes, varieties of spirituality, art forms and idioms, every inward- or outward-bound community needs to possess something to share in the first place. Languages fuse and borrow from one another, but we can still properly speak of Bengali or French, compile separate dictionaries of these tongues, and consider the literatures couched in each, even if we subsequently compare them. The short story form, for example, originated in Bengal and migrated to France.

In such circumstances, acquisition and consolidation become twin aspects of an ongoing and fruitful process. Imaginatively viewed, a nation may be conceived of both as an entity and as a conglomeration; a botanical genus, but simultaneously hybrid. Both visions can be found in English literature, for example in Shakespeare. As an epigraph to this book, I quote a scene from the collaboratively authored play *The Book of Sir Thomas More*, unpublished until 1832 but first drafted between 1601 and 1604 by, it is believed, Anthony Munday (1560–1633) and Henry Chettle, then revised by a number of hands, almost certainly including Shakespeare's. Written at a time of escalating tension caused by the arrival of a wave of Huguenots (French Protestants) in England, the drama takes as one of its persistent themes hysterical xenophobia. In the scene from which the quoted speech is taken, the manuscript of which survives in Shakespeare's hand, More is reprimanding a mob of London apprentices bent on burning to the ground the homes of some economic migrants recently arrived from Lombardy. He asks them to imagine themselves as immigrants to another country—"to France or Flanders/To any German province, Spain or Portugal"—and to treat the arrivals with the sort of courtesy that they would then request and require. The point is taken, and the crowd disperse. We are all more or less natives (even if of more than one country), and we are all potential migrants.

However, Shakespeare also realised, and drew on, a marked and settled sense of national belonging. Twenty years previously, in evoking the roots of the Wars of the Roses which, little more than a century before, had precariously been resolved in the Tudor Settlement, he had written a pivotal scene in *Richard the Second*, and placed in the mouth of John of Gaunt (whose mother, let it be said, hailed from Ghent) perhaps the classic expression of English patriotism:

> This royal throne of kings, this scepter'd isle,
> This earth of majesty, this seat of Mars,
> This other Eden, demi-paradise,
> This fortress built by Nature for herself
> Against infection and the hand of war,
> This happy breed of men, this little world,
> This precious stone set in the silver sea,
> Which serves it in the office of a wall,
> Or as a moat defensive to a house,
> Against the envy of less happier lands,
> This blessed plot, this earth, this realm, this England...[12]

It was during the time of the English Renaissance, and more especially following the English Reformation with its repudiation of papal scope and power, that the tension between territorial sovereignty and continental affinities most dramatically played itself out in English life, and for this very reason I have focused in on the period in three of the chapters that follow. (I am not the first to imply historical parallels between the Reformation and Brexit, and the putative cultural ramifications of both.[13]) In the Renaissance period, English exceptionalism came to an end with the union between the English and Scottish crowns in 1603.

A century later, England had been ruled over successively by Scottish and Dutch monarchs. Such royal migration was not universally popular. In 1700 the Whig journalist and poetaster John Hutchin (1660–1707), who had initially welcomed the arrival of King William III from Holland with his English wife Mary as rescuing the country from popery, published a polemic entitled *The Foreigners* attacking the regal interlopers. The novelist Daniel Defoe read the poem (if such it was) "with a kind of rage", considering it to be a "vile abhor'd pamphlet, in very ill verse". He responded with a much better poem of his own, *The True-Born Englishman: A Satyr*, questioning the very notion of essential Englishness. Who are we English folk anyway if not the products of infiltration and miscegenation?

> Thus from a mixture of all kinds began,
> That het'rogeneous thing, an Englishman:

> In eager rapes, and furious lust begot,
> Betwixt a painted Britain and a Scot.
> Whose gend'ring off-spring quickly learn'd to bow,
> And yoke their heifers to the Roman plough:
> From whence a mongrel half-bred race there came,
> With neither name, nor nation, speech nor fame.
> In whose hot veins new mixtures quickly ran,
> Infus'd betwixt a Saxon and a Dane.
> While their rank daughters, to their parents just,
> Receiv'd all nations with promiscuous lust.
> This nauseous brood directly did contain
> The well-extracted blood of Englishmen.[14]

The English have continued to quarrel about their identity ever since.

"Whither Would You Go?"

In his informative and crisp *International Migration: A Very Short Introduction*, Khalid Koser summarises the consequences of our age-old patterns of migration thus: "Migration has been a critical and influential feature of human history. It has supported the growth of the world economy, it has contributed to the evolution of states and societies and it has enriched many cultures and civilisations."[15] It is with the third of these consequences that the chapters comprising the present book are concerned. In my conclusion I shall attempt to theorise it by drawing on the related fields of philosophy and anthropology. In the meantime, I offer a series of inter-related case studies exploring how migration has assisted bodies of knowledge, schools of literature, art and music. The examples are drawn from England, from mainland Europe, from Israel, Egypt, West Africa, America, India and the Caribbean. In the light of recent events, I return constantly to the matter of Britain, partly because it is best known to me, and partly because Britain is a group of islands whose encircling sea might be expected to have exempted it from some of the influences described. Yet during the chequered course of the country's history, no portion of the earth's surface has been more affected by the movement of peoples, both inward and outward, than this "scepter'd isle".

The object throughout is to assess three competing panaceas. The first—long since discarded—is Arnold's view that human culture represents a single refined entity at which all should aim. The second—call it Burckhardt's paradigm—is the version of cultural nationalism which has it that intellectual formations are inevitably and primarily an expression of the places that produced them. The third is the much more recent idea that globalisation has now diluted this understanding in the interests of an inclusive and heterogeneous norm. By harking back to the classical period, and by negotiating freely between that and the more recent past and present, I demonstrate the partiality of all these beliefs, the first two being a preoccupation of the nineteenth century, the third of the twentieth and twenty-first.

Concentrating for the most part on the complementary arts of literature and music, I attempt to show how the constant movement of peoples and ideas over many centuries has nourished and sustained human culture in a diversity of ways. There are certain constants to this process, tendencies that have spearheaded cultural diffusion and its effects. One is nomadism, a challenging aspect of demography that I examine through a case study of the Roma people as they have wandered across Europe. The second is language, the divagating and yet unifying effects of which I examine by focusing on some uses of Europe's traditional *lingua franca*, Latin, then on English which—even as the English themselves seem bent on "leaving Europe"—appears to have become Latin's modern equivalent. The third is empire, analysed here in a number of different contexts, including colonial administration and education. A fourth is religion, whose disseminating ideological effects are illustrated though four case studies, three from the early modern period and one from the nineteenth century. A fifth is travel and tourism, and the ways in which these are reported and in which they have influenced artistic styles: this I illustrate via a study of the diffusion of Italian music beyond Italy, and another of an American and a Hungarian composer as they witness, and draw on, African drumming. The last is scholarship, and the tendency of academics to group themselves in communities transcending location and language, which I examine under a number of different headings, including the ways in which classical scholarship has shaped our sense both of interdependence and of belonging.

Along the way, I examine certain iconic migrating individuals: the fifth-century Alexandrian mathematician and philosopher Hypatia; the Italian Jewish-born Calvinist scholar Immanuel Tremellius (1510–1580), whose career straddled Italy, England and the Low Countries; the Apulia-born, internationally feted castrato known as Farinelli (1705–1782); the Hungarian-born composer and piano virtuoso Franz Liszt (1811–1886); and the singularly cosmopolitan, and variously talented, writer Violet

Paget (1856–1935) a.k.a. Vernon Lee, each of whom can be seen to have epitomised the cultural plasticity of an age. I end by taking a closer look at Appiah.

All of these factors have combined historically to undermine the centripetal effects of place. And all of them call into question notions of the purism of cultures. The purpose of this volume is to contribute to this ongoing debate about collective cultural identity by placing it in a broad and variegated historical perspective that will, it is hoped, inform discussion across disciplines and fertilise an area of discourse too often confined to the contemporary scene.

In contemporary Europe these issues are very much alive, even more so in the light of the ongoing refugee crisis provoked by events in Syria and Iraq. As I researched this chapter, a boatload of thirty-five refugees came to grief while attempting to reach the Greek island of Kalolimnos from Turkey. In Britain, concern about our long history of migration is very much to the fore, and informs our literature at every point. In Helen Macdonald's 2014 memoir *H Is for Hawk*, the narrator, who is recovering from the death of her father by training Matilda, a goshawk, travels from Cambridge to her parental home in Surrey. With her goes Matilda. They come across a tract of open country haunted by a lone hare and a pack of deer, inhabitants of what to the untrained eye appears to be a changeless and indigenous rural idyll, "the *terra incognita* of our mythical English past". In this dream of apparent eternal authenticity they are joined by an elderly couple out for a walk. "Doesn't it give you hope?" the husband enquires with reference to the landscape that surrounds and seemingly enfolds them. "Hope?" she demurs. "Yes," he persists, "Isn't it a relief that there are still things like that, a real bit of Old England still left, despite all these immigrants coming in."

The stability thus serenaded is an illusion, the countryside as Macdonald invokes it the product of unceasing disturbance and transition. "Ten years ago, there were turtle-doves on this land. Thirty years ago there were corn buntings and enormous flocks of lapwings. Seventy years ago there were red-backed shrikes, wrynecks and skype. Two hundred years ago, ravens and black grouse. All of them are gone." She concludes:

> Old England is an imaginary place, a landscape built from words, woodcuts, films, paintings, picturesque engravings. It is a place imagined by people, and people do not live very long or look very hard. We are very bad at scale. The things that live in the soil are too small to care about; climate change

too large to imagine. We are bad at time too. We cannot remember what lived here before we did; we cannot love what is not. Nor can we imagine what will be different when we are dead. We live out our three score and ten, and tie our knots and lines only to ourselves. We take solace in pictures, and we wipe the hills of history.[16]

The chapters that comprise this book represent a minor exercise in the restoration of scale, of history cleansed of sentiment. I would like to open with a scenario set in that ancient theatre of conflict and migration: the Middle East, as ancient in the tale it has to tell as is the Talmud.

NOTES

1. Matthew Arnold, *Culture and Anarchy: An Essay in Political and Social Criticism* (London: Smith, Elder, 1869), 44–45.
2. Matthew Arnold, *Literature and Dogma* (London: Smith, Elder, 1876), xiii.
3. Edward B. Tylor, *Primitive Culture: Researches into the Development of Mythology, Philosophy, Religion, Art and Culture* (London: John Murray, 1871), vol. i, 1.
4. Kwame Anthony Appiah, *Cosmopolitanism: Ethics in a World of Strangers* (London: Penguin, 2006), 118.
5. Salman Rushdie, *Imaginary Homelands: Essays and Criticism, 1981–1991* (London: Granta, 1991), 394, quoted by Appiah, 112.
6. Quoted in Nicholas Shakespeare, *Bruce Chatwin: A Biography* (London: Vintage, 1999), 219, citing Desmond Morris, *The Naked Ape: A Zoologist's Study of the Human Animal* (London: Jonathan Cape, 1967), 22 and 36.
7. Cited in Khalid Koser, *International Migration: A Very Short Introduction*, Second Edition (Oxford University Press, 2014), 14.
8. Michael H. Fisher, *Migration: A World History* (Oxford University Press, 2014), passim.
9. Ian Goldin, Geoffrey Cameron and Meera Balarajan, *Exceptional People: How Migration Shaped Our World and Will Define Our Future* (London and Princeton: Princeton University Press, 2011), 284. For an equivalent vote of support for migration as a future paradigm for humanity, see Yuval Noah Harari, *Sapiens: A Brief History of Humanity* (London: Harvil Secker, 2014), 231. See also Theodore Zelkin, *The Hidden Pleasures of Life: A New Way of Remembering the Past and Imagining the Future* (London: MacLehose Press, Quercus, 2015), especially his intriguing suggestion that, in future, each of us writes his or her own passport.
10. Fisher, xii.

11. For a summary and critique of this view, see Walter Goffart, *Barbarian Tides: The Migration Age and the Later Roman Empire* (University of Pennsylvania Press, 2006). On p. 14, Goffart sounds a warning note: "The peoples of the north and east of the Roman frontier were no more 'wandering' than the Celts or Greeks or Thracians. They were agrarian villagers like the other sedentaries mentioned, and like them, and us, they moved every now and then."
12. *The Life and Death of King Richard the Second* (First Folio, 1626), page 28. Act Two, Scene One, ll 659–669.
13. Listen, for example, to the conductor David Hill in BBC Radio 3's *In Tune*, Friday, 19 August 2016, http://www.bbc.co.uk/programmes/b07nmqgb
14. *The True-Born Englishman* (1700), in *Satire, Fantasy and Writings on the Supernatural by Daniel Defoe*, vol. 1, *The True-Born Englishman and Other Poems*, ed. W.R. Owens (London: Pickering & Chatto, 2003), 94 (ll. 334–347).
15. Khalid, 2016, 9.
16. Helen Macdonald, *H Is for Hawk* (London: Vintage, 2014), 265.

CHAPTER 2

Is There a Gibbon in the House? Migration, Post-nationality and the Fall and Rise of Europe

At the beginning of Linda Grant's Orange Prize–winning novel *When I Lived in Modern Times*, published on the crest of the millennium, Evelyn Sert, a seventeen-year-old Jewish migrant from London, waits to disembark at Haifa in the then British-mandated territory of Palestine. The period is 1946, one year after the end of the Second World War, two before the inception of the independent state of Israel, and the arrival in Southampton, England of MV *Empire Windrush* bringing immigrants from the West Indies. Evelyn is filled with a sense of an unprecedented event, a *tabula rasa* on which her own embarkation will write an individual and generic story. "I was a daughter of the new Zion," she recalls, "and I felt the ship shudder as the gangplank crashed on the dock. I put on my hat and white cotton gloves and, preparing my face, waited to go ashore at the beginning of the decline and fall of the British Empire."[1]

Several kinds of perspective cross in this carefully worded paragraph. Evelyn's adventure is both private, and part of a politically propelled movement. She is one highly individualistic young Jewish woman, and yet she is also *all* Jewish women, a member of a great and diasporic race. Evelyn's arrival is an act of homecoming that recalls ancient and tragic departures: to Babylon, to Latvia, to England. Appropriately, beneath her tentative celebration there surges a recall of the biblical Lamentations of Jeremiah with its cadences of mourning: "And from the daughter of Zion all her beauty is departed: her princes are become like harts that find no pasture, and they are gone without strength before the pursuer."[2] Against this backdrop of displacement and peregrination, in a gesture that is cosmetic and existential and political, Evelyn now "prepares" her face. *What* face, we are moved to ask, confronting what dangers? Evelyn views herself as an utterly modern, post-war person. Palestine is her opportunity, where she will re-invent her destiny. Yet at the very moment when all links with metropolitan and European culture seem deliberately to have been severed, her testimony makes nodding acknowledgement of that master text of Western deformation and reformation, Edward Gibbon's *History of the Decline and Fall of the Roman Empire*.

Grant's references to the Bible and Gibbon are not mere stylistic flourishes. If Lamentations epitomises her sense of displacement, Gibbon relates importantly to her reading of culture. Published between 1776—the year of the American Declaration of Independence—and 1789—the year of the American Constitution and the official end of the first, transatlantic British Empire, Gibbon's *History* foreshadowed amongst other things the growth, fall from grace and collapse of Britain's second, Asian and African, colonial enterprise. It is at the culmination of this process that Evelyn awaits her uncertain future. Her conjuring with Gibbon's title is itself in a long tradition. For 220 years *Decline and Fall* has been interpreted in the light of society's changing circumstances. It has been seen as an apologia or elegy for empire, even a concerted attack on the imperial ideal. It has been understood to applaud heroic virtue or bemoan human futility, as a reactionary or as a revolutionary text. In the mid-Victorian period it became a cautionary tale of empire. Even when unread, its leather-bound six volumes graced every gentleman's bookshelves. The case of Archdeacon Julius Hare may be extreme. A Broad Churchman and patron of the Christian socialists, he treated *Decline and Fall* as a second Bible. To avoid rising from the dinner table when entertaining guests, he trained his house spaniel to run backwards and forwards from the library to check references to Gibbon's footnotes. In the late Victorian high noon of empire, Gibbon was taken for a jingoist. The young cavalry officer Winston Churchill read him between polo matches in India, imbibing the ignorant lesson that the Romans submitted to decline only because they were not English.

In the twenty-first century we are far more likely to agree with Evelyn's distillation of this classic text: that empires, continents and nations are artificial compounds moulded from shifting sands, from peoples, languages and faiths. Gibbon's theme, after all, is how Rome—at once a *polis* and an empire—was swept away by successive tides of peoples flooding from Asia and Africa across central and southern Europe. It is no accident that, as generations of his readers have attested, Gibbon's narrative recounts no substantial decline, and that the "fall" in his title is difficult to locate, in either time or place. Instead he shows how, as a direct result of successive migrations, displacements and appropriations, there gradually arose that cluster of interests he lauds in his third book as the "One Great Republic" of Europe. Before we turn to address late twentieth-century migrations and their consequences, it is as well therefore to recognise that in the Age of Enlightenment, even as the foundations of the modern world were being laid, there existed this sense of migration as the metal out of which societies are forged. As Gibbon very well knew, and as seventeen-year-old Evelyn Sert obscurely suspects, empires are forever falling to make room for something unexpected. What is more, it is those very factors that sometimes look as if they are about to undermine the empires, nations or cultures that habitually build them up.

There is an additional twist, of course, since Evelyn in the passage quoted is also ironically contrasting herself with that Gibbonian and classical figure: the barbarian at the gates. She is able to question this traditional trope since as a woman she is relatively powerless, and because her purpose is personal discovery, not conquest. Her shifted perspective uncovers what is one essential division between ancient and modern perceptions of migration: the distinction between an invader and a refugee.

Compare two acts of migration at different historical periods but at a common physical crossing point: the narrow stretch of sea between North Africa and Spain. The ancients knew this place as the Pillars of Hercules—the furthest point of the settled world—on the southern shore of which were supposed to lie the Gardens of the Hesperides with their golden apples. We know it, more prosaically, as the Straits of Gibraltar. This is how, in his fifty-first chapter, Gibbon leads up to the invasion of Spain by the Arabs in AD 709, across the straits to the coast of Andalusia:

> In the progress of conquest from the north and south, the Goths and the Saracens encountered each other on the confines of Europe and Africa. In the opinion of the latter, the difference in religion is a reasonable ground of enmity and warfare. As early as the time of Othman their piratical squadrons had ravaged the coast of Andalusia, nor had they forgotten the relief of Carthage by the Gothic succours. In that age, as well as in the present, the kings of Spain were possessed of the fortress of Ceuta; one of the columns of Hercules, which is divided by a narrow strait from the opposite pillar or point of Europe.[3]

The questionable aspects of this passage lie on its surface. All meaningful historical movement is seen as operating from north to south. Religious intolerance is viewed as the prerogative of the Muslims, and this by a Christian sceptic who a few chapters later will tell us about the Crusades. Arab exploration along the southern coast of Spain is interpreted as the work of "piratical squadrons". These barbs are all the more piercing for Gibbon's belatedly expressed recognition that the Spain created by this and other conquests was—and is—culturally part Arab.

Consider now a fragment from the modern fiction of migration. In his short story "Once in the Garden of Plenty", the contemporary Sudanese writer Jamal Mahjoub describes how Majid, an unemployed labourer from North Africa, buys his way to a dream by escaping in an open boat towards the Spanish coast. The boat overturns, and Majid struggles up a beach in Andalusia. He falls among a fellow group of migrant workers without papers living thirty to a shack at the mercy of their Spanish employer. All of these people, he notices, seem haunted by melancholy. At nightfall, he approaches one of the older labourers and asks him why this is so. The man answers that, like the others, he will soon learn how to be sad:

> Majid shifted his weight on the cardboard matting. "But they made it. They made the crossing. They are free. They are working. They are here."
> "Four hundred years ago we ruled all of these lands, from Granada to the gates of Vienna. Now we come here as fugitives begging for a few crumbs."
> "I know nothing about all that. All I want is a chance to make a decent living."
> "You have a wife and child, right? You are blessed. But you are also a fool if you think anything is given away for nothing. You want to feed your family then you have to take what you want. In this world, no one, not even the birds are given something for nothing."[4]

Majhoub's title ironically refers us to the myth of the Hesperides, whose paradisal garden he displaces before pointing us to its non-existence. Majid's reference to migrant birds, meanwhile, points us in another direction: to a categorical uncertainty hovering over the vocabulary of migration. When is a migrant an immigrant, and when is he or she a visitor? Are economic migrants authentic immigrants or birds of passage? Ought we to think of migrant workers as swallows, seasonally returning to a different nesting? What is the exact status of the refugee? When is infiltration investigation, and when is it conquest? When may settlers consider themselves settled? At what point can landowners from a different clime legitimately be treated as interlopers? To what extent does mass migration redefine the host culture? What are personal roots? After how long does a homeland cease to be a homeland?

These questions haunt the world from the Middle East to Ireland, from Serbia to Zimbabwe, Paris, the Greek islands, Dover and London. And yet I would claim they are but sub-compartments of deeper and broader issues: What is a people? What is a nation? What is a culture?

These primary questions are germane to all of our purposes because during the colonial period there existed an effective, and sometimes crushing, collusion between the available answers. A culture was widely held to be embedded within a nation whose ethnic foundations were themselves clear and unambiguous. This was a time-bound triple equation, but it was very widespread during the nineteenth century, lasting well into the twentieth, and surviving into the twenty-first in the rhetoric of both right- and left-wing politics. So pervasive have been its suppositions as to form the ideological bedrock running beneath the varieties of imperialism, and the nationalist movements that opposed and supplanted them. A mere sixty years ago, Sir Antony Eden, Conservative Prime Minister during the Suez crisis in 1956, and Colonel Nasser, the Egyptian leader whose nationalisation of the Suez Canal he so much resented, may have been bitterly opposed to one another, and indeed may have had little in common. Yet on this particular score they would surely have agreed: in the one case, that there existed an English people with its own language, traditions and culture embodied in the English nation; and, in the other, that there was such an entity as the Egyptian people with its language, traditions and culture, effectively enshrined within the country known as Egypt. To this extent the ideological profile of national resistance movements constitutes the mirror image of what it opposes. Attention in each case is focused on what one might call the mirage of essentialism, the Platonic idea or essence of the nation. The hotter the political climate, the sharper the mirage. In places where national groupings are even now forming out of the ruins of crumbling empires, the mirage still retains its allure. Yesterday it was Kosovo, today it is Syria or—to return to the beginnings of this chapter—the running sore of Israel or Palestine. The theoretical position outlined above may be obscure and contingent on circumstances, but in the time you take to read this paragraph, a child somewhere will die defending it.

These are broad historical observations, but it is well worth re-iterating them because they have a deep effect upon—and are in turn fed by—the production and reception of literary texts. Imperialistic nations bring into being an imperialistic literature while interpreting their canon of existing texts imperialistically. Resistance movements then struggle against imperialism to replace it with new nations. These in turn manufacture texts of self-justification while viewing their heritage of folklore as a coherent and supportive tradition.

In 1854, at the height of the Crimean War, the novelist, social activist and priest Charles Kingsley produced a historical romance called *Westward Ho!* It described the resistance of the English of Elizabeth I's reign to the Catholic powers of their own day, and culminated in a stirring description of the defeat of the Spanish Armada in 1588.[5] So effective was it in stimulating patriotic and militaristic sentiment amongst the Victorian reading public that it became a surprise bestseller, on whose financial success the flourishing publishing house of Macmillan was largely founded. In 1968, shortly after Kenyan independence, a postgraduate student at the University of Leeds called Ngũgĩ wa Thiong'o wrote a novel called *A Grain of Wheat*.[6] In graphic and moving detail, it narrated the course of the Mau Mau movement, whose resistance to British imperialism during the 1950s had helped bring the Kenyan nation into being. Very different in style and bearing, these books are both masterpieces, though I would say qualitatively—and from most other points of view—Ngũgĩ's has the edge. They also draw their strength from congruent sources. *Westward Ho!* is a book about Englishness, which it portrays as a property worth defending. *A Grain of Wheat* concerns what it means to be Kenyan, the importance of bolstering that allegiance against all comers, whether from without or within. Despite the considerable merits of each book, neither has much room for insights that might complicate its conception of the nation's essence and will. Migration, and the resulting heterogeneity, plays little part in these works. A people is a people is a people.

To prove how politically driven culture becomes under such pressures, take a look at the evolution of English literature. There is a widespread impression to the effect that the British had a longstanding literature, a stable and teachable canon, that they then exported during the centuries of imperialism to condition and influence subject populations. The history of the subject as investigated by scholars such as Robert Crawford, Chris Baldick, Terry Eagleton, Gerald Graff and Franklin Court, however, presents a somewhat more complicated picture, in the light of which it might be truer to state that the English evolved the idea of English literature in a colonial context, and then imported it. The first chair of "Rhetoric" as it was then known was created in St Andrews in 1720, mid-way between the two Jacobite risings; from Scotland it rapidly spread to colonial America and then to India. At the time of the Indian Mutiny in 1857, English literature was not a subject commonly taught in England. It began to be taken seriously because in 1835 Lord Macaulay, historian and administrator, had prescribed it for Indians. It was examined in no British university until well on in the century, though from the 1890s it was a compulsory element in the qualifying examination for the Indian civil service. English was adopted as a degree course in most colleges in the empire at their foundation; in England it caught on slowly. The University of Ghana appointed its first lecturer in English in the late 1940s. Trinity College Cambridge did not elect a fellow to teach it until 1956, 120 years after one of the college's favourite sons—Macaulay—had passed it for Indian consumption. The University of Oxford did not create a chair in the subject until 1904, Cambridge until 1911.

When the scrutiny of English literature entrenched itself as an academic discipline in the early twentieth century, it was frequently presented as a fleshing out of a perceived core of national identity, one worthy of presentation to foreigners. It is no coincidence that the English folklorist movement headed by figures such as Cecil Sharp coincided in time with the age of jingoism. At much the same period, Ralph Vaughan Williams, whose compositions draw extensively on folk melodies, could entitle a prose exposition of his methods *National Music*. Under such pressures texts, both literary and musical, came to be read as parables of—even manifestos for—the nation. The Bible—that anthology of ancient migrations—was used to keep people in their place. Chaucer, whose most famous poem recounts a journey, became a poet of fixed point, a *terminus post quem*. Shakespeare with his European imagination and affinities became "the Bard". Milton with his wide-ranging and international learning was the English poet *par excellence*.

The resulting regionality of interpretation extended even to classical works. Homer's *Odyssey* and Virgil's *Aeneid*, for example, are poems of physical and spiritual journeying. In the period in question they were frequently refashioned as national myths. The *Aeneid*, of course, is both these things, but the emphasis on the latter produced results that were sometimes inappropriate, and on occasion far more serious. The most notorious instance of such biased reading occurred in the city of Birmingham in 1968 when Enoch Powell, Tory Shadow Defence Secretary, classical scholar and sometime brigadier in the British army in India, cited Virgil during an inflammatory speech on immigration. "I seem", he declared, "like the Roman, I seem to see the River Tiber foaming with much blood." The supposed source of this allusion was a passage in *Aeneid* Book Six. Turn to that passage and you will find, as Powell himself later unapologetically admitted, no Roman, no river and no carnage. Instead you will discover a passage in which the Sybil of Cumae, a Greek prophetess, welcomes Aeneas—a Trojan prince—to Italy. Journey on, she exhorts him, settle in Latium and there you will found a great city with the tribute of your foreign blood. The co-opting of Virgil's meaning for ideological ends meant less to Powell's victims than the insult offered by the speech to their migrant presence. The point I wish to make is that Powell's appropriation of a text and the resulting panic were integrally related. A partisan reading of literature chimed balefully with a partisan reading of culture. It is an object lesson for those who condemn literary criticism as a marginal subject when the misprision of a passage in ancient epic causes havoc on the streets.

It is with such instances in mind that one urges the theoretical and practical consequences of the literature of migration. Migration is one of the main facts of the modern, as it was of the ancient, world. Possibly we migrate more than we ever did: the significant fact for our present purposes is that we have learned to view ancient and modern migrations differently, as sources of continuing enhancement rather than as the crude materials out of which the fortress of nationhood comes to be built. The accession of this fresh insight into human affairs is the latest and arguably the most promising phase in a long process of de-colonisation that has enabled us to see all human culture in a different light. It affects the literature that we write, more and more of which addresses this phenomenon more or less directly. It also liberates our constrained perceptions of the literature of the past. Moreover, it prompts us to interrogate the identities of nations and continents, whose capacity for endless self-invention it highlights. In the process it cannot but enrich of our sense of who we are, and our consequent attitude to others.

The process, however, has been a gradual one. In the year 1948 was published in London a classic of migration: *All About H. Hatterr* by a young Bengali writer, G.V. Desani. It fell stillborn from the press in an England still recovering from the patriotic efforts of the Second World War. In the year 1969 it was revived and won for Desani a brief celebrity. Two writers, both in a sense migrants, played a significant role in this new climate of reception. The first was a polyglot Irishman, born in Manchester: Anthony Burgess, who wrote an introduction for the new edition. The second was a young writer from Bombay living in London: Salman Rushdie, who read the book with eagerness.

Burgess's introduction has much to tell us about the atmosphere of resistance which Desani's novel had faced on its first publication, and the insights which had made it newly acceptable to liberal members of his own generation. Typically he bases his essay on the analysis of a French word: *métèque*. This is not a term commonly employed in contemporary English, but it had recently been used by the British critic F.W. Bateson—Oxford's answer to F.R. Leavis—to describe foreign residents in Britain who had contributed something to the country's culture: people, I suppose, like Joseph Conrad. As Burgess himself was aware, the term had relevant origins in *metoikos*, the Greek for "migration", applied by Athenians to aliens who enjoyed no civil rights but who were permitted to stay within the city boundaries provided they paid a special tax, the *metoikion*. Bateson himself had defined a *métèque* as a "writer with a non-English linguistic, racial or political background" who, ignorant of "the finer rules of English idiom or grammar" was led to "attempt effects of style, sometimes successfully, that an English writer would feel to be a perverse defiance of the genius of the language". If Bateson was describing a British syndrome why, one might well ask, had he used a French word? The reason is evident from the *Petit Robert* dictionary, which defines *métèque* as "wop" or "wog". Having made his point about Bateson's covert racism, Burgess springs to the attack:

> Most of us would say that the "finer rules" are essentially the property of non-creative pundits who, at a higher level, compile manuals of usage and, at the lower, scold children for constructing verbless sentences. As for "the genius of the language", it is doubtful if English has a tutelary spirit or an immanent form. It is plastic, and indeed as ready to yield to the métèque as to Mr Bateson.[7]

Burgess's philippic was, of course, as illuminating of the period in question as Bateson's coy diatribe. Most of us are products of a particular decade: Bateson's had been the 1930s that had also produced Powell; Burgess's was the 1950s that had given us in France Albert Camus's *L'Etranger* and Aimé Césaire's *Cahier d'un retour au pays natal* and, in England, Colin Wilson's *The Outsider*, as well as the Beatniks and the Teddy Boys, originals of the "Droogs" in *A Clockwork Orange*. Burgess's discourse, in other words, is one of insiders and outsiders, and the advantages and positive pain of being one of the latter. It was a binary vision, powerful and liberating at the time. It is not this, however, that inspired Rushdie, who perceived in Desani's work something quite different: the possibility of a culture and a mode of writing lying neither "inside" nor "outside", but in a creative space in between. The possibility, too, of a use of English that in Rushdie's own work would take it way beyond Burgess's plasticity to a molten grace eluding any notion of belonging.

Roll forward twenty years, to 1992. Michael Ondaatje's novel *The English Patient* is about the damage done by nations, and what to do about it. Set in a war-devastated Italy, it centres on a disfigured patient who is not English at all, and whose sense of meaning is gleaned from a systematic re-reading of books that are important to him. One of these is Kipling's *Kim*; the patient persuades Hana, his Canadian nurse, to read it to him. He tells her to take the book slowly and not to jump to conclusions. There is beauty beyond its imperialistic politics, if only she will listen.

Far more important to the patient, however, is an ancient copy of Herodotus's *Histories*, which he uses as a kind of commonplace book, pasting into it snippets and extracts from elsewhere that have caught his fancy. Unusually, Ondaatje specifies the edition and translation used, a matter of evident concern to the patient himself, who has compared the available versions and talks to Hana about the advantages of this one. His care seems excessive until one recognises an important fact which, like so much in this evasive novel, is never spelled out. At the period when the book is set, students of Herodotus who took this classical author at all seriously would have turned not to any of the translations on offer, but to its most celebrated source for exegesis: the *A Lexicon to Herodotus* published in 1938 by Enoch Powell. In 1944, by common consent, Powell—who had resigned his Chair in Classics in order to fight in the war—was the leading international authority on the *Histories*. Had the patient waited another ten years he could have read Powell's own translation, rendered, as its Preface carefully explains, into the antique prose style of the King James Bible in order to give it an air of resonant, archaic Englishness. Throughout, it is couched in that peculiar, rolling rhetoric that fifteen years later would feature in Powell's racist speech in Birmingham.

And what of the patient's own attachment to Herodotus? This is how he explains it to Hana:

I see him…as one of those spare men of the desert who travel from oasis to oasis, trading legends as if it is the exchange of seeds, consuming everything without suspicion, piercing together a mirage. "This history of mine," Herodotus says, "has from the beginning sought out the supplementary to the main argument." What you find in him are cul-de-sacs within the sweep of history—how people betray each other for the sake of nations, how people fall in love.[8]

For the patient, as for Ondaatje, Herodotus is a nomad. He travels between civilisations; he barters insights, he charts failings, he records violence. He is a man of no allegiance. Herodotus with his boundless curiosity into customs and beliefs offers a view of the world that confounds the late war, opening up a new—because an unaccountably old—way of seeing.

The English Patient is a story about the re-invention of Europe written at two removes: by a Sri Lankan writer who had taken his abode in Canada. Its lesson is that the old Europe of boundaries, rivalries and divisions has to die for a new one to be born, a continent fit for the crowd of inspired nomads who people the novel. Its enemy is patriotism, an emotion that nonetheless it struggles to understand. Dissolving old loyalties, it points us towards a serendipity of revelation dependent on travelling, a state of affairs well known to hitchhikers.

As Ondaatje reminds us, people migrate, and so do texts, including his own. In the process they break down barriers between cultures, historical periods and intellectual disciplines. Migrant texts interrogate loyalties and fixed perceptions. Effective subversive agents, they refuse to show their passports. With postcolonial perspicacity, they read one another. Furthermore, they alter and enrich our sense of place.

London, for example, has never looked the same since Samuel Selvon's affectionate but trenchant portrait, *The Lonely Londoners* of 1956. To see the city through the eyes of its protagonist Moses is to glimpse possibilities undreamed of in the metropolitan fiction of the time. Selvon transforms the city, partly by his use of Trinidadian creole, and partly by his evocation of an underclass whose very presence interrogates a confident urban culture, reflecting back to it an image which it was at first reluctant to recognise, but which is now seen as an inalienable aspect of its changing identity. Selvon's book is, of course, a study of the difficult cultural relations in the Notting Hill of the 1950s, but it is also a profound—and at times hilariously funny—love song to London, a hymn to its hybrid essence. The

London of the 1980s found in Ben Okri's stories is a place in which the contingent, the neglected and the apparently squalid have become sources of aesthetic delight, in which the vagrant becomes a seer, a watcher at the city gates.[9] Zadie Smith's *White Teeth*, published in the same year as Linda Grant's novel, possesses something of this same ambivalent quality. It also depicts a town in which a new version of childhood makes its appearance, where memories of shuffling leaves on November afternoons become a possession shared by those whose birth right harks back to Jamaica or Bangladesh. Take all of these Londons, add to them Dickens's London, Defoe's London and Blake's London, and you have a setting where the locale of Peter Ackroyd's *London: The Biography* extends to embrace humankind, without for a moment ceasing to be itself.

Or take that supposed heartland of English ethnic identity: the deep countryside. Perhaps the most moving portrait of rural England written in the closing years of the twentieth century was V.S. Naipaul's *The Enigma of Arrival* of 1987, set near Salisbury.[10] Its migrant protagonist subjects Wiltshire to a scrutiny the more incisive for stemming from one who at first admits his bafflement. As the story progresses he learns to interpret the country through its minutest signs: tiny changes in the landscape, the slow change of the seasons, inflections of voice and attitude, inhibitions, secrets. He reads Wiltshire like a palimpsest, layer upon layer. He perceives the feudal order behind the modern face, the deference or contempt beneath everyday conversations. This is a picture that mirrors something of the protagonist's own reticence and discretion. Like *The Lonely Londoners*, *The Enigma of Arrival* is a searching account of a difficult place that manages also to be an idyll. It is also a panorama of rural life at odds with the acrimonious nostalgia of Roger Scruton: a view larger, more responsive and—for all its alertness to parallels with Trinidad—truer to the actual, rather than the supposed, qualities of Englishness.

The ultimate effect of such texts is to collapse the damaging binaries that sustain ideologies of confrontation: immigrant and emigrant, home and abroad, self and other, town and country, ancient and modern, mainstream and fringe. To embrace migrancy, moreover, is to signal an end of that long procession of stereotypes by means of which cultures protect their self-image against the single or collective challenge of the other: nomad, barbarian, conqueror, métèque, refugee, foreigner, asylum seeker. As all of us know, and the instances already cited suggest, all acts of migration are far more complicated than any such list of arrivants would suggest. To embrace migrancy as a positive force, furthermore, is to propose a way out of the apparently endless reactive cycle described by Gibbon through which empires break down to give rise to new nationalisms, which then re-group to form different amalgamations that in turn dissolve in violence. So that the Roman Empire fragments to give rise to the Byzantine and Holy Roman Empires, which themselves dissolve in rancour. So that the Hapsburg Empire collapses, involving the whole of Europe in war, only to form new balkanised states which then cohere into the Warsaw Pact, this in turn breaking down into the chaos and extremity observable in parts of Eastern Europe to this day. So that the United Kingdom recasts itself in the light of re-born national groupings, and everywhere the Romany is regarded as unwanted. If only we could learn to see the migrant not as the enemy, but as the creator and generator of culture.

Lastly because of the authenticity of its historical perspective, the literature and critique of migrancy help us to read all texts and all cultures in a different way. As a result the present looks different, but so does the past and its literature. Virgil is no longer the champion of heroic nationalism, but a lyrical essence informing the work of, say, Christopher Okigbo, the great African poet, whose proclaimed master he was, and of Ben Okri, who learned Latin in order to read the *Eclogues* and whose novel *Songs of Enchantment* bears an epigraph from the *Georgics*. In Ondaatje's work, Herodotus is released from the bookshelves and becomes a window onto migrant or convergent cultures. Gibbon shakes off his neo-classical dust, providing a clue to the future: to cultural death and renewal. Shakespeare's *The Tempest* becomes a universal allegory of power, and a recurrent ingredient in the literature of the West Indies, rather than the possession of an insular and repressive people.

Viewed through such a lens, perhaps all culture is migrant culture. The fact that we can start to see it like that owes much to the authors or musicians we will be looking at in the following ten chapters. With their assistance, we all become migrant people by virtue of being readers or listeners. For truly regarded, all reading or listening—like all writing—is a kind of travelling.

Notes

1. Linda Grant, *When I Lived in Modern Times* (London: Granta, 2000), 4.
2. *Lamentations* 1:6.
3. Edward Gibbon, *The History of the Decline and Fall of the Roman Empire* [1776–1788] (London: 1820), vol. 9, 468.

4. "Once in a Garden of Plenty", in *Wasafiri* 31 (Spring 2000), 7–8.
5. Charles Kingsley, *Westwood Ho! Or the Voyages and Adventures of Sir Amyas Leigh* (London: Macmillan, 1854).
6. Ngũgĩ wa Thiong'o, *A Grain of Wheat* (London: Heinemann, 1968).
7. G.V. Desani, *All About H. Hatterr* with an introduction by Anthony Burgess (London: Penguin, 1969), 7.
8. Michael Ondaatje, *The English Patient* (London: Bloomsbury, 1992), 126.
9. See especially Ben Okri, *Incidents at the Shrine* (London: Heinemann, 1986), *Stars of the Late Curfew* (London: Secker and Warburg, 1988) and *Songs of Enchantment* (London: Jonathon Cape, 1993).
10. V.S. Naipaul, *The Enigma of Arrival* (London: Viking, 1987).

CHAPTER 3

Roma and Roaming: Borders, Nomads and Myth

The Hungarian-born composer and pianist Franz Liszt was fascinated by Gypsies. In his eyes—part admiring, part contemptuous—they appeared to belong nowhere. More than that, they seemed not to possess, or even to need, any *sense* of belonging. "The Laplander, or the native of Samoa," he wrote in his book *Des Bohémiens et de leur musique en Hongrie* of 1859, "equally with the hunters of the Alps or the Pyrenees, the Cossacks of the Steppes equally with the sailor of Britany, languish and decay if an attempt is made to transport them to scenes other than those in which they have been brought up."

> But with the Gipsies, all this is not so. All notions of country, property and social institutions are specially repudiated by them. They form no local habit, deny the attraction of childhood reminiscence, desire no conquest and, having no past, frankly challenge the future. The entire earth is their country, the ground is their own, while every climate pleases them in which they can wander freely and move without restraint. The tribe, formed and collected by chance though it may be, is their family; a tent, though a mere covering extended from tree to tree, their sufficient habitation, and any object of present momentary enjoyment their undisputed property.[1]

Naturally, for Liszt, the prime "object of momentary enjoyment" was music. In 1853 he had imitated what he took to be the Gypsy or Bohemian style in nineteen "Hungarian rhapsodies" for solo piano, following what he believed to be the essentials of its distinctive form, "divided", as he states in his book, "into two parts: the first corresponding to the slow dance and the second to the animated dance that follows", and flaunting the quiddities of Gypsy melody with its purported minor scale containing an "augmented fourth, diminished sixth and augmented seventh".[2] Added were many a twist and turn suggestive of the movements of the dancer. Thus had Liszt taken Europe by storm.

Yet there lay a paradox at the core both of this music and of his book. At one level, both were expressions of Liszt's own restless temperament. At another, they bodied forth political and aesthetic energies stirred, throughout the Austro-Hungarian Empire as elsewhere across the continent, by the national revolutions of 1848. For Liszt, this was pre-eminently Hungarian music: Hungarian because bestowed and preserved by the Roma. It was also imbued with the spirit of the Roma by virtue of being Hungarian. The contradictions involved in this double view had in turn been aroused by the turmoil of the mid-century. Romanticism, after all, had striven both to express the aspirations of the emergent national state and to move beyond them. In the music of Liszt, a sense of place strains towards the ubiquitous, the itinerant, the universal.

A century later, the foundations of Liszt's thought and practice were vociferously challenged by mid-European musicians and researchers of a differently minded generation, led by Béla Bartók and Zoltán Kodály. Liszt, declared Bartók in 1931, had fallen victim to "false terminology". He had furthermore been deceived by the advertised self-identification of the Roma themselves. What Liszt had been listening to—what he had unwittingly evoked—was not, according to this fresh paradigm, "Gypsy music" at all. It was rather "a recent type of Hungarian popular art music composed practically without exception by Hungarians of the upper middle class" and obligingly echoed by Romany musicians mindful of the tastes of their hosts.[3] Liszt's rhapsodies had, therefore, been imitations of imitations. There existed an authentic Romany music, to be sure, but it was performed in private, for no ears but their own, and certainly not for the likes of Liszt. There was also a bona fide Magyar folk music, on which Bartók and Kodály themselves were resolved to, and did, draw. This, in turn, had little to do with the Roma.

As musicians, the Roma thus flourished in two different capacities. First, they were custodians of their own, jealously guarded, traditions. But they also acted as accomplished absorbers, and gracious purveyors, of certain facets of the musical heritage of the societies through which they passed. The vogue for "Gypsy" music severally evinced by Brahms in his Hungarian dances and Bizet in *Carmen* was therefore one way in which Europe had romantically listened to itself or, more precisely, to a reflection of that otherness, that wild exoticism, that decadent ideal, present within, and epitomised by, the late nineteenth-century cult of "The Bohemian".

* * *

But why "Bohemian" at all? Bohemia was and is both a wild, imagined place—a sort of antidote to urbanity—and a geographical location in the very midst of Europe, in what would eventually emerge successively as Czechoslovakia and the Czech Republic. In the first capacity it has never found a location on any earthly chart; in the second, it has featured in a multitude of maps from the post-medieval period.

All maps, of course, are mental as well as physical projections. Early maps have a strong tendency to assume that physical and political geography are alike static, in which case the clue is where the centre or heart lies. The circular *Mappa Mundi*, kept in Hereford Cathedral and inscribed in around 1290 on one sheet of vellum, admits of three continents: Europe, Asia and Africa, arranged around the main artery of the Mediterranean, above which, drawing on Christian iconography, it situates the centre of the world at Jerusalem, with Christ shown hanging above it on the cross. As the Renaissance dawns with its human and secular preoccupations, a marked shift of attention occurs. Pierre Desceliers's famous World Map of 1550 places the focus somewhere around Mauritania, but with the scale of Europe to the north already discernibly enlarged in relation to its actual size.

Over the next few centuries, the disproportion intensifies. By the late sixteenth century, with the continent's increasing mercantile dominance over the rest of the globe, Europe's appearance is frequently portrayed—or even personified—as regal. On the title page of *geographical encyclopaedia Theatrum orbis terrarum* (Antwep, 1570), as Sir John Hale notes in his *The Civilization of Europe in the Renaissance*, Europe sits sternly on her throne beneath a tree: "In one hand she holds the sceptre of world domination. The other extends over an orb, of globe-like dimensions, marked with the Christian cross. Below, and subservient to her, are three other female characters, a richly clad Asia, a semi-naked Africa, and a nude America holding up a human head in relation to her cannibalism."[4]

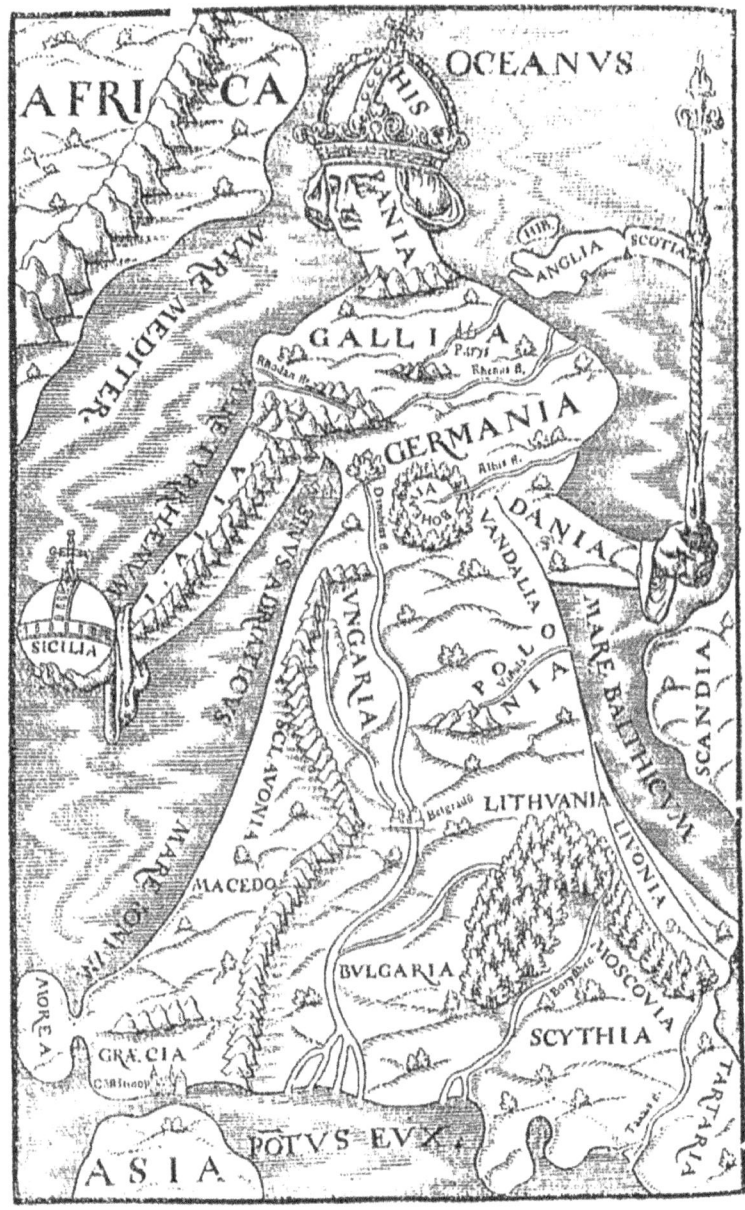

Fig. 3.1 "Queen Europa" from Sebastian Münster's *Cosmographia* (2nd ed., Basel, 1588), B.L.Ac.3838/45

When we come to maps of Europe itself, an analogous mode of allegory prevails. Look at the woodcut of "Queen Europa" featured in Sebastian Münster's *Cosmographia (Fig. 3.1)*, first published in Basel in 1544 and re-issued in 1588, the year of the Spanish Armada.[5] It features an upended topographical design with the shorelines distorted into the figure of a well-proportioned monarch, and the compass bearings re-jigged to place Spain, then at the height of its imperial success, as the crowned head. In her left hand the figure holds the orb of Sicily and in her left—itself composed of Denmark—a sceptre, from which flutters a pennant made up of Scotland, England and Ireland. France composes her upper chest and Germany her stately bosom. The rest of her limbs languish in cartographic uncertainty caused by an absence of national boundaries, not to feature on any map of Europe until 1607. What look like borders in Münster's projection turn out, on closer inspection, to be rivers, each representing an artery feeding Europe's generous body: the Seine her rib cage, the Danube her calves, the Volga her left thigh. The most previous artery of all, the Upper Rhine, springs from her heart, made up of the enclosed grove of Bohemia.

I want us to think about two related consequences stemming from the upright carriage of this figure and the arrangement of her inner organs. Because of her orientation, it is very difficult to form a sense of an East–West axis and, even if there is a compensating North–South fulcrum, it is not where we would put it. Forty years before William Harvey's *De Motu Cordis* (1628), moreover, there is in this analogical body no sense of circulation of the blood. Instead there is a one-way outward flow quite consistent with Tudor notions of the arteries as conduits carrying the vital or intellectual spirits to each and every part. The source of the continuous flux on Münster's chart is the sylvan heart of Bohemia. This is remarkable in itself, since topographical ideas as to the whereabouts and extent of Bohemia were notoriously vague at the time. The most celebrated culprit in this respect was Shakespeare, who set Act Four of *The Winter's Tale* there, but managed in the process to equip Bohemia with a seashore. "Shakespeare in a play", crowed his friend and rival Ben Jonson, "brought in a number of men, saying that they had suffered ship-wrack in Bohemia, where there is no sea near by 100 miles."[6]

Over one fact, however, the Elizabethans were consistent. Bohemia—wherever that was—was the immediate, though not the original, home of a people who had first appeared on the highways of western Europe in the fifteenth century, and in the rural lanes and city streets of England and Scotland from about 1507: the Roma, or as they were then—and are still—commonly called, the Gypsies.[7]

On why the Roma had come to be associated in the public mind with Bohemia, again our best informant is Münster, who had met a troupe of them in Eberach near Heidelberg.[8] When he asked them how they travelled so freely, they showed him a document of safe conduct from the former Holy Roman Emperor, King Zigmund of Bohemia. As it happens, a copy of this document has survived. Signed at Spissky [Spisska Bela] Castle in what is now the Slovak Republic on 17 April 1423, it enjoins all it may concern to treat "Ladislav, Duke of his Gypsy People" and his followers with courtesy: "We recommend that you show to him the loyalty which you would show to Us. Protect them, so that Duke Ladislav and his people may live without prejudice within your walls."[9] Believing the Romas' own explanation that they were Egyptians on a seven-year pilgrimage of penance for having rejected Christ, Zigmund had clearly taken on himself a role as their protector. Indeed, it was on account of this tale of origin, adopted to appeal to late medieval Catholic sympathies, that the Roma were already—and confusingly—known as "Gypsies". Sceptical as always, Münster asked his Heidelberg friends where their homeland was, and was told it lay beyond the Holy Land, beyond even Babylon. He learnedly replied: "Then your Lesser Egypt is not Africa near the Nile but in Asia along the Ganges or the Indus." The Gypsies, who had long forgotten their place of ultimate origin, dissolved into mirth.

From contemporary documents we can follow the progress of the Roma westwards across Europe with a fair degree of precision. Entering Bohemia (that is to say the eastern part of the Hungarian empire, corresponding to what used to be known as Czechoslovakia) from Asia by way of Turkey and the Balkans, they eventually advanced through Germany in dribs and drabs to Holland, Italy and France. In 1420 a band of Gypsy folk were reported at Leiden.[10] On 18 June 1422 a group of about a hundred arrived in Bologna, where their leader Duke Andrea stayed in style at the royal inn while his companions camped before the Galeria gate.[11] On 3 July the Bolognese asked them all to move on. The following year, four from the date on King Zigmund's letter, yet another group produced a copy of this document as a passport in Paris. It was signed by the *roi de Bohème*, and so earned them the nickname *les Bohémiens*. Yet the imperial letter did them little good: outraged by their ragged appearance, the authorities locked them up in La Chapelle.[12] The most successful appearance by any Roma detachment was probably in Scotland. Their reputation had preceded them, since from 1536–7 James V of Scots had spent eight and a half months in northern France, where he had been cured by a

Gypsy woman after his doctors had despaired of him.[13] There is a pen portrait of this sturdy-looking healer in the municipal archives at Arras. James was so impressed by her ministrations that, believing the usual legend about the Roma homeland, he immediately resolved to wage a holy war to wrest Egypt back for his benefactors.

It is clear from these accounts that, wherever they wandered, the uncertainty of their place of origin, and the bizarre and eclectic nature of their language, coloured the way the Gypsies were received. All that anybody could agree on was that they came from the East. This very indeterminacy, on which the Roma themselves could shed little light, proved intriguing as well as worrying. It was in the city and university of Leiden that the mists at last began to clear. In the 1590s a Leiden professor called Joseph Scaliger took to hanging round local taverns, chatting to Gypsies in the only language they had in common: French. His methods of research were haphazard. One evening he approached a carousing Roma and inquired through the hubbub: "How do you say in your language 'Qu'est-ce que *tu bois* [What are you drinking]?'" But the night was far spent and the customers were raucous. The Gypsy tippler thought the Dutchman had asked him "Qu'est-ce que *du bois* [wood]?" and supplied him with *kascht*, the Romani noun for firewood.[14] This error duly appeared under "bibere"—to drink—in the seventy-one-word Romani-Latin lexicon contributed by Scaliger to Bonaventura Vulcanius's *De literis et lingue Getarum sive Gothorum*, published in Leiden in 1597. On the basis of such misinformation, and of the prevailing myth of Gypsy origin, Scaliger concluded that Romani was a branch of Nubian. The truth had to wait until 1763, and another conversation in a Leiden pub. In that year a theology student from the Komorn region of Hungary, István Váli, fell into conversation with three Leiden undergraduates from the Malabar coast of south-west India, and asked them for snippets of their mother tongue. He was instantly struck by the similarity of certain words to the vocabulary of Gypsies he had chatted to at home in Gyor.[15] Váli's inference that Romani was a distant dialect of Malabari was reported in the journal *Wiener Anzeigen* in 1776, though the 1000 items listed there are closer to Malayalam than to the Indo-Aryan group to which he ascribed them. At last, however, the link with India—first casually proposed by Münster two centuries before—existed on an albeit unsteady philological footing.

We must dwell awhile in the immediate pre- and post-revolutionary period, because it is at this moment of the creation of the modern world and the slow consolidation of what were to become Europe's nation-states that the Roma enter European literature as a fully fledged *topos*. There are references before, of course—in Ben Jonson's masks[16] and in Bunyan[17]—but the general impression of exoticism, skill and spasmodic persecution is as yet unmatched by any commanding allure or threat. A change of attitude is already perceptible in a series of decrees passed by the Empress Maria Theresa of Austria between 1758 and 1773. She offered Hungarian Roma full citizenship provided they paid taxes and settled in one place; they were to give up their wagons and horses, and their children for adoption.[18] The policy of enforced integration enjoyed very limited success. Behind it, however, we can discern a drift towards a more constrained, nation-bound notion of belonging. In 1815 the Treaty of Vienna consolidated this presumption by defining Europe's borders in a far more systematic way than ever before. Though Germany and Italy were still to be created as sovereign nations, the principle behind the 1815 settlement was clear: demarcated and rigorously policed borders, a bureaucratic infrastructure capable of interrogating all comers. As Jeremy Black observes in his book *Maps and Politics*, all charts "reflect a society that both seeks to understand and that can create, construct and control"; maps are "instruments of power".[19] On this analogy the European map of 1815 reflected a society that sought to understand culture as a static expression of place. Under this new dispensation all migrants posed a problem. In the legal as well as geographical sense, there was no room for the Roma, or indeed for roaming.

It was against this background that in that year of revolutions 1830, Victor Hugo composed the first of the great nineteenth-century fables of Romany attraction and menace. *Notre Dame de Paris* is a historical romance that projects onto the fifteenth century—the period when the Roma first entered France—the political and cartographic anxieties of the new proto-nationalist age. In it Paris serves as metonym for the French nation, the Ile de la Cité as a metonym for the city and, within that citadel, the cathedral as the repository of France's memory: its proud but compassionate soul. On this pattern of symbols a concentric series of maps is superimposed: the street plan of Paris acting as a miniature of the nation while—on a smaller but still magnificent scale—the architecture of the church becomes as a microcosm of both city and state. On the outskirts of the town—and hence of the nation—dwells a criminal underclass: the Truands, under their leader, the Duke of Egypt and Bohemia. The relationship of this Romany rabble to the rest of society is manifest in a climactic scene in Book Ten when they attempt to rescue the Gypsy dancer la

Esmeralda from the cathedral, where Quasimodo is guarding her as a fugitive from French justice. As the hunchback stares from the great west towers, the darkness of the unlit *quais* beneath him heaves: it is the Romany mob, who then attempt to batter down the door. The outrage is possible because, as Hugo is obliged to pause in his narrative to explain, late medieval Paris has no police force. When the royal troops arrive, the crowd is dispersed, and la Esmeralda arrested and hanged. A fourth topography is then carefully laid onto these culminating events: a map both ethical and ethnic. Hugo reserves his moral approbation for those capable of a noble, self-sacrificing love. La Esmeralda is as capable of this feeling as is Quasimodo, whom she spurns. However, the narrative builds up to the moment when it is predictably revealed that the beautiful street performer is not a Gypsy at all, but Agnès, lost daughter of the French recluse la Sachette. *Notre Dame de Paris* is perhaps the first nineteenth-century novel to depend upon that territorial phobia: the kidnapping and spiriting away of the community's children.[20] Agnès's true identity is revealed just before she swings on the rope, at which point Hugo is free to compare her to the Angel of Humility from Dante's *Purgatorio*: "La Creature Bella Bianco Vestita".[21] The girl, the church and the city are one.

In *Notre Dame de Paris* Europe, once seen by Münster as one large and confident body, is envisaged as a cluster of cells, such as had been observed by Hugo's fellow liberal, the hygienist and revolutionary François Vincent Raspail, who described them in the very year of the novel's composition in his *Essai de chimie microscopique*. During the following decade the physiological metaphor was explored in greater detail by the Prussian polymath and radical Rudolf Virchow. Virchow was a doctor, an energetic research scientist and a political liberal who had experience fighting on one particular frontier, the Silesian border of Prussia, during the uprising of 1848. A close associate of the archaeologist Schliemann, he also had a strong amateur interest in anthropology, a study that he did much to encourage in Germany. He was in his later years a member of the Prussian Diet, where he argued strongly against emerging German nationalism.[22]

As a physiologist Virchow concentrated on the structure of and interrelationship between cells, compared by him to the individuals composing a nation, or the nations that make up a continent. The body, he wrote, was itself "a republic of cells, each one living its own life". He was in strong agreement with the view earlier stated in Latin by Raspail: *omne cellula e cellula*, "every cell originates in another cell". Virchow attributed this independence both to sound and to diseased organisms. Correspondingly, as an anthropological amateur, Virchow believed all cultural manifestations to be the products of movement and borrowing. Politically, he was a potential federalist who thought the newly clarified borders of Europe to be not merely permeable, but doomed. Doomed too was any attempt by a nation-state to enforce discipline and ethnic uniformity within its geographical boundaries. In an article written in 1847, a year before serving in Silesia, Virchow used ethnic cleansing as a metaphor for a reactionary and anachronistic pathology. Outbreaks of xenophobic zeal were like puss; like puss, moreover, they were powerless to ensure health. "Puss formation", he wrote, "is no longer the struggle of the organism to heal itself, by filling up this or that hole; the corpuscles are no longer the *gendarmes* whom the police state orders to escort over the border this or that foreigner who has entered without a passport; scar tissue no longer holds an imprisoning wall, in which such a prisoner is enclosed, when it pleases the Police-Organism."[23]

This insistence on the pointlessness of population control exasperated Bismarck, the architect of the new Germany, who once challenged Virchow to a duel. Yet the questions raised by the medical argument became central to Europe's evolving view of itself. If boundaries are analogous to membranes separating cells, how permeable are these walls, and what happens when they are breached? In the 1840s these worries were given memorable expression in the second and third of our nineteenth-century parables about the Gypsy presence: Prosper Mérimée's misogynistic novella *Carmen* (1845)[24] and Emily Brontë's romance *Wuthering Heights* (1847). Both distil powerful myths; like Hugo's story they were soon to enter middle-brow and then popular culture through operatic and cinematic adaptations. In all three cases, the popularising entailed a sentimentalisation of what in the literary original was a vivid, destabilising menace. Mérimée's tale is of special interest because this professional archaeologist and amateur writer had some knowledge of the Spanish Gypsies, whom he had observed during a tour in 1830.[25] In 1847 he added an extra chapter to the book, summarising his research. Two of the salient characteristics of the Roma, he stated, were "patriotism"—by which he meant loyalty to their kind—and absolute marital fidelity. His story demonstrates the very opposite. A sort of emotional vagrant, Carmen destroys the peace of the workplace, the lives of lovers and friends. After she has cathartically played out the reader's fantasies of masochistic freedom, her Basque lover Don José brutally stabs her. In Bizet's opera of 1875, she lies crumpled and humiliated on the stage before an audience whom she has musically and sexually excited for three hours. They are rid of her, and can safely go back home.

Heathcliff's origins have sometimes been seen as ambiguous, without that ambiguity being properly understood. One twentieth-century editor of *Wuthering Heights*, Ian Jack, encapsulates this blind spot when he announces: "Speculation about the racial origins of Heathcliff are futile because Emily Brontë deliberately leaves the matter uncertain." Jack goes on to state that "the key word in descriptions of him is 'gipsy'".[26] This looks like a contradiction, but is it? A relevant insight may be gleaned from an apposite study in international relations: Iver Neumann's *Uses of the Other: "The East" in European Identity Formation*.[27] Neumann's thesis is that European nations derive their separateness by contrasting themselves with cultures that lie to their east. His own preoccupation is with static "easts" or "others": Turkey or Russia. We might add that since the fifteenth century the Roma have played out the role of a permanent, shifting repository of "Eastness", eerily identified by the very indeterminacy of its origins. In *Wuthering Heights* Heathcliff, the Gypsy outsider, is the alien presence against which an agrarian, property-owning community defines itself. The housekeeper Nelly Dean puts a shrewd finger on the demographic problem when she tells of Mr. Earnshaw's arrival with the foundling: "I was frightened, and Mrs. Earnshaw was ready to fling it out of doors: she did fly up—asking how he could fashion to bring that gipsy brat into the house, when they had their own bairns to feed and fend for? What he meant to do with it, and whether he were mad?"[28] Brontë's answer to Mrs. Earnshaw's question about the sanity of granting the boy asylum is provided when Heathcliff infects the daughter of the house with erotic insanity, resulting in her death and in the potential ruination of this close-knit group of families.

The tragic consequences of Heathcliff's domestication pose an interesting problem. These stories by Hugo, Mérimée and Brontë are not usually branded as racist, yet racialism is strongly encoded into each. The reason has, I believe, less to do with the dilutions of popular culture than with a phenomenon integral to the original texts. In these books a remarkable transformation is occurring before our very eyes: the myth of the vagrant Gypsy is being annexed by the cult of the vagabond artist. The clearest evidence of this change at the time is the appropriation of the term Bohemian to cover dissident behaviour by impoverished, and normally young, poets, painters and musicians. The initiation of this neologism is easy to date, since it occurs in Henry Murger's portrait of Left Bank

Parisian life, *Scènes de la Bohème* [Scenes from Bohemia] of 1851, later to form the basis of a famous opera by Puccini. In his Preface, written in May 1850, Murger stresses the novelty of his coinage. He is equally at pains to stress that the borrowing entails no cultural obligation or debt. Though the dissident artist may now be considered a Bohemian, he is free from infection by—and from occupations traditionally associated with—the Roma. "The bohemians I am dealing with here", Murger begins, "have nothing to do with those bohemians who serve in popular drama as synonyms for rogues and murderers. You will not find them amongst bear-leading gypsies, sword-sharpeners, vendors of safety-chains, practitioners of the quick buck, black market racketeers, and a thousand other suspect and ill-defined professions whose principal purpose is their apparent dereliction and willingness to do anything as long as it's up to no good." Murger's subjects are not nomads; they are settled. Turning Hugo's townscape inside out, he places his new Bohemians in the Quartier Latin, in the very shadow of Notre Dame. By the end of Murger's humorous Preface the appropriation and relocation are complete: "Bohemia", he announces with deliberate half-irony, "only exists—indeed is only conceivable—in Paris."[29]

The isolationism, and severance from suspect foreign connections, implied by this careful paradox were in step with the cultural ambience of the closing decades of the nineteenth century, during which a renewed imperial impulse on the part of the chief European powers went along with intensified nationalism at home. Cartographically and anatomically too, the relative openness to extraneous influence implied by Virchow's cellular structures with their semi-porous walls gradually gave way to the régime of medical and political thought associated in Germany with Virchow's arch-enemy, the bacteriologist and political reactionary Robert Koch.[30] The driving force behind this change was disease. The cholera epidemics of 1832, 1849 and 1853 had concentrated medical inquiry on the problem of diffusion. Previously assumed to be the result of contiguous unhealthy environments, from the 1860s such outbreaks were increasingly attributed to micro-organisms that could be carried across borders. It was Koch who identified the tuberculosis bacillus in 1882; in 1883 he traced cholera back to India, from where it had advanced along an itinerary coinciding with that attributed to the Gypsies. The prophylactic measures Koch proposed—in Europe, an increased emphasis on documentation, medical screening and quarantine, the establishment of *cordons sanitaires* between indigenous and settler communities overseas—reinforced the dividing lines between ethnic and social groupings. Already pestilence was commonly employed as a journalistic metaphor for unwelcome migration or revolution. The year after Koch published his findings on cholera, the British-held Sudan suffered the Mahdist rising, widely interpreted as an outbreak of religious dementia. A right-wing French satirist caught the mood of the moment when he compared the rising to a plague, the need to suppress which spelt the end of Virchow's liberal republic of permeable and mutually supportive units. He continued: "Cellular pathology has had its day. Our body is no longer that 'republic of cells' each leading its healthy life...so dear to the German professor Virchow. Dethroned is your cellular republic, Grand Master...Down with cells, long live independent beings, infinitesimal but prolific...coming from outside, penetrating the organism like Sudanese, ravaging it by right of invasion and conquest."[31]

Inevitably the new dispensation impacted backwards on historical readings of culture. Virchow's insistence on the interdependence of all civilisations gave way to a vision of each society as the unique expression of local conditions within a home- or fatherland. Advanced nations, it came to be argued, were end results of the supplanting of hunter-gatherer societies by agrarian and then industrialised communities. Increasingly culture came to be defined as a condition of settling down. Adopted by German ethnology, this orthodoxy was eventually to become the cornerstone of Nazi anthropology. Its corollary was a view of all mobile groups as regressive, degraded or deviant. In 1936, Martin Block, a leading German authority on the Roma—and a relatively sympathetic observer of them—wrote: "Gypsies are different from us. One realises that as soon as one meets them."[32] The incorrigible indifference towards sedentary life displayed by his subjects intrigued and exasperated Block. "It may be," he rhetorically observed, "that they are stronger than civilisation. But even if they are, why do they exercise that strength so relentlessly, rejecting all attempts to change them?"[33]

The incomprehension, sentimentalising and plain prejudice that mark attitudes towards the Roma in the late nineteenth and early twentieth centuries are exactly contemporaneous with the enshrining of Bohemianism as a defining feature of artistic life in the West. Verdi's *La Bohème* epitomises a cult growing ever more tenacious and alluring as Romanticism reaches its decadent late phase. Interestingly, the most moving moment in the opera is Mimi's death from tuberculosis, the less virulent of the two diseases identified by Koch, already softened by *fin-de-siècle* myth into "consumption". In 1894 George du Maurier's novel *Trilby* glamorises the casual and transgressive life of the "Bohemian" Left Bank in much the same terms as Murger, adding an acceptable frisson of mesmerism and sex. In 1908 Augustus John, *enfant terrible* of British painters, portrays his wife in a Roma-style dress, starting a vogue for Gypsy accessories that grips European capitals even as the models for the fashion are limited to—or expelled from—their margins.[34] As Bloch memorably puts it, "the carts move on."

By now the equation between illness, madness and migration was firmly fixed in the European mind. Perhaps the haunting expression of it—certainly the most learned—is Thomas Mann's *Der Tod in Venedig* [*Death in Venice*] of 1912. Situated in a sea port and historic gateway to the East during a cholera epidemic, it describes how the fastidious and celibate Bavarian writer Gustav von Aschenbach, the epitome of *Mitteleuropa*, is infected, inspired, maddened and finally killed by a strain of the disease originating in the Ganges Delta. The agent of his mental and, symbolically at least, of his physical intoxication is a young Polish boy of a certain Gypsy-like grace, with whom he falls in love. Mann of course is playing with motifs that go right back to the *Bacchae* of Euripides, with its evocation of cultic possession sweeping across from the East to stir up and then destroy the genius of royal Thebes. The East, to extend Neumann's argument backwards, is both the historical other and, paradoxically, the source of Western art.

The fact that Aschenbach's condition, with its oriental aetiology, coincides with active political suppression of the East is not one that Mann cares to explore. As the twentieth century progresses, however, that paradox—though seldom remarked upon—grows more glaring. The successive fads for Eastern art that gripped colonial capitals during this period are only one instance of this. More relevant to our purpose is the continuing rage for Bohemianism in Western culture, then as now. By mid-century, the very moment when the historical Bohemian—the Gypsy—came to be identified by governments everywhere as a "problem", an artistic and a "Bohemian" way of life had largely become synonymous. In the 1940s, as Hitler's final solution condemned thousands of Roma to the death camps, a new vogue for Bohemianism erupted in Britain. Its epicentre—the new, temporary Latin Quarter—was Soho and adjoining districts. "During the war", enthuses Andrew Sinclair without a hint of irony in his study of 1940s London, *War Like a Wasp*, "Fitzrovia was a true bohemia as it never was before or after it."[35] This comparative freedom —comparative, that is, to Nazi-occupied Paris—did much to relax the British painters and poets who frequented local pubs alongside the expatriate Free French. As far as I am aware it did little to console the 1.5 million originals of this "true" condition languishing in concentration camps at Auschwitz-Birkenau, Lety, Hodonín and elsewhere. The extermination decimated the Gypsy population of Eastern Europe, and of Czechoslovakia in particular. By 1945, out of 6500 Roma who had been rounded up for imprisonment in historical Bohemia, 583 were left alive.[36]

What I seem provocatively to be proposing is that there exists not simply a logical connection between the cult of the Bohemian artist and the persecution of the Roma, but a causal link as well. The implications are disturbing. The myth of Bohemia, for example, is now the birth right not simply of Western artists, but of a range of alternative and radical social groupings.[37] It has also provided a role model for generations of students and dropouts. Over the same post-war period, the map of Europe has been re-drawn twice: at the post-war settlement of 1945, and after the collapse of the Warsaw Pact in 1989. At much the same time, migration of various kinds and from various sources has become a dynamic feature of the European scene. Have these new realities done anything to relieve the Roma from their historical burden of glorification and denigration? How much light is shed on Europe's oldest society of travellers by our postcolonial understanding of the world, our new emphasis on hybridity and the migrant nature of cultures?

One clue is provided by a key migrant novel: *Le thé au harem d'Archi Ahmed* (1983), Mehdi Charef's affectionate and humorous study of young North African migrants and their friends set on a high-rise housing estate near Paris. In one scene the gang saunter past an encampment of Spanish Gypsies. Majid, a second-generation Algerian settler, stands entranced: "Majid can't take his eyes off the gypsy women. He thinks they're amazing, the way they're always dressed in technicolour like an arrangement of Japanese flowers. They wear long-brightly coloured skirts—a blinding yellow with bright pink roses...he wonders how on earth such beautiful women can have ended up here in the middle of nowhere, surrounded by filthy pots and pans. If he had his way, he'd haul them off to a fancy patisserie, and he'd make them a bed among the coloured candies—the round white ones, the blue oval ones and the red flat ones that he remembers from when he was a kid with his mouth watering at the shop window."[38] Charef's novel is an expression of the migrant gaze as it re-interprets the city, a perspective present here in Majid's memory of himself as a poor child staring wistfully at the delicacies inside a

Paris cake shop. In this passage, however, we also encounter another, far more unsettling gaze: the migrant staring upon the vagrant. The resulting perception of Romany life—beauty amid filthy pans—is indistinguishable from the centuries-old desire and contempt I have been describing.

So much for the glorification. To observe the denigration, I offer an early twenty-first-century scenario. The scene is set aboard a crowded carriage attached to a late evening train to the suburbs from London Victoria. I am on my way home after watching a revival of Jonathan Miller's production of *Carmen* at the English National Opera.[39] My neighbours are a Polish couple who, I gather from their conversation and the programme they are reading, have been enjoying *Notre Dame de Paris* at the Dominion Theatre, with Dannii Minogue as a scantily clad Esmeralda. We are approaching Gipsy Hill, a suburban station named after a Roma encampment cleared in 1866 to make way for a church.[40] As we draw level with Romany Avenue, the door at the end of the carriage slides open. Down the aisle a Roma woman of East European extraction slowly advances with a baby on her shoulder. One hand holds a piece of cardboard with an appeal in blue biro; the other is cupped and imploring. As this real-life Carmen reaches us, the couple opposite me stiffen. The boy's face has hardened: he is repeating in a manic undertone, "I hate them. I hate them. I hate them." Then, at the very end of the carriage, a Lonely Londoner of the Windrush generation rises to his feet. His trilby hat trembling with indignation, he harangues us. "It is", he enjoins, "important that we British do not give to these people."

He has, of course, spoken for several people in the carriage, and for many in the nation. The late lamented historian Raphael Samuel once called the Roma "those age-old pariahs of British society".[41] But, of course, the taboo was and is Europe-wide; all the signs are that these peripatetic folk are little better understood now than they were in the sixteenth century. Indeed, the evidence suggests that they were more hospitably received in the fifteenth.

There are, moreover, important theoretical issues at stake. In the closing decades of the twentieth century, postcolonial theory added a different kind of map to those found in conventional cartographies: a chart drawn by the memories of peoples as they criss-cross continents and oceans. Paul Gilroy's reading of the Atlantic as a kinetic cultural space provided us with one such reshaping.[42] Yet Gilroy does not mention the Roma, and neither do most of the experts on the international phenomenon of migration cited in our opening chapter. One reason for this relative neglect is suggested by the scenario above. A superficial but inevitable assumption is that nomads and migrants, as travelling folk, possess a common cause. Yet, as the reactions of my fellow commuters on that late evening train suggest, this is very far from being the case. Migrants by and large have a deep desire to settle; most nomads have a deep desire to move on.

Yet both groups have acted as conveyors and purveyors of culture; both have enriched their host societies, even as they sometimes fall victim to their own precarious mystique. The Hungarian rhapsodies of Liszt made very little difference to the social and political position of the Roma of his own time, in Hungary or anywhere else in Europe. The continuing cult for Bohemian fashion and manners leaves the plight of present-day Roma almost untouched. As nomadic culture is absorbed sideways into the mainstream, the effect on those who generated it in the first place is too often to strand them high and dry.

NOTES

1. Franz Liszt, *The Gipsies in Music*, trans. Edwin Evans (London: William Reeves, 1926), vol. i, 78–79.
2. Frantz Liszt, vol ii, 300.
3. Béla Bartók, "Gypsy Music or Hungarian Music?", *The Musical Quarterly* 33, no. 2, (April 1947), 240–41.
4. Quoted in John Rigby Hale, *The Civilization of Europe in the Renaissance* (London: Harper Collins, 1993), 10–11.
5. The first edition of this work, issued in Basel in 1540, was an updating of Ptomely's *Geography*. Ten years later Münster published a much improved edition incorporating twenty-seven woodcut maps after Ptolemy and twenty-one of his own design, including this one, as well as townscapes and maps. "Queen Europa" is reproduced from the edition of 1588 (BL Ac.3838/45). She is also to be found in Hale, 11. I am grateful to Professor Ken Parker for drawing my attention to this remarkable map.
6. Quoted in Shakespeare, *The Winter's Tale*, Variorum Edition, 139.
7. A fine account of Gypsies in Elizabethan England is to be found in Gāmini Salgādo, *The Elizabethan Underworld* (London: Dent, 1977), especially his Chap. 7: "Minions of the Moon", 151–162. The publication of Salgādo's book—and his teaching—had a profound effect on scholars and writers of my generation.
8. Münster's experience is first recounted in the 1550 edition of *Cosmographia*. The Latin text is reproduced in D.M.M. Bartett, "Münster's *Cosmographia Universalis*", *Journal of the Gypsy Lore Society* 3 (1952), 83–90. See also Angus Fraser, *The Gypsies* (Oxford: Blackwell, 1992), 64–65.

9. The full text is reproduced in "The History of the Roma Minority in the Czech Republic", http://romove.radio.cz/en/clanek/18913, 1. It seems, however, that there must have been several copies of the original document carried at various times and in varying versions by different groups of Roma.
10. Fraser, 70. The sighting does not seem to have been entirely trustworthy.
11. An account of their stay is given in *Rerum Italicarum Scriptores*, ed. L.A. Muratori (Milan, 1730), vol. xviii, 611. "Their women", it recounts, "went about in shifts and wore a coarse outer garment across the shoulder, rings in their ears, and a long veil on their head." Eventually they departed in the direction of Rome. The visit is also mentioned in Martin Block, *Zigeuner* [1936], translated as *Gypsies: Their Life and Customs*, trans. Barbata Kuczynski and Duncan Taylor (London: Methuen, 1938). See also Fraser, 72–73.
12. Salgãdo, 152. They were imprisoned as *cajoux* or undesirables.
13. Fraser, 118–20 and plate 10, 121.
14. Fraser, 187.
15. Block (1938) 39. Block, however, takes Vály's discovery very much at face value. A more critical account can be found in Fraser, 193.
16. Especially his *Masque of the Gypsies Metamorphosed* presented before James I (James VI of Scotland) in London during August 1621. A stage direction reads: *Enter a Gypsy, leading a horse laden with stolen poultry*. Quoted in Salgãdo, 151. From Jonson and contemporary authors we learn that the Gypsies of Elizabethan England held an annual get-together at the mountain still known as "The Devil's Arse" in Derbyshire. (This is in the Peak District, a few miles outside Buxton.) From at least the eighteenth century there seem to have been similar gatherings on Blackheath and Penge common, both just south of London.
17. In his *A History of the Gipsies* (London: 1865), Walter Simson makes a strong case for Bunyan having been of Gypsy stock. Seepp. 206, 309, 402, 507–523, 530, 535–36. The case is based on Bunyan's father having been a Bedfordshire tinker. However, though many Gypsies have been tinkers, not all tinkers have been Gypsies. With others Simson believed that the itinerant programme of *Pilgrim's Progress* (1678) was inspired by the author's family background.
18. Fraser, 157–59, 191, 196, 211, 262.
19. Jeremy Black, *Maps and Politics* (London: Reaktion Books, 1997). Quoted in Richard Horton, "The key to life—Or a dead molecule: Unresolved questions about the practical value of the genome", *The Times Literary Supplement* March 9, 2001, 13–15. Like Münster and Virchow, Horton is concerned with parallels between geographical and anatomical maps: in his case the emerging "map" of DNA.

20. Though a passing reference to this common fear occurs in Act One of Richard Brinsley Sheridan's farce *The Critic* (1779), where the analogy is to literary plagiarism: "Steal! to be sure they may; and egad, serve your best thoughts as gypsies do stolen children—disfigure them to make them pass for their own."
21. Victor Hugo, *Notre Dame de Paris* (Paris, 1831), Book XI, chap. ii, quoting Dante, *Purgatorio*, xii, 89–90. Though, oddly from Hugo's point of view, Dante's angel is male.
22. An informative and incisive account of Virchow's career, and of his analogies between physiological and political structures, can be found in Laura Otis, *Membranes: Metaphors of Invasion in Nineteenth-Century Literature, Science, and Politics* (Baltimore and London: The John Hopkins University Press, 1999), 8–25. See also Neal Ascherton, "International Space", Darwin Lecture Series on "Space", Lady Mitchell Hall, University of Cambridge, 23 February, 2001.
23. Rudolph Virchow, "Über die Reform der pathologischen und therapeutischen Anschauungen durch die mikroskopischen Untersuchungen." *Archiv für pathologische Anatomie und Physiologie und für klimische Medizin* 1 (1847). Quoted and translated in Otis, 22.
24. The depth of the book's misogyny can be gauged from its punning Greek epigraph from the poet Palladas. It might be rendered: "A woman has two decent positions: in bed and dead."
25. Another source of information and ideas was Pushkin's poem of 1824, *Tsygany* (*The Gypsies*). In 1852 Mérimée made a prose translation of Pushkin's work with a title seemingly influenced by Murger: *Les Bohémiens*.
26. Emily Brontë, *Wuthering Heights* [1847], ed. Ian Jack (Oxford: The World's Classics), 344.
27. Iver Neumann, *Uses of the Other: "The East" in European Identity Formation* (Manchester: Manchester University Press, 1999).
28. Brontë, ed. Jack, 35.
29. Henry Murgher, *Scènes de la Bohème* (Paris: Lévy brothers, 1851), Préface, 1.
30. For a shrewd analysis of Koch's science in relation to his politics, see Otis, 31–36.
31. Quoted in anger by Virchow in "Der Kampf der Zellen und der Bakterien", *Archiv für pathologische Anatomie und Physiologie und für klimische Medizin*, 101 (1885), 1–13. Cited and translated by Otis (p. 23), who, however, renders "chaqu'une d'une vie propre" as "each one (living) its own life".
32. Block (1938), 2
33. Block (1938), 247.

34. Augustus John's "Woman Smiling" hangs in the portrait section of Tate Britain in London. There are earlier romanticised likenesses of Gypsies themselves by Murillo in Spain and Sir Joshua Reynolds in England.
35. Andrew Sinclair, *War Like A Wasp: The Lost Decade of the Forties* (London: Hamish Hamilton, 1989), 66.
36. "The History of the Roma Minority in the Czech Republic", http://www.romove.cz/history.html, 3–5.
37. For a comprehensive guide to the spread of the cult of Bohemianism, see Elizabeth Wilson, *Bohemians: The Glamorous Outcasts* (London and New York: I.B. Tauris, 2000).
38. Mehdi Charef, *Le thé au harem d'Archi Ahmed* (Paris: Mercure de France, 1983). English translation *Tea in the Harem* trans. Ed Emory (London: Serpent's Tale, 1989), 59.
39. The Coliseum, 15 March 2001. The production revival was by David Ritch. Carmen was sung by Sally Burgess and Don José by David Rendall.
40. Alan R. Warwick, *The Phoenix Suburb: A South London Social History* (London: The Blue Boar Press in association with the Beulah Group, 1982), 25–32.
41. *Patriotism: The Making and Unmaking of British National Identity*, ed. Raphael Samuel (London: Routledge, 1989), vol. II (Minorities and Outsiders), xiv.
42. For which see Paul Gilroy, *The Black Atlantic: Modernity and Double Consciousness* (London: Verso, 1993).

CHAPTER 4

Of Sirens, Science and Oyster Shells: Hypatia the Philosopher from Gibbon to *Black Athena*

Why in 1975 did Tony Harrison, forthright and classically learned British Northerner, elect to translate the *Epigrams* of Palladas? I suspect that it was because of their terse music and hard-boiled attitude. All the same, there is one of his translations that stands out from the rest by reason of its limpid serenity of tone. It is entitled simply "Hypatia":

> Searching the zodiac, gazing on Virgo,
> Knowing your province is really the heavens,
> Finding your brilliance everywhere I look,
> I render you homage, revered Hypatia,
> Teaching's bright star, unblemished, undimmed.[1]

Palladas, an Alexandrian poet of the fourth century AD and hence her contemporary, was the first contributor to the literary legend of Hypatia—philosopher, mathematician, lecturer, astronomer—and Harrison via his translation is one of the more recent. A present-day authority on her life and work, the Polish classicist Maria Dzielska, states that the epigram may be about a different Hypatia altogether,[2] but in view of the specificity of its references this seems unlikely. Meanwhile Hypatia's legend has spread far and wide, from her Greek homeland and Egyptian abode, to England, Italy, Quebec, the United States, then through the postcolonial world to South India and thence back to Egypt. There is a journal of feminist philosophy named after her in Indiana, and she has 101,000 references on Google. She has become a film, a minuet, a waltz and a gavotte, a time-traveller,

© The Author(s) 2018
R. Fraser, *Literature, Music and Cosmopolitanism*,
https://doi.org/10.1007/978-3-319-68480-2_4

an asteroid, a shipboard computer, a pioneer of women in science, a role model and a sex symbol—sometimes at one and the same time. In the process, she has sometimes changed colour and sex, and she has provided a banner for a multitude of causes. Seldom has cultural migration carried any figure quite so far and so wide.

But the Palladas poem certainly captures one of the recurrent images: staring up at the night sky, ignorant of her terrible fate, an impression captured in a recent novelistic treatment from Italy, Caterina Contini's *Ipazie e la notte* [Hypatia and the night].[3] Dzielska considers this wide and proliferating diffusion a distraction from the facts. In this chapter I want to take it seriously as a study in cultural translation and cross-interpretation. It is certainly both rich and full.

To give the facts their due, what do we know for sure? That she was the daughter of Theon the mathematician, that she taught publicly in Alexandria, both in the streets and at the Museum, that she wrote commentaries on the *Arithmetica* of Diophantus and Apollonius's study of conic sections, and that she edited her father's book on Ptolemy. All of her works are now lost, but we can glean something of her teaching from seven letters written to her by her most successful pupil, Synesius, who converted to Christianity and became Bishop of Cyrene.[4] From these we gather that she made for Synesius an astrolabe and a diagnostic instrument later identified by the famous Fermat as a hydrometer. Another of her pupils, and a personal friend, was Orestes, prefect and governor of the city, and nominally an adherent to the official Christianity of the Empire. Hypatia herself, though, was a follower of Plotinus and the neo-Platonic tradition; in the eyes of the Church, and especially of the city's patriarch Cyril, she was a pagan.

The date of her birth is uncertain. Most encyclopaedias give the year 370, though Charles Kingsley, with an eye to her sex appeal, seems to put it around 390[5] and Dzielska, after trawling though the evidence, places it at 355, which means that Hypatia was around 60 at the time of the one fixed point that we do have: March 415, set in horror. What exactly occurred on that day of doom depends which source you believe: the tenth-century *Suda Lexicon*, the fifth-century *Ecclesiastical History* of Socrates Scholasticus, or the *Chronicle* of John, Monophysite Bishop of Nikui, who claims that she deserved everything that she got.[6] It is the version by Socrates Scholasticus that has burned its way into the legend, principally because Gibbon's account in *The Decline and Fall of the Roman Empire* is an almost word-for-word translation of it. A mob, certainly devoted to—and possibly acting under the orders of—Bishop Cyril, entered her house, carried her through the streets to a church called the Caesarion, stripped her and scraped the flesh from her bones with—well, what?—Socrates's dative noun is *ostrakois*, which Gibbon unforgettably translates as "with oyster shells", though it can also mean with potsherds or even with roof tiles.[7] On two matters all of the sources agree: Hypatia was not a Christian, and a Christian crowd, fearing her influence over the governor, did her in. Her remains were buried in the church.

But even here there is an ironical twist, for Hypatia was not the only Alexandrian woman in those violent centuries to have been butchered for her beliefs. Roman Catholic tradition speaks of a young woman called Catherine who, almost a century previously—before the official conversion of the Empire under Constantine—opposed the persecution of Christians by the co-emperor Maxentius. She was strapped to a spiked wheel—the original Catherine wheel—and then beheaded. Her feast day is 25 November. Yet sometime, somehow, the two legends became intertwined: Hypatia's death seeped via the public imagination into Catherine's, and vice versa. So that there were now two martyrdoms—a Christian and, if you like, a contra-Christian—facing one another, and at times touching.[8] Hypatia for one has been a focus for nationalist, feminist, Afro-centric and postcolonial aspirations, but in all of these it is her vexed relationship with authority that has shaped the successive re-workings of her tale. And never more so than at the historical moment when her legend really gathers pace: at the Enlightenment.

Anticlericalism is the unsurprising fulcrum around which eighteenth-century treatments of Hypatia swing. The first tremor is marked by a pamphlet of 1721 by the notorious and intemperate deist and freethinker, John Toland (1670–1722). The illegitimate son of an Irish Catholic priest, Toland was brought up in Derry and educated at the universities of Glasgow, Leiden and Oxford, where he wrote his first work, *Christianity Not Mysterious* (1695). He was befriended by John Locke who, however, considered that Toland had an "exceedingly great value of himself"; for all that, on 9 September 1697 the House of Commons voted that the book be burned by the public hangman. Toland soon fled to the continent, where he seems to have lived principally on an allowance of £30 a year provided by the Earl of Shaftesbury. He descended into penury and, almost on his deathbed, penned a 2/6d pamphlet entitled *Hypatia, or, the History of the Most Beautiful, Most Virtuous, Most Learned and in every Way Accomplished Lady; who was Torn in Pieces by the Clergy of Alexandria, to Gratify the Pride, Emulation, and Cruelty of the Archbishop, Commonly but Undeservedly Titled St. Cyril.* Toland's target is the cult of sainthood and—more broadly—the integrity of the clergy. He has learned the hard way not to attack Christianity itself. Thus in an honourable deist tradition he applauds the moral example of Christ, but deprecates his followers: "No, no, they were no Christians that killed Hypatia; nor are any Christian clergymen to be attacked through the sides of her Murderers, but those that resemble them; by substituting precarious Traditions, scholastic Fictions, and usurped Dominion to the salutiferous Institution of the holy Jesus."[9]

It is against this background that we must view Gibbon's celebrated account of the story. Whether he had read Toland or not, he draws on exactly the same sources, and benefits from a controversy that had been kept alive in France by Voltaire, both in his *Examen important de Milord Bolingbroke ou le tombeau du fanatisme* (1736) and his *Dictionnaire philosophique*. Despite these incisive influences, there is a danger of simplifying Gibbon's interpretation of Hypatia's murder in line with his reputation as an unreconstructed anticlerical polemicist, or of seeing him as plugging some standard Enlightenment line. There is a certain amount of justice in this view, but Gibbon is also an historian with a judicious sense of the wider context. It is against the backdrop of the "cobwebs" of fourth-century theological controversy, and the personality cult surrounding Bishop Cyril, that he broaches his theme. The relevant passage, from Chap. 47 of *The History of the Decline and Fall of the Roman Empire*, is careful and dramatic. Not content with the title Patriarch of Alexandria, Cyril has usurped the role of Civil Magistrate of the city, in which capacity he expels the Jews from Alexandria. The act is flagrantly illegal but, "in a feeble government [i.e. Orestes's] and a superstitious age", he gets away with it. Orestes complains, whereupon his chariot is attacked by monks, one of whom, Ammonius, wounds him. When Orestes has the assailant executed, Cyril confers on his votary the moniker of "Thaumasius" or "Marvellous", and ascends the pulpit:

> to celebrate the magnanimity or an assassin and a rebel. Such honours might incite the faithful to combat and die under the banners of the saint; and he soon prompted, or accepted, the sacrifice of a virgin, who professed the religion of the Greeks, and cultivated the friendship of Orestes. Hypatia, the daughter of Theon the mathematician, was initiated into her father's studies; her learned comments have elucidated the geometry of Apollonius

and Diophantus; and she publicly taught, both in Athens and Alexandria, the philosophy of Plato and Aristotle. In the bloom of her beauty, and in the maturity of her wisdom, the modest maid refused her lovers and instructed her disciples; the persons most illustrious for their rank or merit were impatient to visit the female philosopher; and Cyril beheld with jealous eye the gorgeous train of horses and slaves who crowded the door of her academy. A rumour was spread among the Christians that the daughter of Theon was the only obstacle to the reconciliation of the prefect and the archbishop; and that obstacle was speedily removed. On a fatal day, in the holy season of Lent, Hypatia was torn from her chariot, stripped naked, dragged to the church, and inhumanly butchered by the hands of Peter the reader and a troop of savage and merciless fanatics: her flesh was scraped from her bones with oyster shells, and her quivering limbs were delivered to the flames. The just progress of inquiry and punishment was stopped by seasonable gifts; but the murder of Hypatia has imprinted an indelible stain on the character and religion of Cyril of Alexandria.[10]

Typical Gibbon this: antithetical, barbed. "Modest", for example, conflates bashfulness and humility, neither of which qualities is stressed in the sources. And "inhumanly" is a nice touch. How exactly does one butcher someone "humanly"? Hypatia, we notice, "professed the religion of the Greeks"; in Gibbon's eyes, that makes her a disciple of Julian the Apostate, Constantine's nephew, who in the previous century had briefly returned the Roman Empire to the "pagan" religion of its ancestors. Ultimately the experiment had failed. Gibbon's account is touched by the pathos and grandeur of that *débâcle*, against the backdrop of which Hypatia herself features as a tragic victim literally torn between competing ideologies. In effect, she is a victim of history.

Gibbon sets his mark on much of what follows; the tendency to view Hypatia as a female apostle of Julian, for example, is evident in a number of subsequent versions. With the dawn of the nineteenth century, however, something else enters the scene: an impulse to construct a Christianised recital of her story that rises beyond denunciation of her, or collusion with her murderers. It is often accompanied by something equally vibrant: a desire to recruit Hypatia to the causes of nationalism and anti-imperialism. The 1820s, for example, saw the birth of a minor cult of Hypatia in Italy, inaugurated in 1829 by Diodata Saluzzo Roero's verse-drama *Ipazia ovvero delle filosofie*. This is a twenty canto *terza rima* poem, drawing on—while romantically amplifying—the classical sources with an eye to the first stirrings of national revolt in Western Europe, in Greece,

Italy and elsewhere. Hypatia here is no celibate and passive dedicatee of Plotinus, but a passionate activist with a sort of live-in lover in the temple of Serapis. Her fortunes change when she becomes involved with a dynamic character called Isidore. Some of the original sources actually name this individual as her "husband"; here however he is an Egyptian nationalist fighting against Roman domination in a variety of anticipatory Risorgimento. Hypatia herself is saved from the crime of bigamy by the intervention of Cyril, whom Saluzzo, perhaps as a result of her deep and residual Catholicism, is almost unique in post-classical literary tradition in viewing in a sympathetic light.[11] From that moment on, Hypatia's destiny recalls that of her *alter persona*, St Catherine. Joining the Christian church, she dies at the foot of the cross, felled by a heterodox priest, her example serving to commend the future of a Christian Egypt, united under God. Her fate and her commitment thus echo the destiny of Italy as the poet evidently regards it. "Ma 'l patrio amor nasce e ritorna in Dio" runs the last line of the poem: "But love of country is born and returns towards God."[12]

It is to the revival of Roman Catholicism in England at mid-century that we owe the most extended Victorian account of Hypatia and her story. Published in 1851, Charles Kingsley's *Hypatia, or, New Foes with an Old Face* is best viewed as an expression of the anxieties provoked in the national psyche by the so-called Papal Aggression, the re-establishment of the Roman Catholic hierarchy in Britain the previous year. As an Anglican Broad Churchman, anticlerical priest and committed Christian Socialist, Kingsley was prone to worry over such issues, and to agonise about the consequences of Catholic emancipation and empowerment for the nation as a whole, especially for the established Church. As his subtitle suggests, he is just as keen to use this ancient story to expound a contemporary national-cum-religious allegory as, in her very different context, Saluzzo had been. Cyril, in his reading of events, is very much a proto-Papist, and the Church of Alexandria a mirror turned forwards to the presumptions of the See of Pious Ninth. As for Hypatia herself, Kingsley cannot seem to make up his mind whether to admire her, admonish her, or shamelessly to lick his lips over her. Certainly he wishes to co-opt her spiritually, since in a scene reminiscent in its echoes of that complementary figure St Catherine, Kingsley has Hypatia —in an intriguing variant of one mid-Victorian novelistic trope—suffer a crisis in her neo-Platonic faith, and then embrace Christianity. At her death, it is eroticism of a somewhat sadomasochistic variety that wins through. A pack of monks career round the corner wielding "flints, shells, fragments of pottery"—Kingsley is hedging his linguistic bets here—and drag her into the church where

> She shook herself free from her tormentors and, springing back, rose for one moment to her full height, naked, snow-white against the dusky mass around—shame and indignation in those wide, clear eyes, but not a stain of fear. With one hand she clasped her golden locks around her; the other long white arm was stretched upward towards the great still Christ, appealing—and who dare say in vain?—from man to God. His lips were opened to speak; but the words that should have come from them reached God's ear alone; for in an instant Peter struck her down, the dark mass closed over her again...and then wail on wail, long, wild, ear-piercing, rang along the vaulted roofs, and thrilled like the trumpet of avenging angels...[13]

The publication history of Kingsley's novel is itself instructive. By the time of his high-profile quarrel with Cardinal Newman in 1864, it had already been reprinted twice. That ecclesiastical *contretemps* was memorably to give rise to Newman's *Apologia Pro Vita Sua*; in the context of Kingsley's own religious development it can best be construed in terms set out in the novel, since Kingsley seems to have considered his Catholic adversary very much in the light of a latter-day St Cyril: not murderous perhaps, but cunning certainly. "Truth, for its own sake," the novelist had notoriously complained, "had never been a virtue with the Roman clergy."[14] There is then a gap of some thirty-five years before a flurry of new editions at the *fin de siècle*, by which time I suspect *Hypatia* was already being read in ways that Kingsley might have found objectionable: not so much as an anticlerical as a secularist text.

That opens the door on the ample history of twentieth-century interpretations, most of which desert the nineteenth-century Christian synthesis to adopt Hypatia as a secular cause: feminist, nationalist, Afro-centric by turns. Interestingly a couple of them come from Quebec, and I will begin with one of them: a delightful spoof. Andrée Ferretti's *Renaissance en paganie* (1987) is set in Montreal where Hubert Aquin, a blocked writer and Quebequois nationalist, encounters the shade of the Alexandrian philosopher when he inadvertently taps in her name into a computer terminal in the national library. They immediately understand one another: she has the Church to content with, he has the Ottawa parliament. Hypatia discerns his problem immediately: there is a new hegemony in the world, not of bishops and priests this time but of remote, unresponsive metropolitan bureaucrats and technocrats. "Il y a quinze siècles", she instructs him, "c'était l'Eglise chrétienne qui cherchait a imposer universellement son nouveau pouvoir...Il semble que, à l'inverse, ce soit aujourd'hui ceux qui commandent l'essor scientifique qui postulent à l'hégémonie absolue"[15] [Fifteen centuries ago it was the Christian Church that sought universally to impose its new power...It seems to me that nowadays by contrast it is those who command scientific and technological know-how who aim at absolute hegemony]. So manifest is their mutual sympathy that, in mock remembrance of Hypatia's death, Aquin puts a bullet through his brain and spends the rest of the book as a disembodied pantheistic spirit stalking the St Cyril of the piece: no Christian dignitary, but the treacherous Quebec-born Prime Minister of Canada, Pierre Trudeau. Hypatia's ghost keeps her soulmate company, telling him to be patient.

Jean Marcel's *Hypatie ou la fin des dieux* presents us with a less frivolous but no less playful set of variations on our classical theme. In fact I would say that it is the most resourceful and nuanced of the twentieth-century deployments of her story, all the more so because, though it takes considerable risks with the classical sources, it ballasts its postmodern liveliness with a responsive feeling for the manifold possibilities visibly contained within the past. In form, for example, it echoes one of the classical documents that I have already mentioned, consisting of a set of letters between Hypatia and her favourite pupil Synesius, and between Synesius and Palladas, who has metamorphosed from a poet into an amanuensis and devotee of the female philosopher. But the account given of her death digresses from Socrates Scholasticus, the familiar story on which Gibbon, Kingsley and others drew. Instead Palladas witnesses his mentor and friend broken on the wheel and then beheaded—in other words, she suffers the same fate, physically speaking, as Catherine. However, when he gets wind of the saint's own death, Palladas determines to have his revenge on the Church who murdered his beloved Hypatia by deliberately conflating the two stories so that his teacher becomes the ironic object of Christian veneration. "Ma détermination était de fer", he notes grimly. "Ils avaient détruit celle que j'avais adorée; ils allaient enfin adorer celle qu'ils avaient détruit"[16] [My resolve was iron-hard. They had destroyed her whom I adored; they were going to worship her whom they had destroyed].

Marcel underscores this antiphonal reversal of two related legends by a sub-plot that has to do with the authenticity and vulnerability of texts. Coming right forward in time, he introduces a priestly scholar: a latter-day *bollandiste*, or official compiler of saints' lives, entrusted with the difficult task of authenticating the cult of St Catherine. He seems utterly convinced of the evidence for her sanctity, prominent among which is the survival of her decapitated corpse in a shallow grave on Mount Sinai. In fact the body is Hypatia's, placed there by Palladas who, centuries previously, had humped her remains across the desert and mischievously buried them on the holy mountain. We are privy to this subterfuge thanks to the present-day monk in whose safekeeping resides a manuscript in which Palladas confesses to his hoax. In this learnedly and richly paradoxical novel, truth is a secret shared between perpetrator, novelist and reader. Everybody else, including the authorities of church and university, are completely taken in.

In the closing years of the twentieth century, the tendency to back-project the circumstances of modern academic life onto fifth-century Egypt proved irresistible. Caterina Contini's *Ipazia e la notte* opens in what would appear to be Freshers' Week 414. It offers us a Hypatia who is squeamish, fastidious, highly strung and deeply devoted both to her students and to the Greek pantheon. When the pagan shrines of Alexandria are closed on the orders of the emperor, and Orestes the Prefect lamely accepts the edict, Hypatia is appalled: "Chi governa questa città," she asks Orestes, "tu o Cirillo?"[17] [Who governs this city, you or Cyril?] In the subsequent power struggle between Christians and the now persecuted pagans, society rapidly bifurcates, producing a state almost of civil war. Hypatia knows that she is in danger. From the tower of her house—a kind of ivory tower—she watches the stars for the last time, and then descends to lecture to her students. "Abbiate cura di voi e continuate a filosofare," she enjoins them: "Look after yourselves and continue to philosophize." The following day she meets her death, a martyr for that profoundly twentieth-century cause: the integrity of the intelligentsia at a time of glowering extremes. It might be Hitler's Germany, Mussolini's Italy, Pol Pot's Cambodia. What Contini offers us is a parable of the liberal academic as responsible victim.

Italia Morici's *Conversazioni con Ipazia* (1982) ups the ideological stakes even further by staging a series of what amount to weekly research seminars at Hypatia's house, with a programme of relevant topics and a visiting speaker from Ravenna. This ardent group discuss the respective advantages of monotheistic and polytheistic systems, the nature of spirituality and the rights of women. In place of Contini's impartial and serene heroine, Morici presents us with a committed ideologue, her mind and speech filled with the urgency of some proleptic Women's Movement.

As the speaker from Ravenna remarks: "La sua eloquenza e sempre fluente ed appassionata, ma...quando fra discepoli si discute della condizione femminile, Ipazie diventa pui aggressiva del solito e passa con disinvoltura dall'ironia scherzanda al sarcasmo pungente"[18] [Her eloquence is always fluent and passionate, but...when she gets to the topic of the condition of women, Hypatia passes by turns from playful irony to cutting sarcasm]. Her Platonism, it has to be said, is of a somewhat reversionary sort; ignoring the misogyny of the *Timaeus*, she delivers a paper demanding a re-organisation along egalitarian lines responsive to the complementarity of genders. The person from Ravenna is impressed. "Avresti meritato di vivere in un'epoca migliore di questa" [You deserve to have lived in a better age than this], he informs her. As if to emphasise the point, the narrative of Hypatia's death places the blame squarely on Cyril's shoulders. A monk appears from nowhere and unceremoniously dumps what is left of her in the garden, before the astonished eyes of her students. Somewhat surprisingly under the circumstances, several desert to the Christian cause.

From Hypatia the feminist to Hypatia the racial icon is but a short step. It was taken in 1987 with the publication of Martin Bernal's *Black Athena: The Afroasiatic Roots of Classical Civilization*. Bernal's book is a concerted and scholarly attempt to place the argument for ancient Greece's debt to Egypt—and hence by extension to Africa—on firm empirical foundations. Undoubtedly it is a response to the *zeitgeist*, but it also answers back to certain elements in legend, exemplified in the case of Hypatia by Kingsley's description of her death. Remember her "snow-white against the dusky mass around"; remember too her "other long white arm" and how "the dark mass closed over her again". Bernal opens his second chapter with his own account of this episode, understandably complaining about an "Aryan tradition" that has construed the lynching of the philosopher in terms of "a resurgence of Egyptian fanaticism against Hellenistic rationalism". For Bernal it is quite otherwise: an act of violence marking "the end of Egypto-Paganism and the beginning of the Christian dark ages".[19] Maria Dzielska remarks at one point that Charles Kingsley would dearly like Hypatia to have been some sort of proto-Protestant. One might equally speculate that Bernal would dearly love her to have been black or Berber. He also wants to view Ptolemaic Egypt not as the product of the superimposition of Macedonian manners on a subject indigenous population—or even of a blending of the two—so much as an expression of an authentically African intellectuality that was exported to, rather than imported to, Greece. In the process he benefits from a tendency in several of the twentieth-century accounts to expand the meaning of the term "paganism" whilst endowing it with a strongly positive ideological charge. As a response not so much to the documented case history of Hypatia as to certain unpleasant elements in her culturally transmitted legend—the theme, after all, of this chapter— Bernal's argument was both timely and just.

The twenty-first century has led Hypatia in some radically new directions, bridging both space and time. Paul Levinson's *The Plot to Save Socrates*, for example, begins in Athens in the year 2042, where Sierra Waters, an American postgraduate student, sets out on a long journey that will lead her through many embodiments, the last and definitive one of which is the historical Hypatia of Alexandria. In *Azazeel* by Egypt's own Youssef Ziedan, Hypatia's murder is observed by a monk, physician and disciple of Nestorius, who tells his and her tale in thirty scrolls supposedly translated from the Syriac. Ziedan's controversial purpose was seemingly to remind the Egypt of the Arab Spring of its forgotten Christian past. In stark contrast, the use to which Hypatia's legend has been put in the United States remains in line with the anticlerical bias of Tolland and Gibbon. This tendency was already marked in Carl Sagan's 1980 TV series *Cosmos*, where her fate—that of a martyr to reason and science—was collated with the destruction of the library of Alexandria, reputedly by Philistine Christian monks. The 2014 version of the series re-iterated the rationalist message, more flamboyantly depicted in the 2009 film *Agora*, in which Hypatia, fetchingly played by the then thirty-nine-year-old Rachel Weisz, is publicly confronted by an intemperate and fanatical Cyril with the accusation that she "believes in nothing". "I believe in Philosophy," she retorts, whereupon Cyril whips up his monkish followers into an orgy of bloodlust. They are about to stone Hypatia to death when, in a telling concession to twenty-first-century squeamishness, she is humanely suffocated by her disciple and lover, Davus.

This leads one towards some tentatively phrased conclusions. Martin Bernal interpreted Hypatia as existing at the great divide between one age, one cultural phase, and another. He was far from alone in this. From Gibbon onwards she has been offered up, not as one might expect as a marginal, but as a defining figure. The definitions fluctuate, of course, but it is scarcely surprising that she has appealed on the one hand to Catholic and post-Catholic societies and on the other to colonial and postcolonial conditions. Imperialism and its decline, of course, are central to Gibbon's theme; he had also, let it be remembered, briefly been a Catholic before turning to his own particular brand of humane scepticism. Charles

Kingsley, descended though his mother from white plantation stock in the Caribbean, returns over and over to questions of race; his anti-Catholicism was also fairly rabid, and his deep love–hate relationship with the Church of Pio Nono is a matter of his intimate biography.[20]

That Hypatia has repeatedly appeared in various guises in the literature of Italy and Quebec—both languishing under a colonial yoke in the early modern period, in the case of Italy somewhat longer, and both marked by the presence of Catholicism—is therefore no coincidence. There are other continuities. Bernal's argument may seem modish, but it is rooted in a much older debate concerning the meaning and content of Hellenism, stretching from Matthew Arnold and Johann Winckelmann through Walter Pater, then Gilbert Murray and the Cambridge Ritualists, right up to the present day. It is a debate the beginnings of which even Kingsley would have recognised and which, towards its latter end, touches on the work of Wole Soyinka and Derek Walcott.

My lasting hunch is that that Hypatia has proved an attractive and resurgent figure insofar as she embodies the divide between what we regard as "reason" and what we have come to mean by the "irrational". Time and time again she exposes just how we line up other urgent or topical polarities—sexual, religious or political—in relation to that sometimes quite arbitrary underlying binary. In the process, Hypatia has been thoroughly dismembered by our critical cutlery, be it roof tiles, shards or oyster shells. But whenever and wherever women intellectuals, secularists and rationalists of various affiliations require a pattern and example, Hypatia will be waiting at the departure gate, hand luggage packed, willing and able to travel.

NOTES

1. Palladas, *Poems* a selection translated and introduced by Tony Harrison (London: Anvil in association with Rex Collings, 1975), 67 with note. The case for and against Palladas' authorship of the Hypatia poem is put by G. Luck, *Harvard Studies in Classical Philology* (1958), vol. lxiii, 462–66.
2. Maria Dzielska, *Hypatia of Alexandra*, trans. F. Lyra (Harvard University Press, 1995).
3. Caterina Contini, *Ipazia e la notte: romanza* (Milan: Longanesi, 1999).
4. *Epistolae Synesii Cyrensis*, ed. A. Garyza (Rome: Instituto Polygrafico, 1979).
5. Charles Kingsley, *Hypatia, or New Foes with an Old Face* Re-printed from *Fraser's Magazine* (London: Macmillan, 1853).

6. Damascius, *The Life of Isidore* in *Suidae Lexicon*, ed Ada Adler (Stuttgart: Teubner, 1935); Socrates Scholasticus, *Ecclesiastical History* in *Patrologia Graecae* (Paris, 1857–66), vol. 67; *The Chronicle of John, Coptic Bishop of Nikui*, ed. R.H. Charles (Amsterdam, 1916).
7. It is one of the many ironies of the situation that Socrates' word is related to "ostracism", the process by which the ancient Athenians voted to banish unpopular people by writing names on shards. I am grateful to Dr Emily Greenwood for confirming this observation.
8. Mindful of the contagion, the Church in the early twentieth century removed Catherine from the calendar; not that this has made much difference to the respective myths that have grown up around two sets of uncertain facts.
9. John Tolland, *Hypatia, or, the History of the Most Beautiful, Most Virtuous, Most Learned and in Every Way Accomplished Lady; Who was Torn in Pieces by the Clergy of Alexandria, to Gratify the Pride, Emulation, and Cruelty of the Archbishop, Commonly but Undeservedly Titled St. Cyril* (London: 1720, second ed. 1753), unpaginated. A year later Toland's diatribe was unctuously answered by Thomas Lewis in his *The History of Hypatia, A Most Impudent Schoolmistress of Alexandria. In Defence of the Alexandrian Clergy from the Aspertions of Mr. Toland* (London: 1721). From the partiality of Lewis's tone, a strong impression is created that it is the Anglican—rather than the Alexandrian—clergy that he is defending, and bluestockings of his own age whom he is bringing to book.
10. Edward Gibbon, *The History of Decline and Fall of the Roman Empire* (London, 1776–83), chap. 47.
11. However, for another sympathetic treatment of Cyril see Charles Leconte de Lisle's poem "Hypatie". There are two versions: the first in 1847, the second in 1874. [For a decent recent edition covering both, see Charles Leconte de Lisle, *Poèmes antiques*, ed. Claudine Gothot-Mersche (Gallimard, 1994)]. See also Leconte de Lisle's verse drama *Hypatie et Cyrille* (1857).
12. Contessa Diodata Roero si Saluzzo, *Ipazie ovvero delle filosofie*, 2 vols (Torino: Chirio E. Mina, 1827), vol. ii, 215.
13. Kingsley, *Hypatia*, 320.
14. This provocation had been offered in Kingsley's review of J.A. Froude's *History of England from the Fall of Wolsey to the Defeat of the Spanish Armada*, vols. vii and viii. The review appeared in the issue of *Macmillan's Magazine* for January 1864, and was signed 'C.K.'. It dealt with Froude's coverage of Henry VIII's divorce crisis, concerning the role of the papacy in which Kingsley had notoriously remarked that, in the early Tudor period, "The Roman religion had, for some time past, been making men not better, but worse."

15. Andrée Ferretti, *Renaissance en Paganie; récit* (Quebec: Saint Leonoard, 1987), 23.
16. Jean Marcel, *Hypatie, or la fin des dieux* (Montreal: Leméac, 1989), 214.
17. Caterinia Contini, *Ipazia e la notte*, (Milan: Longanini, 1999), 116.
18. Italia Morici, *Conversationi con Ipazie* (Milan: Nuove Editioni, 1990), 39. For other late twentieth-century fictional treatments, see Mario Luzi, *Libro di Ipazie e Il messaggero* (Milan, 1978) and Arnulf Zitelmann, *Hypatia* (Weinheim and Basel, 1989). For an academic treatment of Hypatia as viewed from a feminist perspective, see M.R. Leftkowitz, *Women in Greek Myth* (Baltimore, 1986) and U. Molarino, "A Christian Martyr in Reverse: Hypatia 370–412AD", *Hypatia: A Journal of Feminist Philosophy*, 4 (1989), 6–8.
19. Martin Bernal, *Black Athena: The Afroasiatic Roots of Classical Civilization* (New Brunswick, New Jersey: 1987), vol. i, 121–2.
20. For Kingsley's youthful agonising over the attractions and repulsions of Catholicism, see especially Susan Chitty, *The Beast and the Monk: A Life of Charles Kingsley* (London: 1975). As a young man Kingsley had once fantasised about visiting a monastery in France where, after making his public confession, he would offer his naked body to the monks to be "scourged by them". See letter to his future wife Fanny, December 1843, BL Add Ms. 62552.

CHAPTER 5

Cultural Migration as Protestant Nostalgia: (1) British Listeners in Italy

An important aspect of cultural migration is the reality of assimilation. An equally evident by-product is the fact of resistance. In the case of England, the insularity of which observers sometimes complain was for at least three centuries—from say the Elizabethan Church settlement to the re-establishment of the Roman Catholic hierarchy in 1850—bolstered by religious prejudice. To all intents and purposes England was a Protestant country; much of the rest of Europe, with the notable exceptions of Holland, certain Swiss cantons and large parts of what is now northern Germany, were stoutly Roman Catholic.

No episode in the history of the British Isles epitomises more vividly the recurrent love–hate relationship with Europe characteristic of the nation than the trauma of the English Reformation. The severance it caused represented both a source of conflict and affront and, especially in the cultural sphere, a stimulus to mutual curiosity. The severance of sensibility recorded by the Catholic historian Eamon Duffy in his books *The Stripping of the Altars* and *Saints, Sacrilege and Sedition* inflicted a running wound on the mentality of the English people.[1] Arguably from the time of the dissolution of the monasteries in 1538 to at least the last half of the nineteenth century, England possessed a Protestant consciousness combined with a subconscious mind that was romantically Catholic, constantly welling up in music, stories and poems. Shakespeare compared his middle-aged condition to that of the "bare ruin'd choirs, where late the sweet birds sang", remnants of the Roman Catholic monastic foundations that

© The Author(s) 2018
R. Fraser, *Literature, Music and Cosmopolitanism*,
https://doi.org/10.1007/978-3-319-68480-2_5

surrounded him in his youth.[2] John Donne was born a Catholic and spent his childhood among dedicated Jesuits, of whom both his mother and his brother were strong defenders; after becoming Dean of the Anglican Cathedral of St Paul, his sermons were still peppered with allusions to Catholic thinkers.[3]

In the following three chapters I would like to examine three linked instances of the religious split personality in England, of what I contentiously style "Protestant nostalgia", during the early modern period. The first concerns the cult of Italian, especially ecclesiastical, music as experienced by successive English visitors to Italy. The second involves the veiled "longing" evident in several ardently Protestant writers from Milton to Ruskin for Catholic literature and art. The third relates to the persistence of Latin as an ecclesiastical and scholarly vernacular.

For much of the period in question, a tidal pull seems to be operating from the south to the north of Europe. Both poles were visibly affected by the resulting attraction and the resistance which it so often provoked. The ensuing complex of feelings has much to tell us about the ways in which the sort of cultural migration of which we are speaking mirrored, and still mirrors, migration of the demographic kind. I begin in the reign of James I of England—that is, of James VI of Scotland—son of a devout Catholic mother and, during his occupation of the English throne, the continual target of Catholic plots, of which the Gunpowder Plot of 1605 was only the most flagrant.

THE IMPORTANCE OF IMPORTS

My first story begins, famously, with a pair of shoes. The shoes adorned the feet of one of most inquisitive eccentrics to grace the England of the royal Stuarts. Thomas Coryate was a clergyman's son from Odcombe in Somerset, a Wykehamist and Oxford graduate and sometime jester in the court of Prince Henry, elder son of James I. But in 1608, wanderlust struck him, and he set out to journey from his native Somerset across France and onwards to Venice, travelling by a mixture of ship, horseback and footslogging with the famous shoes. The shoes survived and so did he to tell a strange tale, and start several minor revolutions.

His specialism was to introduce into England from Italy a few objects and habits now thought of as quintessentially British. Every time a cloudburst obliges us to seek cover, we are indebted to Coryate, who had noticed the way in which the citizens of Turin, Milan and Venice protected themselves from the broiling sun. "Many of them", he observed, "doe carry other fine things…which they call in the Italian tongue 'umbrellaes'. They are made of leather somewhat answerable to the form of a little canopy and hooped on the inside with divers little wooden hoopes that extend the umbrella in a pretty large compass."[4]

And every time we sit down to dinner, we are indebted to him for another import, until then unique to Italy. He had observed the Italians eating (though not the kinds of food now associated with them, since tomatoes—those culinary migrants from the New World—were not to be adopted into Italian cuisine for a further century[5]). "The Italians and also most strangers that are commorant in Italy", he had perceived, "doe always at their meales use a little forke when they cut their meate. For while with their knife which they hold in one hand, they cut the meate out of the dish, they fasten their forke which they holde in their other hand upon the same dish, so that whatsoever he be that sitting in the company of others at a meale, should unadvisedly touch the dish of meate with his fingers from which all of those at the table doe cut, he will give occasion of offence to the company, as having transgressed the lawes of good manners, in so much that for his error, he shall be at the least browbeaten, if not reprehended in words."[6] When Coryate returned to England he had this exotic implement re-created for him, doing much to tame the traditional and uncouth hands-on approach of his countrymen to foraging.

"Supernatural…for Clearness"

Apart from the assisted migration of forks and umbrellas, Coryate also achieved subtler effects.

The Feast of Saint Roche: Saturday, 16 August 1608. In the upper hall of the Scuola Grande di San Rocco in Venice, beneath a ceiling of biblical scenes gorgeously painted by Tintoretto, a concert is being held in honour of the fraternity's saint: none other than the aforesaid Roche, frequently invoked to secure the city from one of its regular visitations of plague. The programme this evening consists of motets by Giovanni Gabrieli accompanied by a consort of sackbuts, cornets and violas de gamba, and of solo songs by Bartholomeo Barbarino, a forty-year-old former organist of Pesaro Cathedral and an accomplished falsettist, performed by the composer himself with chitarrone continuo. Barbarino thinks his own voice "raucous", but our English visitor disagrees. Coryate is sitting in the audience beneath those Tintoretto frescoes. As Barbarino starts to sing, he is charmed. The soloist, he later reported, had a "peerless and (as I may in a manner say) a supernatural voice for clearness...I always thought he was an Eunuch which if he had been, it had taken away some part of my admiration, because they do most commonly sing passing well, but he was not, therefore it was the more admirable. It was nothing forced, strained or affected, but came from him with the greatest facility that ever I heard."[7]

Coryate, though, was in a quandary. The son of an Anglican clergyman, convinced of the exclusive merits of the Christian Reformation, he spent much of his time in Italy fulminating against the gaudy excesses of its Catholic architecture. On one or two occasions, with dire results, he attempted to convert local Catholic congregations to the merits of the true reformed faith, and he even went as far as to enter the Synagogue and harangue the Jews of the Ghetto. He narrowly escaped with his life since, chased out onto the canal bank, he was only saved from the wrath of the Hebrews by the English ambassador Sir Henry Wotton, who happened to be passing by in his gondola.[8] After returning to England and preparing his book, Coryate was on his travels again: again largely on foot, this time through Turkey to India, where he perished in Mandu, Madhya Pradesh, in December 1617. His comments on Indian music would have been worth having.

With his account of that Saint Roche–day concert, however, there enters into the literature of cultural reception an observation frequent among post-Reformation English visitors to Italy: a wary admiration for the elusive serenity associated with upper voices the tessitura of which the hearer cannot quite place. The epitome of this vogue was perhaps to be the cult of the castrato, whom Coryate calls a Eunuch, concentrated with peculiar tenacity on the person of the singer whom the English called Farinelli.

"Auditui meo dabis gaudiam et laetitiam"

He was actually Carlo Broschi, though the Italians called him Farinello. Of the quality of his voice we have the expert testimony of that German flautist Johann Joachim Quantz, who heard him in Naples in 1725. Farinello, he reported, possessed a "penetrating, full, rich, bright and well-modulated soprano voice...His intonation was pure, his trill beautiful, his breath control extraordinary and his throat very agile, so that he performed even the widest intervals quickly and with the greatest ease and certainty."[9] Handel tried to lure him to England and failed. It took the offices of the English ambassador to Turin, Lord Essex, eventually to persuade Broschi to London, where he joined a company run by his old singing teacher—reputedly the best voice coach in Italy—Nicolò Porpora. After a season Porpora's company failed, but for a further two years Farinelli remained in London, feted and indulged. In 1734, however, he received an offer he could not refuse to cure the Spanish king's blues by singing to him every night in Madrid. It was yet another British ambassador, Benjamin Keene, who secured this move, and the English public, which had grown besotted, resented the desertion sorely. Complained *The Daily Post*, Farinelli "gets at least £5000 a year in England, yet he is not ashamed to run about like a Stroller from Kingdom to Kingdom, as if we did not give him sufficient encouragement".[10]

By 1771, Broschi was long retired and living in relative seclusion on his estate outside Bologna. Yet he could not keep the English at bay. In that year, 162 years after Coryate, the musicologist and author Charles Burney was visiting Venice to collect materials for a *General History of Music*. Again it was Assumption-tide, and in early August he attended a concert of sacred music in the Ospedaletto a Santi Giovanni e Paolo. As he entered the church, a fifteen-year-old soprano from Ferrara called Adriana Gabrieli was singing an aria from a "Salve Regina" by Antonio Sacchini. She was later to make an accomplished Susanna in *Le nozze di Figaro* and Fiordiligi in *Così fan tutte*. What amazed Burney was Gabrieli's range: she had, he wrote in his account of his travels, "an extraordinary compass of voice, as she was able to reach the highest E on our harpsichords, upon which she could dwell for a considerable time, in a fair, natural voice".[11] Much Italian vocal practice, as he confessed, lay beyond Burney's experience: he had, for example, never before heard a contralto take the bottom line of a trio of girls' voices, a frequent practice in the city's four female orphanages where, as he puts it, "many of the girls sing in the counter-tenor as low as A and G, which enables them always to keep below the *soprano* and *mezzo-soprano*, to which they sing the bass". (The effect is heard with particular poignancy in that object of a later English musical craze, the Pergolesi *Stabat Mater*.) In Milan, in his quest for the deepest roots of European tonality, Burney twice visited the Duomo to experience the wimpling wing of Ambrosian chant with its four prescribed modes, a subject that he also researched from manuscripts in the famous Ambrosian library. In Florence, he followed a company of Laudisti, itinerant psalm singers, down from the hillside of Fiesole: "They stopt at every church in their way, to sing a stanza in three parts; and when they arrived at their own church, into which I gained admission, there was a band of instruments to receive them who, between every stanza that they sang, played a symphony." Castrati evidently fascinated him, since he made a lengthy detour to Bologna to talk with Farinelli, whom he heard sing in his house on Tuesday, 23 August. A week later, on 30 August, Burney attended a day-long recital of sacred music at the church of Santo Johanni in Monte, and in the interval he chatted with another musical visitor: the fifteen-year-old Wolfgang Amadeus Mozart.

For such visitors, diverse musical experiences were as essential an aspect of the Grand Tour as the viewing of art and, as there, what they do not say is often as illuminating as what they do say. There is often an implied contrast between what they are used to and what they find, with the result that their accounts are frequently as revealing about English musical life at the time as Italian. For many, used to the vocabulary of scores and habituated to Italian opera in London or Dublin, Italy was quite simply the land of music. This was clearly the case, for example, with the tenor Michael Kelly, later a manager of the Theatre Royal, Haymarket. In the 1770s Kelly had studied under Italian singing teachers in Dublin and then Naples, and by his late teens was taking on minor roles in smaller Italian opera houses. He was thus in a position to render a double account of Italian musical life: from the point of view both of a performer and of the audience. The reactions of the audiences he encountered in both capacities were emphatic and sometimes dramatic, echoing his own stormy temperament. In 1781 he was present in the Teatro Argentina in Rome when a tenor named Gabrieli, a brother of the celebrated soprano Caterina Gabrieli, was booed off the stage within five bars of his debut. Disinclined to brazen it out, the unfortunate young man came to the front, publicly congratulated the critics on their taste and then quitted the opera stage, never to darken it again. The following year in Brescia, Kelly re-created the title role in Cimarosa's opera *Il pittore parigino*, but so convincing were the transports he directed towards his *prima donna* in the second act that he was forced to flee the town later that night in face of threats issued by her lover, who had been in the audience. The incident propelled Kelly towards Venice, where he was recruited by the Austrian emperor for his opera house, and thus to a brief fame as Don Curzio and Don Basilio in the first production of *Le nozze di Figaro* in Vienna.

In his *Reminiscences* dictated late in his life, Kelly recounts his musical activities in both Italy and Austria. As a cradle Roman Catholic, it is clear for instance that he had a strong personal affinity for the music of the

Italian church, observing of his visit to Rome that "when the Pope chants the *Te Deum*, assisted by the choir, and in some parts by the whole congregation (generally possessing good voices and fine ears), the effect produced is certainly fine, but it is in the Pope's chapel that one can hear to perfection the divine music of Palestrina".[12]

Already the English preoccupation with the agility of Italian voices had found a focus in one work: Allegri's setting of the *Miserere*, officially a monopoly of the Vatican where it was performed exclusively on Good Friday. Six months prior to meeting Burney, Mozart had heard it in the Sistine Chapel and famously transcribed it from memory, but it was Burney who had secured a copy from the composer Battista San Martini in Milan, and published it in London the following year, complete with re-created ornamental *bellimenti*.[13] In Rome the work remained a major tourist attraction through the nineteenth century, attracting amateurs like the not especially musical John Leland Maquay, manager of the Irish bank in Florence. In March 1825 Maquay heard the work twice, once in the chapel itself and once in a private house.[14] In March 1860 George Eliot, who was on tour with her consort G.H. Lewes, attended the annual performance in the Sistine, standing in awe at its beauty and, as she wrote in a letter, with a feeling of affinity for other worshippers that transcended religious differences. In her account she mixes aesthetic delight with the kind of inbred suspicion that in *Middlemarch* she was to attribute to Dorothea Brooke, like her the product of a constrained Protestant Midlands upbringing, standing before the statues of the Vatican museum. Later still, Eliot transposed similar reactions into the mind of Daniel Deronda as, re-discovering his Jewish faith, he stood in the synagogue in Frankfurt and "gave himself up to that strongest effect of chanted liturgies which is independent of detailed verbal meaning—like the effect of an Allegri's *Miserere* or a Palestrina's *Magnificat*".[15] Almost despite themselves, Jew and Protestant gentile alike are transported by the power of this distinctively Catholic music.

Music and Its Lovers

At the *fin de siècle* it is possible to observe a reversal of the formula whereby performance dictated and provoked reception. As in the closing years of the nineteenth century an interest in and concern with historical authenticity took hold, more and more recorded reception from earlier periods contrived to inform performance. To begin with the practice was uncertain, and the reactions very mixed. Witness the audience response to an afternoon concert held at the Teatro della Pergola in Florence on 16 January 1897, attended by many of the city's culturally curious English residents. The Pergola is Florence's most prestigious concert venue, associated with the premiere there of Verdi's *Macbeth* on 14 March 1847. Half a century later, it hosted a recital of what we would now call early music, vocal and instrumental, by, among others, a French harpsichordist and recent addition to one of London's leading musical émigré families. Elodie (inevitably "Mélodie") Desirée was soon to marry the manufacturer of early musical instruments and champion of the recorder, Arnold Dolmetsch; in the meantime she had prematurely taken his surname while they lived in sin in Dulwich, whence Elodie had set forth on this proselytising Italian tour. In the stalls sat the twenty-three-year old socialite Lina Duff Gordon, later Waterfield, who reported on the scene to a friend: "I have not yet told you of the music. It was a 'concerto di musica antica' with the old instruments—arpsichordo, Viola d'Amore e violin, and the Viola Tenore, and everyone was interested, though I cannot say *charmed* by the sounds produced by these strange forgotten instruments. The harpsichord resembles nothing so much as the spinnet of our grandmothers, and nearly drove us all mad with its tinkling tones. The Signora Dolmetch played a fugue in re minore, and it never changed but stuck at the re minore for about half an hour. Can you imagine anything more disastrous to the nerves?"[16]

Not everybody was this unimpressed. For much of that evening the judgmental Lina had been hiding behind her fan to avoid catching the eye of the city's most illustrious Early Music Enthusiast: the forty-one-year-old, Boulogne-born English expatriate Viola Paget, who wrote ghost stories and music and art criticism under the *nom-de-plume* Vernon Lee. Lee not only appreciated the harpsichord, but owned and played one in her fourteenth-century villa, the Residenza del Palmerino, out on the old Fiesole road. For her, this recital of "music not heard for a century" was manna from Heaven. Paget was a kind of template of *fin-de-siècle* cultural migration: mother from a planter's family in Jamaica, father the son of an émigré French nobleman, fluent herself in four European languages. Seventeen years previously, at the age of twenty-four, she had written the extensively researched *Studies of the Eighteenth Century in Italy* that contained lengthy chapters on the musical scene and opera of the period. Her main source for both was Burney, and there she recounts it all with exemplary empathy: the Venetian street and gondola music, the cult of Farinelli, "the exclusive and passionate worship of the human voice, which formed the mainspring of Italian music".[17]

Differences in musical style fascinated Lee, as did the varieties and psychology of listener response. So much so that fifteen years later, in 1912, she compiled a lengthy questionnaire that she sent round to 150 music-loving friends throughout Europe, posing such questions as:

QUERY IV
In actually listening to harmonies do you:

(A) Distinguish the constituent notes? Always or often?
(B) Distinguish the simultaneous movements or parts? Or (always in listening to harmonies) do
(C) The harmonies seem something vague, a sort of halo around a single thread of melody?
(D) Do the notes *which are not the melody* become a sort of *sound colour*, like the *quality* of a single instrument or voice? Etc

Published in 1932 in her book *Music and Its Lovers: An Empirical Study of Emotion and Imaginative Responses to Music*, the results of this survey represent an incisive guide to listener responses in the first third of the twentieth century.

The Top C That Never Was

Throughout Europe in any case, attention to the changing interface between audience psychology and the realities of performance was beginning to clarify distinctions between what was heard and what was thought to have been heard. Thus in the following century interpretations of historical Italian music increasingly took the form of revivals or rediscoveries, conducted in the light of existing listener accounts, taken either as guides to performing and editorial practice, or as indications of what might be enhanced, or even avoided.

The growing cult around Allegri in England in the late twentieth century, to take one stark example, drew on just this sort of informed re-imagining. In 1951 the Welsh-born organist of Worcester Cathedral, Ivor Atkins, collated editions of the *Miserere* by Burney and Mendelssohn to produce a version of his own and, reaching for the sort of elusive ethereality described by early listeners such as Coryate, inserted a top C towards the end of the treble part of the smaller of its two antiphonal choirs.[18] In little more than a decade this idealised high point became an inalienable aspect of the work's appeal. The inception of the modern British cult of Allegri can actually be pinpointed to a particular moment in listening history: 4.30 on the afternoon of Wednesday 27 February 1963 towards the close of a broadcast of Choral Evensong, then on the BBC Home Service. The choir was that of King's College Cambridge and the Master of the Choristers, David Willcocks. As they launched into the *Miserere* in Atkins's questionable edition and Roy Goodman's treble voice reached for that uncanny top C, I cannot have been the only one who rushed to a nearby upright piano in an attempt to locate the authentic pitch of this inauthentic note. The contemporary vogue for performing the *Miserere* on Ash Wednesday begins with that shared experience, and a Decca recording of the work made the following month with the same vocal forces. It is now as essential an element in an English Lent as hot cross buns.

A counter-example is provided by Monteverdi. Burney for one was baffled by him. Though he recognised his superiority as a madrigalist, he could make little sense of the operas. Used to the strict division between recitative and aria in works by Handel he had heard in London, the free generic flow of *Orfeo* quite took him aback. "It is", he complains in his *History*, "as difficult to distinguish airs from recitative, as in the operas of Peri and Caccini"[19]; he then devotes five pages to proving that in his works, whether secular or sacred, Monteverdi broke every precept, including the rational ban on consecutive octaves and fifths. It was this very formal freedom, however, that was to inspire the great post-war rediscovery of Monteverdi during the twentieth century in England. The development that set this off was the late re-discovery of *L'incoronazione di Poppea*. Unperformed between 1561 and 1913, it first emerged in modern British consciousness in 1948 when Michael Tippett directed a performance at Morley College. The popular craze for the work, however, is almost contemporaneous with that for Allegri, since the production that brought it into the limelight was that directed by Raymond Leppard at Glyndebourne in 1962, interposing between Monteverdi and us an English libretto and a large, inauthentic orchestra. The distance travelled between that and the Glyndebourne production directed from the keyboard by Emmanuelle Haïm in 2008 is marked by a systematic re-examination of manuscripts, but it also benefitted from closer attention to a Renaissance aesthetic to which one sure guide is provided by early listeners such as Coryate. The same sort of re-positioning in time was to inform twentieth-century interpretations of the Vespers such as that recorded by

Eliot Gardiner in St Mark's in 1989. An additional factor was a renewed respect for the acoustic qualities of a church which, with his preference for a dry sound over a resonant one, Burney castigates in 1770 as "breaking up" the music before it reaches the ear.

Yet the most spectacular instance of such systematic re-imagining must surely be Vivaldi. For centuries before the mid-twentieth century, in England as elsewhere, he was largely forgotten. By the time Burney reached Venice, Vivaldi's star had long been eclipsed by the recently deceased Tartini and the sociable and persuasive Galuppi. Hence, though he describes at some length the musical activities at the Ospedale della Pietà where Vivaldi had taught violin in the 1720s, on the subject of the red priest himself Burney is almost silent. In his travels, though anxious to air his knowledge of the local music scene in all its aspects, he does not accord Vivaldi a single mention. In his *History* he briefly alludes to the fact that Vivaldi had composed fifteen operas, yet does not appear to have heard any of them. The only work of Vivaldi's of which he had direct experience seems to have been the Cuckoo concerto that he could dimly recall a lay clerk in Hereford Cathedral, a man reputedly of Italian extraction, performing at rural concerts in his distant youth. On the question of Vivaldi's extinct reputation he is obliged to rely on an earlier traveller, Edward Wright, who, following three tours of Italy during Vivaldi's lifetime, had reported that in Venice "it is very usual to see Priests in the orchestra: the famous Vivaldi (whom they call the *Prete rosso*) very well known amongst us for his concertos, was a topping man among them".[20] Fifty years later, to Burney himself, Vivaldi appeared to be a has-been whose sole virtue had resided in the opportunity he had provided for virtuosic display. Vivaldi's *La stravaganza*, Burney acerbically remarks in his *History*, formerly occupied the highest favour among "flashy players", but the "chief merit" of these lively concerti "was their rapid execution". "If acute and rapid tones are evils", he censoriously concludes, "then Vivaldi has much of the sin to answer for."[21]

Yet, ironically perhaps, it was these very causes of eighteenth-century dissent that were to form the foundations for Vivaldi's twentieth-century revival. Scholastically speaking, this begins with Marc Pincherle's *Vivaldi: Génie du Baroque* in 1948, but his popular cult decidedly commences with LP (long-playing record) technology. Following a Decca recording of 1959, *Le quattro stagioni* became by the mid-1960s an integral ingredient in middle-brow musical taste right across the English-speaking world. Soon, in a thousand bookshops from Surbiton to San Francisco, bibliophiles were being seduced into unpremeditated purchases by baroque insinuations of spring. What beguiled these listeners, or half-listeners, was precisely the apparent exhibitionistic display that earlier offended Burney's insular Augustinianism. Vivaldi as musack, Vivaldi as kitsch, even, in the hands of Nigel Kennedy, Vivaldi as rap were products of a motorised consciousness which relished precisely that busy quality of relentlessness that repelled an English traveller in 1770. Nowadays in Venice, the city that so quickly forgot the red priest, you will find a performance of The Seasons advertised every evening of the year. For today's English tourists therefore, Vivaldi *is* the sound of Venice, though what is heard, and the manner in which it is heard, are arguably as much products of the modern age as the compositions of Luigi Nono who lived down the quayside. Which only goes to show that, when it comes to the cultural migration of established works, preconception and habit are frequently as active agents as actual observation.

Notes

1. Eamon Duffy, *The Stripping of the Altars: Traditional Religion in England, 1401–1570* (New Haven, CT and London: Yale University Press, 1992); and *Saints, Sacrilege and Sedition: Religion and Conflict in the Tudor Reformations* (London: Bloomsbury, 2012).
2. In Sonnet 73. For Shakespeare's lingering debt to Catholicism, see A.D. Nuttall, *Shakespeare the Thinker* (New Haven, CT and London: Yale University Press, 2007), 17–19, 34–7, 59, 96, 110–11.
3. For the long-term consequences of Donne's Jesuit upbringing, see Francesca Bugliani Knox, *The Eye of the Eagle: John Donne and the Legacy of Ignatius Loyola* (London: Peter Lang, 2011). See also Robert Fraser, "Riddling Soul: John Donne, Theatrical Performer of His Various Selves and Maker of an Oddly Modern Music, *The Times Literary Supplement*, no. 5653, August 5, 2011, 3–4.
4. *Coryate's Crudities. Hastily gobbled up in five moneths travels in France, Savoy, Italy, Rhetia commonly called the Grisons county, Helvetia alias Switzerland, some parts of High Germany and the Netherlands; newly digested in the hungry aire of Odcombe in the County of Somerset, and now dispensed to the nourishment of the travelling members of this Kingdom* (1611) (Glasgow: James Maclehose and Sons, 1905), vol. 1, 257.
5. See David Gentilcourt, *Pomodoro! A History of the Tomato in Italy* (Columbia University Press, 2010).
6. Coryate, *Crudities*, i, 236.
7. Coryate, *Crudities*, i, 391.

8. Coryate, *Crudities*, i, 374–76.
9. Quantz's account is in Freidrich Wilhelm Marpurg, *Historische-kritishe Beyträge zur Aufnahme der Musik* (Berlin, 1754). See entry for 11 May 1726.
10. *Daily Post* (London), 7 July 1737.
11. Charles Burmey, *The Present State of Music in France and Italy* (London: T. Becket, 1771), 143.
12. Michael Kelly, *Solo Recital: The Reminiscences of Michael Kelly*, ed. Herbert van Thal, Intro. J.C. Trewin (London: The Folio Society, 1972), 51.
13. *La Musica che si canta annualmente nelle funzioni della settimana santa, nella cappella pontificia da Palestrina, Allegri e Bai*. Raccolta e pubblicata da C. Burney (London: Robert Bremner, 1771). The text is taken from the Vulgate version of Psalm 50, and verse 8 as sung reads "Auditui meo dabis gaudiam et laetitiam: et exultabunt ossa humiliata." In the Anglican *Book of Common Prayer* of 1662, the Psalm is re-numbered as 51, and the translation given is Giles Coverdale's: "Thou shalt make me hear of joy and gladness: that the bones that thou hast broken may rejoice." A fine recording of the work, though with a slower tempo than is sometimes the case, by the Choir of New College, Oxford may be heard at https://www.youtube.com/watch?v=36Y_ztEW1NE
14. British Institute in Florence, Harold Acton Library, *The Journals of John Leland Maquay* (1791–1868), *Journal for January 1825–December, 1835, Folder 1*, pp. 14–15.
15. George Eliot, *Daniel Deronda* (Edinburgh: Blackwood, 1876), vol. ii, 300.
16. British Institute in Florence, Harold Acton Library, Correspondence of Lina Waterfield (1874–1974), Letter to Madge Symmonds, January 16, 1897, p. 4.
17. Vernon Lee, *Studies of the Eighteenth Century in Italy* (London: Fisher Unwin, 1907), 115.
18. Ivor Atkins, ed. *Miserere, Psalm 51, Music by Gregorio Allegri, with Traditional abbelimenti sung in the Sistine Chapel in Rome* (London: Novello, 1951). The complex evolution of this work, from bare fauxbourdon to the haunting but fraudulent modern embellishments, has recently been uncovered by the musicologist Ben Byram-Wigfield. An edition incorporating his researches is available through Ancient Groove Music, and a CD recording by the Sixteen demonstrating all of its successive phases can be found at COREPSIN01.
19. Charles Burney, *A General History of Music from the Earliest Ages to the Present Period* (London: Payne and Son), vol. 4, 27.
20. Edward Wright, *Some Observations Made in Travelling through France, Italy etc. in the years 1720, 1721 and 1722* (London, 1730), 84.
21. Burney, *A General History of Music*, vol. 3, 561.

CHAPTER 6

Cultural Migration as Protestant Nostalgia: (2) Milton, Ruskin and Religious Longing

The English Reformation inflicted a severe wound on the national mind. The construction of an insular religious consciousness severed from the main body of continental Christendom involved multiple kinds of re-adjustment. Christianity had been traditionally Catholic and pan-European. In successive works the historian Eamon Duffy has recorded the theological, liturgical and even architectural consequences of this condition of severance.[1] What I am concerned with here are its broader cultural effects: specifically in literature and art appreciation. I offer two case studies: one from the seventeenth century, the other from the nineteenth, one a poet and controversialist, the other an art critic and social prophet; both learned and well travelled from their earliest years, both profoundly—even dogmatically—Protestant. Both of them attempted in their respective spheres to purge an inherited Christian culture of its Roman Catholic associations, with very mixed results. Their polemical writing protests their intentions, but their creative work usually gives the game away. During the centuries in which they flourished, as for the many centuries that preceded them, many of the most resourceful elements in imaginative culture migrated from the south towards the north. My two authors were minded to stem this flow: in effect they were party to it.

Proserpin Gathring Flours

One of the most moving passages in English poetry occurs in Book IV of *Paradise Lost*. Milton is eulogising the perfect garden that Adam and Eve are about to forfeit by disobeying God. He does this by means of an epic simile, all the more stirring for being negatively phrased:

> Not that faire field
> Of *Enna*, where *Proserpin* gathring flours
> Her self a fairer Floure by gloomy *Dis*
> Was gatherd, which caused *Ceres* all that pain
> To seek her through the world; nor that sweet Grove
> Of *Daphne* by *Orontes*, and th' inspir'd
> *Castalian* Spring might with this Paradise
> Of *Eden* strive…[2]

In the twentieth century, these lines featured in a famous altercation between the poet T.S. Eliot and the critic F.R. Leavis over the merits of Milton, whose supposed prettiness had been blamed for the stilted quality of much English verse in the century after him. The passage is a negatively phrased epic simile in which a classically conceived version of Paradise is pitted against the biblical one, to the former's disadvantage. It is also a kind of excursus into the world of Graeco-Roman learning, genuinely pathetic in its effects. Leavis's way of putting this is that the reflective and reflexive tone here is "smuggled in", the effect being one of enrichment lending classical resonance to what might otherwise have been a somewhat bare, and spare, account.[3] Milton is sometimes an elaborate poet, and the passage under examination allows us some insight into why, and to what effect, he elaborates. He does so because he wishes certain parallels to echo, musically and theatrically, from a source—catholic with a small "c"—extraneous to, and wider than, the doctrinally loaded one in which he is explicitly operating.

The twentieth-century stylistic debate over the merits of this passage had a tendency to obscure its subject matter, which concerns loss, displacement and longing. A set of comparisons is established between one system of reference and another: what academics call a "typology". The analogous systems are biblical and classical: Eve is the equivalent of Proserpine or Persephone, and Satan of Dis or Pluto. Who then stands for the heart-broken Ceres or Demeter? I shall come to this point in a minute. Meanwhile I offer a conjecture concerning Milton's mind, and the culture it inhabited. The object of regret in this passage is, I believe, neither Eve nor Proserpine, Satan or Dis, human beings or gods. It is the field of comparison itself.

In the Middle Ages classical analogy was a way by which the Catholic Church rooted itself in the Graeco-Roman world. The habit of mind went back to the fourth century AD after the re-imposition of Christianity following the apostate regime of the Emperor Julian. It represented a kind of counter-Paganism, a means of heading off the surviving ancient cults by integrating them into the renovated faith. After the collapse of the Empire in the West, the policy gained ground as a way of bolstering the papacy as a substitute imperium. The Pope became an updated, Christianised Flamen Dialis. The Virgin Mary, Mother of God, was enshrined as a new Isis. Christ was a second Adonis, slain and resurrected for the world's salvation. Later, the colonnade of reference supported the political and cultural vaulting of Christendom, while its allusions enriched its poetry. The permeation was anathema to the Protestant reformers, who with limited exceptions made to expunge it. As a young scholar-poet, a pious Puritan deeply versed in the classics, Milton had attempted to cleanse the Doctrine of the Incarnation from any such contagion. In his "Hymn on the Morning of Christ's Nativity", composed in 1629, he banishes the Roman gods, a rejection resembling that in his epic masterpiece, written three decades later as retired Latin Secretary:

> In consecrated Earth,
> And on the holy Hearth,
> The *Lars* and *Lemures* moan with midnight plaint,
> In Urns and Altars round,
> A drear and dying sound
> Affrights the *Flamins* at their service quaint;
> And the chill Marble seems to sweat,
> While each peculiar power forgoes his wonted seat.[4]

The tone of this Hymn seems torn between celebration and regret. The expulsion of the classical tutelary spirits of Catholic Christendom is a necessary cleansing, but its consequences for a poetic mind nourished by these very sources are "drear". What we seem to observe at such moments is a classically learned poet—one immersed in the traditional literary culture of Europe—tearing at the roots of his own inspiration. In the lines that I quoted earlier from *Paradise Lost*, it is Milton as much as Ceres who is mourning.

Sermons in Stones

The division in the sensibility of Protestantism manifest here has been a recurrent—even a chronic—aspect of English life. A fresh bout occurred in a mid-Victorian Britain that was experiencing both a revival of classical—especially Greek—learning and the effects of the Oxford Movement. It was in 1851, one year after the re-establishment of the Roman Catholic hierarchy in England, that John Ruskin began publishing his extended study *The Stones of Venice*. The book is a portrait of a city, and at the same time a diatribe against cultural decline. Ruskin's twin *bêtes noires* were the Counter-Reformation, and its painterly and architectural concomitant, the Baroque. Strictly, the work is not so much anti-Catholic as anti-Tridentine and—in a literal sense—Pre-Raphaelite. It is the art of the High Renaissance that Ruskin believes to have been the ruin of Italian painting; it had also, he believed, destroyed the integrity of the Venetian Republic. The besetting characteristic of Counter-Reformation culture is idolatry, a communal prostration before false gods that, Ruskin believed, had been the political and artistic undoing of Venice.

Ruskin regarded this phase of European culture with disapprobation laced with horror. The response had personal origins in a nonconformism imbibed at his mother's knee. As an adolescent he had spent whole summers travelling with his parents around southern Europe. After a day visiting galleries and Catholic churches, they would return to an atmosphere of Bible reading and energetic prayer. In the eyes of Mrs Ruskin, the Roman Church was the Whore of Babylon. Yet, thanks to the education she and her thrifty, sherry-importing husband gave their son, Italy became his mental home, and Fra Angelico and Giotto his patterns among painters.

In the first volume of *Modern Painters*, written in his early twenties, Ruskin attempted to resolve this tension by presenting truth, naturalness and simplicity as the handmaids of art. By praising "the truth of colour", "the truth of chiaroscuro" and "the truth of clouds", he could yoke aesthetic appreciation to a universal mimesis, hence presenting early Italian art as a proto-Protestant form of natural reverence. In the later volumes, this balancing act comes unstuck. Here he is in Volume III inveighing against the "false ideal" of "the profane":

> As long as men sought for truth first, and beauty secondarily, they cared chiefly, of course, for the *chief* truth, and all art was instinctively religious.

But as soon as they sought for beauty first, and truth secondarily, they were punished by losing sight of spiritual truth altogether, and the profane (properly so called) schools of art were instantly developed...Little thinking this, they gave themselves fearlessly to the chase of the new delight, and exhausted themselves in the pursuit of an ideal now doubly false. Formerly, though they attempted to reach an unnatural beauty, it was yet in representing historical facts and real persons; *now* they sought for the same unnatural beauty in representing tales which they knew to be fictitious, and personages who, they knew, had never existed. Such a state of things had never before been found in any nation.[5]

The last sentence is a violation of history, and the entire passage an implied attack on the foundations of art and fiction. By such methods did Ruskin, the Puritan aesthete, reconcile his Protestant revulsion against artifice with his private longing for a visual ideal. Turning his back on the "profane"—on Athens and Rome as much as on Bellini and Tintoretto—he entered with suspect rejoicing into the camp of the Philistines.

The violence that Ruskin wrought on his own temperament led first to arid dogmatism, finally into madness. In Milton's case, his renunciation of his imaginative birth right effected a dissociation of the sensibility combined with an incurable sense of loss. Both writers had been taught to regard the Graeco-Roman legacy of Christendom as a malign tumour growing within the matter of Europe. Paradoxically, their attempt to perform a surgical operation led, in one instance, to a supreme poem and, in the other, to some of the most alert art criticism ever written. Both men found it in themselves to compensate for their dismantling of the traditional grand design by the erection of large-scale, architectonic works in poetry or prose. Both were attracted to the myth of Eden, which each saw as a place too innocent for disputation, too wholesome for mere doctrine. At the close of Milton's epic, Adam and Eve stand at the gates of Paradise, looking back. With them pauses Milton, missing his kin, free—like Ceres—"to seek her through the world".

Notes

1. See especially Eamon Duffy, *The Stripping of the Altars: Traditional Religion in England c. 1400 to c. 1580* (New Haven, CT: Yale University Press, 1992) and *Saints, Sacrilege and Sedition: Religion and Conflict in the Tudor Reformations* (Yale University Press, 2012).

2. *Paradise Lost*, iv, ll 268 sq. *The Poems of John Milton*, eds. John Carey and Alastair Fowler (London: Longman, 1968), 628–29.
3. F.R. Leavis, *Revaluation: Tradition and Development in English Poetry* (1936) (London: Chatto and Windus and Penguin, 1964), 58.
4. *The Poems of John Milton*, 110.
5. John Ruskin, *Modern Painters* (Orpington: George Allen, 1888), vol. iii, 63–64.

CHAPTER 7

Cultural Migration as Protestant Nostalgia: (3) Purcell, the Popish Plot and the Politics of Latin

The tensions caused in the fields of literature and art appreciation by the hiatus of the Reformation were arguably even more extreme in the area of music, if sometimes less easy to verbalise, and hence to pin down. The music of northern Europe, including that of England, had been begotten in—and nourished by—the Roman Catholic church. Its modes and scales, derived from medieval ones (which had in turn been derived from the Greek), melodic contours that followed the curves of Gregorian chant, a harmonic finesse honed by elements of choral performance within the ordinary of the Mass: all attested to this point of origin, even if the political and ecclesiastical context within which these arts were now practised had lurched away from Rome. Under these circumstances, composers in every genre were obliged to ply their trade in an atmosphere sometimes mildly, frequently vocally, unsympathetic to its deep historical roots. In the case of Germany one could wax loud and long, as John Eliot Gardiner has recently done, on the effect of this split cultural personality on the work of J.S. Bach.[1] In this chapter I wish to focus on one of Bach's contemporaries, an English musician whose family possessed strong Catholic connections, and whose musical idioms hark back to France and Italy, even as he pursued a highly successful career in the heart of the Carolingian Anglican establishment. Arguably the greatest, as well as the most European, of all English composers, he confronts us with the third of our stories of Protestant longing: one that involves a Protestant king with a

© The Author(s) 2018
R. Fraser, *Literature, Music and Cosmopolitanism*,
https://doi.org/10.1007/978-3-319-68480-2_7

Catholic wife, and a court conspiracy that nearly unseated both. To make my point, I will concentrate on one short work of this composer, the text of which involves us in a mystery. The solution to this introduces us to the fourth of my high-profile migrants: a scholar and refugee of very great, though sometimes overlooked, importance.

Restoration and Relaxation

In many respects Henry Purcell was an exceptionally lucky musician. Born the son of a Gentleman of the Chapel Royal a year before the Restoration of the monarchy, he grew up in an atmosphere that was newly beneficial to his art. After more than a decade in which the composition and performance of church music, for example, had been quite exceptionally restricted—with the disruption of liturgies, the dispersal of choral establishments, the active destruction of pipe organs—the climate at court and in the sanctuary had been suddenly transformed. Charles II liked music, and he liked it where and when he worshipped. Following his years of exile abroad, he was also exceptionally open to French and Italian cultural influences, which had migrated with him. He paid for what he liked. With the efficiency and enthusiasm of the freshly empowered, Captain Henry Cooke, the new Master of the Children, rode out into the shires and dragooned or persuaded promising boy choristers into the ranks of the royal choir. The Italian and French styles were now encouraged alongside the English, and violins graced holy places. Pelham Humfrey was sent forth to the continent to pick up cosmopolitan skills and returned to train amongst others the growing Purcell, whose verse anthem with string accompaniment "My Beloved Spake", composed at the age of seventeen, with its clashing string harmonies, triple dance rhythms, chirruping refrains and sense of sheer nervous release, bodied forth a rite of spring, exultant, European in its idioms even if the words are English.[2]

The openess and toleration did not last, and the darkening of the skies after 1679 is my theme here. Before turning to this, it is worthwhile contemplating some of the co-existences that had flourished in the early Restoration sunshine. There were, for example, two chapels royal. The king's, over the musical dispensation of which Cooke at first presided, followed by Humfrey and then John Blow, was in Whitehall, and naturally it was Anglican. Meanwhile the long-suffering Portuguese-born queen, Catherine of Braganza, had her own Roman Catholic establishment, for which Purcell's acquaintance Giovanni Battista Draghi served as Director of Music, assisted until his death in August 1677 by Purcell's even closer friend Matthew Locke, himself a probable Catholic convert, who played the smaller of two available organs. Until 1671 this existed in the dowager Queen Henrietta Maria's former palace at Somerset House; afterwards it moved west in closer proximity to its Protestant equivalent in Whitehall. James, Duke of York, the king's overtly Catholic brother, would have attended mass there. In the honeymoon ambiance of the times all this seemed natural and inevitable, nor until the very late 1670s does there seem to have been much evidence of official conflict or stress.

The *entente cordiale* that these arrangements evidenced represented a lull in a century of intense religious strife. Another facet of it was the verbal medium of worship over which, again until the late 1670s, considerable toleration was exercised. Consider how far attitudes had travelled in a century. In the England of the Tudors, liturgical language had clearly been coded. Thomas Tallis, who worked through several reigns, had needed to cut his stylistic coat to a series of linguistic and liturgical cloths, from Latin to melismatic—followed by austerely syllabic—English word setting. When William Byrd writes Latin motets in the latter years of Queen Elizabeth, we are entitled to conclude that the man was working *sub rosa* for clandestine Catholic households, and that he himself may have remained secretly Catholic.

Few of these inferences are appropriate to the honeymoon period of the 1660s and early 1670s, when cosmopolitan tendencies experienced a short heyday. In her 1995 biography of Purcell, Maureen Duffy observes that in the Royal Peculiar of Westminster Abbey settings of Latin words were acceptable at this time, and Blow, organist until 1679, produced several, notably his anthem "Salvator Mundi". To some extent such ecclesiastical usage of the Roman tongue closed the gap with its secular use. Latin, after all, was still the medium of international scholarship and of natural philosophy or science, in which Isaac Newton wrote as inevitably as did his mathematical rival Leibniz in Germany. Administrative Latin too had remained the language of diplomatic communication right through the Commonwealth when, as we have already seen, that arch-Puritan John Milton had been exclusively employed to correspond through it. For Milton at least, then, secular Latin was a medium with no political baggage. I very much doubt, however, whether he would have appreciated church services that employed Latin at any time. At least to begin with, Charles, and even more his brother James, were happy to be known to think otherwise.

Papism and Paranoia

When Blow stepped down in favour of Purcell in 1679, his successor might well have enjoyed the same breadth of toleration. But 1679 was an odd, watershed year, and so we need to take stock. This was the year when the mocking and divisive terms "Whig" and "Tory" entered the language, when the precarious understanding between Protestant and Catholic England started again to come apart, when differences of religious affiliation, with their respective linguistic affiliations, became once more the subject of political concern, and deep disagreement. From now on, it seems, a court that had cast a benign eye on the cosmopolitan way of life of the queen and the king's flamboyant brother was no longer inclined to behave so generously. The problems began in December 1677 when an anonymous pamphlet accused the Catholic elements in the kingdom of planning to seize power. It escalated the following August when the king was informed of a manuscript written by the scabrous scandalmonger Titus Oates claiming there was a Catholic and Jesuit plot on his life.[3] It has to be said that at no time did Charles believe any of this, but the queen found herself implicated that November when Oates instigated the further slander that she and the royal physician were jointly attempting to poison the king. Quarters were searched, and the officials of Catherine's household remained under some suspicion at least until the early months of 1680; that would have included the staff of her chapel. Catherine herself was vocal in her loyalty throughout, and was eventually exonerated when Oates's story collapsed under questioning. But the hysterical and trumped-up "Popish Plot" marks in several respects the turning of the political and religious tide.

It was in the very midst of this crisis that Blow stepped down as organist at the Abbey. The twenty-year-old Purcell took over, and looked about him. It cannot have been a comfortable sensation. Several members of his own family were practising Catholics, and he had just married a girl of Flemish Catholic descent.[4] His personal connections with the small Catholic community in London ran very deep. He was close to Draghi, and when Locke had died two years previously had composed a lament for him—"What hope for us remains now he is gone?"—to grieving words that were probably his own. To some extent Locke, thirty-seven years Purcell's senior, had been a mentor and an exemplar, someone who, when he had published his harmonic treatise *Melothesia* in 1673, had unproblematically styled himself on its title page as "Composer in Ordinary to His Majesty, and Organist of Her Majesty's Chapel". The uncontroversial conjunction joining these two job descriptions was part of the ambiance in which Purcell had been raised: religious and cultural accommodation was what he was used to. Though people around him inevitably discussed the Civil War, he had no personal recollection of it. Many of those he knew most intimately had conducted their professional and family lives across communities of different ecclesiastical affiliation that seem for once to have been uncomplicatedly compatible. If Duffy is correct, Henry's uncle Thomas, born in 1627, had been Groom to the Queen Mother and to the Queen in Somerset House, though his children had been baptised in Anglican fashion at nearby St Mary-le-Strand. This sort of comfortable straddling of divides would soon become a thing of the past.

It was under these circumstances that in 1680 Purcell, whose responsibilities were rapidly expanding, opened a new manuscript book, now in the British Library, in which he made fair copies of completed anthems (Fig. 7.1). Amongst them is a deeply moving setting of a biblical text voicing the dismay of a much earlier king beset by his enemies.[5] Psalm Three is traditionally interpreted as a response by King David to an insurrection against his authority mounted by his son Absalom, as recounted in the Second Book of Samuel. "Lord," runs the text in the Authorized King James Version, "how are they increased that trouble me! many are they that rise up against me." That Purcell should have elected to set this particular psalm at such a time of court intrigue and national emergency is sufficiently interesting; even more remarkable is that he should have chosen to set it not, like the overwhelming majority of his church motets, in English, but in Latin.

It is a distinctive kind of Latin too, from a source that modern scholars have experienced some vexation in identifying. The standard Latin translation of the Old Testament employed since the first millennium is the Vulgate text prepared by the peripatetic St Jerome in the fourth century AD. "Domine", runs its version of this psalm, "quare multiplicati sunt hostes mei multi consurgunt contra me." It is evident from the very first

Fig. 7.1 "Jehova, Quam Multi Sunt Hostes Mei". Henry Purcell's fair copy holograph from B.L.Add.Ms, 30930, *The Works of Henry Purcell* (Dom, 1680)

verse that Purcell is drawing on a quite different text, the words of which run as follows (I have given the Authorized Version's translation in the endnote):

> Jehova, quam multi sunt hostes mei!
> Quam multi insurgent contra me.
> Quam multi dicunt de anima mea;
> Non est ulla salus isti in Deo plane;
> At tu Jehova, clypeus es circa me;
> Gloria mea, et extollens caput meum.
> Voce mea ad Jehovam clamanti,
> Respondit mihi e monte sanctitatis suae maxime.
> Ego cubui et dormivi, ego experge feci me;
> Quia Jehova sustentat me.
> Non timeo a myriadibus populi,
> Quas circum disposuerint metatores contra me.
> Surge, Jehova, fac salvum me deus mi;
> Qui percussisti omnes inimicos meos maxilliam,
> Dentes improborum confregisti.
> Jehova est salus:
> Super populum tuum sit benedictio tua maxime.[6]

For a long time, musicologists scratched their heads over the provenance of this text. As late as 1992, John Caldwell, who calls Purcell's anthem a "masterpiece of the Italian style", conceded that its setting of an "unidentified Latin text" represented "an inexplicable artefact".[7] It was not until 2000 that the definitive source for the words was winkled out.[8] The story revealed in the process takes us deep into the cultural migrancy of the early modern period.

A Case of Translation

The personal origins of the translator, Immanuel Tremellius, are themselves cloaked in uncertainty. We know that he was born in around 1510 in Ferrara and that he was Jewish, presumably one of the small Ashkenazi community in that city.[9] As such he would have been well schooled in Hebrew, which accounts for the fidelity with which he translated the Psalms. By 1530 he was living in the household of Cardinal Farnese in Rome, and had presumably become a Roman Catholic

Christian. He was not to remain one for long. By 1542 he had been drawn into the fold of Calvinism, and was forced to flee Italy when Farnese, raised to the purple as Pope Paul III, decided to revive the Inquisition. Tremellius settled in Strasbourg, became a teacher of Hebrew and married. By 1547 he was on his travels again, since the Habsburg Emperor Charles had restored Catholicism to his German dominions. Tremellius came to London, where the newly crowned Edward VI was resolved to pursue the Protestant Reformation instigated by his father, Henry VIII. Tremellius took up residence in Lambeth Palace at the invitation of the Archbishop of Canterbury, the ardently Protestant Cranmer. Two years later he was appointed Regius Professor of Hebrew at Cambridge. But in July 1553 Edward died, to be succeeded on the throne by his passionately Catholic half-sister Mary. Tremellius was obliged to uproot himself yet again, this time for northern Germany, where he took up a Professorship in Theology at the University of Heidelberg. It is possible that he had already begun on his greatest work, a complete Latin translation of the Old Testament scriptures. It was not, however, until 1579 that, with the assistance of his collaborator Franciscus Junius, he published the first part; the whole was issued in London in 1580, the year of his death. It is from this translation, as we now know, that Purcell derived his text.

Purcell's "Jehova, Quam Multi Sunt Hostes Mei", therefore, is a setting of an ancient Hebrew complaint rendered into Latin by an Italian scholar of Jewish extraction who had spent the whole of his earthly existence in a condition of serial flight: from Ferrara to Padua (where he seems to have attended the university) to Rome to Alsace to London to Cambridge, and thence to one of Germany's oldest and most prestigious academies.[10] It is a history of multiple migrancy: physical, linguistic, theological, cultural and even textual, which partly explains the pertinacity of Tremellius's text, and Purcell's adherence to it. By the late seventeenth century, the Tremellius/Junius version had become the Latin Old Testament of choice, not simply for Calvinists but for English Protestants in general. As such it was commonly bound together with a Latin translation of the New Testament by the French Calvinist Theodore Beza, Calvin's successor in Geneva, to constitute a complete Latin Bible, a Protestant alternative to the Vulgate. Milton possessed a copy and so, apparently, did Purcell, who turned to it in a moment of national crisis.

A Catholic Queen

But why set the psalm in Latin at all? The answer can only lie in the nature of the first performance, which in turn begs the question of the congregation for which the anthem was written. Given its date, there are reasons for supposing it may have been composed for the Abbey, where Purcell was trying his strengths. The principal reason for thinking this is musical. It is notably solemn and dramatic, and its full choral sections would have been much enhanced by the resonant acoustic of a large building, such as an abbey or cathedral still provides, but which neither of the necessarily small and intimate royal chapels of the period could have supplied to quite the same extent. There is a problem with his theory, however, namely that in the circumstances of the emergency of 1679, the tide was turning against Latinate and pan-European idioms and forms. To have performed so eloquent a piece as this in Latin in a church so closely associated with the vulnerable crown at this moment would almost certainly have been viewed as an act of provocation by a very young musician anxious for official recognition.

There is, however, another possibility that has attracted some scholars, and this is that "Jehova, Quam Multi Sunt" was written for the queen's chapel, where Latin was the liturgical idiom commonly in use. With this in view, I suggest that we look briefly at that demurely pious yet complex personality, Queen Catherine of Braganza. She was, for a start, the product of a remarkably rich and well-endowed religious and musical culture. Her father Juan de Bragança, Duke of Barcelos, had succeeded to the Portuguese throne as Juan IV when she was two. He was no mean composer, and his Latin motet "Crux Fidelis" is sung during Lent to this day. He was the author of treatises in Latin on Palestrina and on harmonic style. He was furthermore the creator of one of the most extensive musical libraries in the Europe of his time, the contents of which were destroyed during the Lisbon earthquake of November 1755. By the time she married Charles in May 1662, Catherine would therefore have had almost a quarter of a century of immersion in Catholic musical culture behind her. By all accounts her religion was a mainstay of her vulnerable temperament, one that supported her through all of her husband's successive *amours*. The queen is very unlikely to have taken the arrangements for her private chapel lightly. And she is also liable to have taken the wild accusations flung at her and her co-religionists during the Popish Plot very hard.

"Jehova, Quam Multi Sunt" was written at the climax of that emergency. It is, furthermore, a work the choice of whose text is likely to have been made in the light of public events. David was a common trope for the English king, one to which the male Stuarts and their Hanoverian successors were both deeply attached. Charles himself was partial to the analogy, and it was forever being applied to him, notably by the Catholic Poet Laureate Dryden, who two years later would take the story of Absalom and his advisor Achitophel as the archetype for a celebrated cautionary poem about the deleterious influence of the Earl of Shaftesbury on the king's natural son, the Protestant Duke of Monmouth, later a pretender to the throne. Bearing this in mind, some commentators have gone as far as to connect Purcell's anthem with the tension caused by the rise of Monmouth's party at court. The trouble is that it was written at least a year too early to apply to this particular scandal, four years before the Rye House Plot in which Monmouth was formally implicated, and a good six years before the Monmouth Rebellion itself. Besides, despite their religious differences, the queen had at the time quite a soft spot for Monmouth, whom she was warmly to defend when his integrity was being traduced, by Dryden among others, in 1681.

The question as to where and for whom this dramatically satisfying motet was first performed may never be fully resolved. It is, I submit, far less important and interesting than what the choice of text—and the way it is set—have to tell us, first about Purcell, and second about contemporary views of Latin. Manifestly the anthem represents a vocal expression of loyalty to the king at a time when he was beset by pressures on all sides, principally from those anxious to suppress the Catholic connection. It is also strongly empathic in mood. This is one of the psalms in which David, who for once is unambiguously identified as the poet, speaks in the first person. Hemmed in by calumny and mistrust, the king is enabled to speak.

Moreover, in choosing to set this psalm neither in English, nor in the canonic and community-specific words of the Vulgate, Purcell is obviously implying something about the Latin tongue itself. Despite the pressures of the moment, and despite the ecclesiastical associations it possesses in some quarters, it clearly represents for him a medium that is available, suggestive and ideologically neutral. An attractive medium too for a composer newly and unexpectedly trapped between competing religious and cultural camps. "Jehova, Quam Multi Sunt" is that rare thing: a sacred work that comments, however obliquely, on the shifting politics of Latin.

Notes

1. John Elliot Gardiner, *Bach: Music in the Gate of Heaven* (London: Penguin, 2015).
2. For Purcell's holograph, see BL Add. Ms. 30932, f.87. For Humfrey's travels in Europe, see Maureen Duffy, *Henry Purcell* (London: Fourth Estate, 1994), 34–35.
3. For the course and development of the Popish Plot, see John Kenyon, *The Popish Plot* (London: Heinemann, 1972).
4. Duffy, 61.
5. BL Add. Ms. 30930, ff.9–12. A recording in which the Latin text is especially clear is that by the choir of St John's College, Cambridge with organ and string accompaniment, which may be heard at https://www.youtube.com/watch?v=6cLiAR7qZHA
6. The Authorized Version runs: "Lord, how are they increased that trouble me! many are they that rise up against me./ Many there be which say of my soul, There is no help for him in God./ But thou, O Lord, art a shield for me, my glory, and the lifter up of my head./ I cried unto the Lord with my voice, and he heard me out of his holy hill./ I laid me down and slept; I awaked; for the Lord sustained me./ I will not be afraid of ten thousands of people, that have set themselves against me round about./ Arise, O Lord; save me, O my God; for thou has smitten all mine enemies upon the cheek bone; thou has broken the teeth of the ungodly./ Salvation belongeth unto the Lord: thy blessing is upon thy people."
7. John Caldwell, *The Oxford History of English Music from the Beginnings to c. 1715* (Oxford University Press, 1991), 569.
8. See *Early Music Review* No. 65 (November, 2000), 28 and No. 67 (February, 2001), 27. I am indebted to the late Anthony Hicks for pointing these out.
9. Kenneth Austin, *From Judaism to Calvinism: The Life and Writings of Immanuel Tremellius (c.1510–1589)* (Aldershot: Ashgate, 2007), 8.
10. Tremellius's translation of Psalm 3 is in *Testamenti veteris Biblia Sacra*, trans. Immanuel Tremellius and Franciscus Junius, Second Edition (London: Henry Middleton, 1581), 58. Apart from one or two minor variants—"insurgentes" for "insurgunt"; "scutum" for "clypeus"—it is, to all intents and purposes, identical to the text that Purcell employs.

CHAPTER 8

Migrant Consciences in the Age of Empire: Charles Kingsley, Governor Eyre and the Morant Bay Rising

British imperialism as it emerged through the eighteenth and nineteenth centuries may be regarded in two different lights: as a system of explicit and implicit domination, or as an act of international co-operation and collaboration. An interpretation of the matter from the former point of view may be found in Edward Said's forceful, though sometimes inaccurate, book *Culture and Imperialism*.[1] A nuanced reading more sympathetic to the latter viewpoint intermittently emerges in *Revolutionary Empire* by that ardent poet, cultural historian and Scottish nationalist, Angus Calder.[2] Whatever view one takes, however, the imperialistic project as a whole involved multiple cross-currents, synchronicities, odd and sometimes contradictory directives. In such circumstances, to understand history aright it is necessary to view it through the widest of lenses: taking in both the purported centre and neglected corners and margins. The story I am offering in this chapter involves a colonial administrator, an island in the Caribbean, some Australian Aborigines, a Christian socialist and priest, a Scottish seer, revolution in Ireland, and a British novelist and advocate of social reform. None of these elements can properly be understood in isolation from the rest. The events portrayed echoed around the globe, as did the consequences. Like most of the best stories, it is local and universal at one and the same time, and so are the lessons that may be derived from it.

The English in the West Indies

Amongst the oddest titles in West Indian literature is that of John Jacob Thomas's diatribe of 1889 called *Froudacity*.[3] The suggestive title is a pun, and refers to the work of one of England's leading historians, the elderly James Anthony Froude, onetime fellow of Exeter College, Oxford, former editor of *Fraser's Magazine*, and chief disciple and biographer of Thomas Carlyle. The target of Thomas's angry riposte, however, is none of these irreproachable activities, but an innocent-seeming travelogue which Froude had published in the previous year called *The English in the West Indies*.

Subtitled "The Bow of Ulysses", this book was an impressionistic account of a tour made by the author in 1886–7 around the principal English-speaking islands of the Caribbean.[4] A century later, it is difficult to discover what in this gentlemanly peregrination had made Thomas quite so indignant. True, Froude seems woefully ignorant about day-to-day realities in the islands, and displays a risible tendency to generalise about the lives of the inhabitants whilst sipping cocktails on the Governor's verandah. His rapidly written account is admittedly somewhat stilted, even a little geriatric. Thomas, however, peers beneath this sedateness, where he discovers a purpose of "deterring the home authorities from granting an elective local legislature, however restricted in character, to any of the colonies not yet enjoying such an advantage". He goes further. Behind Froude's mild and suave self-deportment, he claims, lurks an even more sinister intent: "the dark outlines of a scheme to thwart political aspiration in the Antilles".[5]

Froude's intentions, and Thomas's retort, can best be appreciated if we bear in mind the circumstances in which both men were writing. Both were reacting to the Imperial Conference in London in 1887, called to celebrate the Golden Jubilee of Queen Victoria, with the purpose of determining future patterns of representation in a fast-growing empire. Froude had explicitly invoked this background, starting his book by describing the delegates leaving, some by the same boat in which he is himself about to journey to the West Indies. Were these colonial dignitaries better off, he had asked, for resolutions proposing limited self-government for the larger and more important colonies? Were they fit possessors of such additional powers, if granted? He had then pointedly inquired whether such freedom would ever be appropriate to smaller colonies, more especially to struggling Caribbean islands.

Midway through his leisurely tour, Froude had visited Jamaica, where he had stayed on an estate called Cherry Hill, owned by the manager of the Colonial Bank. The estate interested him because it had once belonged to George William Gordon, a businessman and radical politician hanged by court-martial in October 1865 on a charge of inciting insurrection in the Parish of St Thomas-in-the-East. The insurrection, known to history as the Morant Bay rebellion or rising, but referred to by Froude as the "Gordon riots", its brutal suppression under Governor Edward John Eyre, and Eyre's subsequent cashierment and disgrace, were vivid in Froude's memory since they once divided his generation bitterly, striking along ideological fault-lines until then invisible to many. At the time of the controversy, Froude had been editor of *Fraser's Magazine*. Fearful of offending that periodical's proprietors, he had held back from taking too active a role in the dispute, as had his more famous brother-in-law, the novelist and Anglican priest Charles Kingsley, who nonetheless had been vocal in Eyre's support. But in *The English in the West Indies* Froude airs his persistent conviction on two matters: Eyre's actions, culminating in his suppression of the island's ancient House of Assembly, had been extreme but justified; they had also placed, and continued to place, the restoration of democratic rights in the island in question.[6] It is this inference, indeed, that lies at the core of Froude's much-resented book.

Morant Bay: The Roots of a Rising

Even now, any account of the Morant Bay rising, and of the Eyre controversy that followed it, is complicated by the fact that these events are interpreted variously in different places. The rebellion itself occupies a legendary place in Jamaican politics, a role most vividly depicted by the Jamaican novelist V.S. Reid in his novel of 1949 *New Day*, the narrator of which, the eighty-seven-year-old John Campbell, has witnessed the disturbances as a young boy, and counterpoints his still urgent memories of them with an account of the creation in 1944 of a new constitution establishing universal adult suffrage on the island.[7] Campbell's narrative, couched in an irresistible patois, is compelling, as well as beautifully composed. For a slightly earlier generation of readers, the events of 1865 were reviewed in *The Myth of Governor Eyre* by one of Eyre's successors to the governorship, Lord Olivier, Fabian Socialist and uncle of a celebrated actor.[8] Olivier had a very low opinion of his predecessor's conduct, a view once shared by many influential Victorians, led by John Stuart Mill.[9] Considering the terrible retaliation inflicted on the islanders, it is hard to dissent from their distaste. The question is how did the opposing view once gain credit, not simply with Froude and Kingsley, but with Dickens, with Ruskin, with Tennyson and with a whole host of nineteenth-century writers and intellectuals of marked humanitarian concern?

The uprising and its aftermath raised, and continue to pose, moral, legal and constitutional questions, none of which is easy to comprehend without a consideration of its causes. In the 1860s Jamaica's economy had been in decline for some time: the value of its sugar exports, for example, being a little over a third of what it had been before Emancipation in 1833. Not surprisingly, few liberated slaves had wished to return to work for their former masters as wage-earners, preferring to acquire plots of land and survive precariously as smallholders. Despite widespread absenteeism among longer-established landlords, the amount of available land was limited; persistent causes of discontent were the level of rents demanded and the reluctance of the Crown to release lands confiscated from tax defaulters, the so-called back lands, for general use. As Gad Heuman remarks, the year 1865 in particular had been cursed by drought.[10] What is more, the recently concluded American Civil War had disrupted trade in the region, and the price of foodstuffs such as codfish had risen in consequence. On the other hand, in 1865 St Thomas, the site of the rising, was better off than most parishes, and the ringleaders of the rebellion were not among its poorer residents.

These economic considerations, however, are meaningless unless viewed against the political circumstances of the island. For over 200 years Jamaica had been administered by a constitution granted under Charles II which provided for a two-chamber assembly to regulate most matters, apart from defence and the civil law. In fiscal affairs, for example, the legislature had a fairly free hand, its principal brake being the power of the Governor, resident in Spanish Town, appointed by, and answerable to, the British monarch. But in 1853, Britain had come to the rescue with a half-million-pound loan; as a condition it had demanded a modification of the constitution, strengthening the Governor's hand by setting up an Executive Council nominated by himself.

Though in theory the interests of the Governor and the Assembly were identical, in practice little love was lost between them. Membership of the Assembly was confined to those with property valued at over £3000. For years this corrupt and vexatious body had acted as the mouthpiece of the old plantocracy, but as the older planters had deserted their estates it had increasingly come to be dominated by a *nouveau riche* class far more reactionary than those whom they replaced. The Assembly had resisted both the abolition of the slave trade in 1807 and Emancipation itself. In the 1840s and 1850s several covert attempts had been made by its members to have Jamaica admitted to the United States, thus re-introducing slavery by the back door. It remained acutely unrepresentative because, although all citizens with incomes over £6 per annum were entitled to vote provided they could raise a registration fee of ten shillings, the property qualification for candidates ensured that few blacks stood for the chamber. As a result, the electoral process was dismissed as an irrelevance: at the election of 1862, only a thousand or so Jamaicans of African descent had participated out of a total of almost a million. The new plantocracy were acutely aware that, should an economic upturn enable more blacks to stand, or should the property threshold be lowered to bring Jamaica into line with a Britain then on the threshold of a Second Reform Act, the complexion of the Assembly would alter radically. The only precedent for such rapid democratisation in the region was nearby Haiti, where Toussaint L'Ouverture's revolution of 1791 had been followed by a widespread slaughter of the planting families. It is no exaggeration to say that the Haitian Revolution still figured in the imagination of white Jamaicans much as the French Revolution featured in the minds of middle-class Britons, ensuring caution through fear.

In 1865, one of the few men of African descent who had managed to be elected to the chamber was Gordon.[11] He was one of seven illegitimate children of Joseph Gordon, a Scottish plantation owner who had acted as attorney for absentee landlords, and his slave mistress. At emancipation, Joseph had liberated his mistress and offspring, married and raised a second family. George William had quickly availed himself of the economic opportunities of the new dispensation. By 1843 he was reputedly worth £10,000; three years later he had purchased the Cherry Hill estate from his father and, though its value had recently fallen, he had soon added to it three more substantial landholdings, including Rhine Hill, a few miles from Morant Bay, where for several years he sat as a magistrate. When in the 1850s he was elected to the Assembly, he joined the Town Party which sat in opposition to the Country Party, representative of the planting interest. He continued to take an active part in the debates when re-elected after a short gap in 1862. Both as representative and as magistrate he championed the cause of the black majority with vigour. Such advocacy had soon brought him into conflict with Charles Darling, the Governor.

It was to continue a source of contention when, in 1862, Darling took leave and was replaced, first temporarily and then permanently, by Eyre.

EDWARD JOHN EYRE, AUSTRALIAN EXPLORATION AND ABORIGINE RIGHTS

Eyre is the other chief antagonist in the Morant Bay tragedy. "Bloody Eyre", Reid's narrator calls him, and Olivier excoriates him as a racist. The problem for any viable reconstruction of events, however, is that, had he been a simple combination of these traits, his conduct and fate would not have divided England so sorely. He was certainly a highly unusual colonial official. Born a mere parson's son in Yorkshire in 1815, he had emigrated to Australia at seventeen because, as he later admitted in a psychologically telling phrase, you could "be your own man there".[12] In his early twenties he had been among the first, perhaps the very first, to discover the possibilities of driving sheep overland from the farms of New South Wales to the recent settlements in South Australia. He owed his rise in the world to an even more dramatic feat of endurance. In June 1840 he had gained the support of the Governor of South Australia, Sir George Grey, for an expedition into the interior north of Adelaide. Setting off with a team of companions, Eyre had found the way blocked off, as he believed, by the salt flats of Lake Torrens. Undaunted, he had dismissed most of his party and, with an overseer called Baxter and three native Australians, had made his way westwards along the Great Australian Bight. On the way, Baxter had been murdered and two of the Aborigines had absconded. Eyre and one remaining Aborigine had persevered. Though reduced to killing their horses for meat, and sometimes to collecting dew laboriously drop by drop from the long grass to slake their thirst, they had eventually walked the 1000 miles to King George's Sound.

Journals of Expeditions of Discovery into Central Australia, the book of 1845 in which Eyre recounts this journey, demonstrates vividly the streak of stubbornness in his make-up which doubtless made his feat possible, but which a quarter of a century later in the West Indies was to be unleashed to such frightening effect. It also gives evidence of more paradoxical qualities: a level-headedness in crisis, for example, and an ability to detach himself from standard settler attitudes. Eyre had passed through Port Lincoln, in what is now the Eyre Peninsula, when the twelve-year-old son of a missionary was speared to death by marauding Aborigines. His reaction to this harrowing episode is to condemn settler expansion in Australia, and to defend Aborigine land rights:

> Without laying claim to the country by right of conquest, without pleading even the mockery of cession, or the cheatery [sic] of sale, we have unhesitatingly entered upon, occupied, and disposed of its lands, spreading forth a new population over its surface, and driving before us the original inhabitants.
> To sanction this aggression we have not, in the abstract, the slightest shadow of either right or justice—we have not even the extenuation of endeavoring to compensate those whom we have injured, or the merit of attempting to mitigate the sufferings our presence inflicts.[13]

It is impossible to understand the furore caused by Eyre's disgrace in 1865 after his treatment of the Morant Bay rising without taking such statements into account. They also make his reaction to protest in Jamaica all the more surprising.

Governor Eyre and Politics in Jamaica

It had been Eyre's supposed capacity for tolerant leadership that had encouraged Grey to appoint him magistrate responsible for the Murray river, where he seems to have been a notable success. He had then served as Deputy Governor in Wellington, where he had finally fallen out with Grey, who had himself been transferred to Auckland and, as Eyre's superior officer, used every means at his disposal to strip his subordinate of effective authority. Eyre's most perceptive biographer, Geoffrey Dutton, ascribes his eventual overreaching of his authority in Jamaica to this earlier setback. Transferred to Antigua, he applied for the coveted governorship of Guyana, but was turned down by the Colonial Secretary of the day, the Duke of Newcastle, who commented in a confidential minute: "He is not strong enough for the place." After eighteen months of unemployment back in England, he had accepted the job as Darling's substitute on half pay, with the ominous explanation that Jamaica would give him a chance to "distinguish" himself.

Eyre's first tiff with Gordon was not long in coming. One of Gordon's duties as magistrate was to inspect the gaols of Morant Bay. He submitted a report to Eyre claiming that the Rector had caused a sick prisoner to be detained for three months in the privy. Eyre checked up with the Custos of

St Thomas, Barclay, who replied that the poor wretch had been permitted to stay in the lavatory all of this time because he had nowhere else to live. Since the integrity of the Rector was at stake, this preposterous explanation was accepted by the devoutly Anglican Eyre, who instantly dismissed Gordon as a magistrate on the grounds that he was a troublemaker.

As a result, Gordon also lost his place on the Parish Vestry and, with it, all vestige of municipal power. In order to regain admission to this useful body, he now stood as churchwarden, and in July 1863 was duly elected. There was, however, an impediment since, raised a Presbyterian, Gordon had long ago joined the ranks of the Baptists. Having undergone adult immersion, he had gravitated to the local, black branch of this church where he was now a Deacon, a rank into which he also ordained two other men who were to play a significant role in subsequent events: the brothers Paul and Moses Bogle. His membership of the sect had augmented his local power base: it had not, however, endeared him to the island establishment, who regarded the Baptist communion, especially the black variety of it, with scarcely veiled suspicion. The black Baptists had been active on the island since 1815; they had been instrumental in the struggle against slavery and, as Edward Brathwaite remarks in his book on early nineteenth-century creolisation, attracted an enthusiastic popular following "because their ideas and their style of preaching contained strong, syncretised African elements".[14] As Heuman asserts, the sect had long been regarded as a channel for political dissent.[15] In any case, Gordon's membership of the denomination technically disqualified him from being churchwarden, as the Rector was not slow to inform him.

Religion, which had always played a decisive role in the history of the island, exercised a vital function in the build-up to the rising. The Baptists might be scorned by the establishment, but they could not be ignored. In January 1865, Dr Underhill, Secretary to the Baptist Society in England, dispatched a warmly phrased letter to the Colonial Secretary Edward Cardwell, complaining that large sectors of the population were near to starvation. Suspecting that Underhill was exaggerating, Cardwell consulted Eyre, who promptly circularised magistrates in every parish seeking information. Unsurprisingly they replied in numbers discounting Underhill's claims. Governor Eyre was satisfied. The principal cause of the poverty of which the Baptist Secretary complained, he wrote in an official dispatch, was "the idleness, improvidence, and vice of the people".

Undaunted, the people of the Parish of St Ann decided to contact the Colonial Secretary directly. They phrased a letter in which they outlined every deprivation: the high taxes, the absentee landlords, the vacant and idle Crown lands. When Cardwell replied, he directed his response as if it had come from the Court of St James's. His communication hence became known as the Queen's Advice, and its words have echoed down Jamaican history. In the words of Reid's elderly narrator, recalling the commonly felt indignation across eighty years:

> Hear the QUEEN'S ADVICE;
> THE MEANS OF SUPPORT OF THE LABOURING CLASSES DEPEND ON THEIR OWN LABOUR. HER MAJESTY WILL REGARD WITH INTEREST AND SATISFACTION THEIR ADVANCEMENT THROUGH THEIR OWN EFFORTS.
> *Wait!* plead the good pastors from their pulpits, *Her Majesty has been wrongly advised!*
> *Wait*, says Mr. Gordon at his Underhill meetings, *We will take the case to Whitehall ourselves.*[16]

The Governor's response to the Queen's Advice was characteristically decisive. On 5 July, he ordered that 50,000 copies of it be made, and posted as bills on the church door of every parish in Jamaica.

Gordon's reaction to this provocation was equally prompt. He called a meeting at St Elizabeth's and St Ann's for 29 July, employing in the invitation words that would later be used against him: "This is not the time when such deeds should be perpetrated, but, as they have been, it is your duty to speak out, and act too! We advise you to be up and doing on the 29th." In alarm, the Custos of St Elizabeth, a Thuringian aristocrat by the name of Baron Maximilian von Ketelhodt, sent a panicky letter to Eyre who, mindful that the anniversary of emancipation fell on 1 August, sent round a ship of war. An uneasy peace prevailed.

Prominent among those who had attended the meeting on 29 July were the Bogle brothers, who possessed a secluded yet accessible power base at Stony Gut, the 500-acre estate which Paul Bogle farmed in the Blue Mountains above Morant Bay. In mid-September, the brothers journeyed further up into the hills to consult with Major Sterling, leader of the Maroons at Hatfield, as to the possibility of Maroon support in the event of a rising. Paul later claimed that the Maroons, descendants of escaped Spanish slaves, had agreed to support him and subsequently changed sides. At the commission of inquiry, Sterling would claim that he had never promised Bogle assistance, though, bearing in mind the circumstances under which his evidence was given, it is difficult to know how much weight to put on this disclaimer. In any case, Bogle retreated to Stony Gut and was soon levying men. On 7 October, he led a party down to the court house, where a routine case of assault was being heard. When the accused was fined with costs, a member of Bogle's party called out that the amounts were excessive; the police made to arrest him for contempt, but Bogle and the others fended them off. Two days later, a group of constables visited Stony Gut, where they attempted to deliver a warrant to Bogle, but were driven back. As soon as Ketelhodt got wind of this incident, he issued a general call-out of the constabulary and immediately wrote to Eyre in Spanish Town, ending his appeal: "I am of the opinion that no time ought to be lost in dispatching a sufficient military force."

In England meanwhile, Eyre was appearing before the reading public in a contrasted, and flattering, light. In the October issue of *Macmillan's Magazine* an article had just appeared by Henry Kingsley, younger brother of the Revd Charles, under the title "Eyre, the South-Australian Explorer". This eulogistic piece drew both on admiring rumour picked up by its author during a sojourn in Australia in the 1850s, and on an appreciative reading of Eyre's own memoirs. It recounted its subject's travels, and emphasised his self-effacing treatment of native Australians. It praised his work among the inhabitants of the Murray river and, though conceding that he was "high-strung", went on to commend him as an example of gentlemanly and humane distinction.[17] But what was more impressive than the article's substance was its style: jerky, enthusiastic, abstruse, the very prose of Thomas Carlyle's influential lecture series *On Heroes, Hero-Worship, and the Heroic in History* which, when published in 1841, had so influenced a generation's notions of male virtue. The audible implication was that Eyre had been, and arguably still was, the embodiment of the rugged and sublime ideal extolled in those lectures. *Macmillan's* was widely read: by Carlyle himself, by Charles Kingsley, by Froude, by virtually everybody, that is, who subsequently took a prominent part in Eyre's defence. The form which that campaign was to take can best be understood by reference to the vivid transformation, in Henry Kingsley's sometimes stumbling sentences, of the individual Edward John Eyre into the likeness of a Carlylean hero.[18] Thus, a few days before the first shot was fired in anger in the square at Morant Bay, the grounds on which the report of it would be received by a certain section of the English intelligentsia had already been prepared.

October 1865: The Rising Erupts

That week, in Spanish Town, the object of Henry Kingsley's fervour received the latest of Ketelhodt's alarmist pleas. He convened the Executive Council, who advised sending the frigate *Wolverene* round to St Thomas's. The following day, Bogle's men again entered the square with fife and drum. They were met on the steps of the court house by the apprehensive Custos who read the riot act and then, upon being pelted with stones, permitted his troops to shoot, killing seven of the protesters. Later that evening the school house was torched, and the fire soon spread to the court house. By nightfall, Ketelhodt, one of the Rector's sons and sixteen other citizens lay dead.

In Kingston itself, among the first to receive the news was Gordon. He had been spending the day engaged in business, and in the evening returned to Cherry Hill and told his wife about the incident. Eyre heard later that night and instantly convened the Council, who advised him to declare martial law throughout the County of Surrey, with the exception of Kingston. The few regular troops on the island were under the overall command of General L. Smythe O'Connor; Eyre as Governor, however, was responsible for specific troop movements. Eyre placed 100 men from the 2nd Battalion, 6th Regiment and the 1st West India Regiment under the command of Captain Lewis Hall, responsible for scouting and subduing the area immediately inland from Morant Bay.[19] He rapidly appointed a police inspector called Ramsay, who had earned the Victoria Cross during the Crimean War by taking part in the Charge of the Light Brigade, to the post of Provost Martial, responsible for the administration of the emergency provisions in Morant Bay itself, where courts martial were to be convened to try suspects.[20] Convinced that Gordon had incited, if not fomented, the disturbance, Eyre determined to bring him to book. There was one problem: Kingston, where Gordon was staying, was specifically excluded from martial law. Undaunted by this technicality, Eyre confronted Gordon in person before personally signing a warrant for his arrest and escorting him by ship to Morant Bay, where he delivered him into the hands of the tribunal. Found guilty, Gordon was hanged beneath the arch of the gutted court house on 23 October. The following day, Bogle, and several of the ringleaders, were executed at the *Wolverene*'s yardarm. Ever afterwards, folklore was to give Bogle and his mentor a symbolically identical fate. "Do no' go down, Father," calls out Reid's narrator in his agony of reminiscence, "Mr Gordon and Dean Bogle are hanging by their necks from the court-house steps."[21]

Anxious to assert his authority, Eyre claimed that the rising was contained after three days. Substantially this was true since, though small detachments of rioters went on the rampage north and west, none strayed beyond the boundaries of the parish. Despite this reassurance, Eyre maintained martial law for another three weeks. Later, a Royal Commission of Inquiry would discover the full severity of the measures taken: 439 people were put to death, 354 of them by court martial, the rest shot by soldiers, sailors or by the Maroons who soon joined in the chase. Furthermore, 1005 dwellings were razed to the ground. The military commanders, two of them certifiably demented, did nothing to restrain the sadistic impulses of their men. Ramsay stood by while men and women were flogged: on one occasion fifty lashes were meted out to a bystander for not wearing a hat; a witness at one court martial was given twelve for winking at the accused. On finally declaring an amnesty, Eyre addressed a full session of the Assembly. The unusual circumstances of the last few weeks, he argued, rendered the suspension of the constitution necessary. He then persuaded the members to dissolve the house permanently. Jamaica was declared a Crown Colony; it would remain without effective representative institutions for another seventy-nine years.

The Case of Governor Eyre: The Victorian Debate

News of the severity of the executions was now slow to reach England, where opinion was quickly divided between those who believed that Eyre had exceeded his legitimate functions, and those who thought that he had behaved with necessary and commendable dispatch. Scandals concerning governors of Caribbean islands who had overstepped their authority were not, of course, entirely new in the metropolis. Perhaps the most notorious case had been the legal proceedings in 1801 following the torture, on the signature of the irascible Welshman Thomas Picton, first British Governor of Trinidad, of the fourteen-year-old mulatto girl Luisa Calderon, vividly recreated for our generation by V.S. Naipaul in his history *The Loss of El Dorado*.[22] Picton's prosecution through the English courts by Colonel William Fullarton, former First Commissioner of Trinidad, had smacked of a personal vendetta, however. Besides, there is no evidence that Fullarton had ever enjoyed much popular support, and Picton had ended his life in glory, as a hero of the Peninsular War. What was relatively new about the case of Edward John Eyre was the groundswell of public revulsion that promptly succeeded news of his acts, a surge of feeling that had much to do with the pervasive influence, in certain quarters of British opinion, of a philanthropically inclined Evangelical Movement, then at its height. The first anti-Eyre demonstration was held in Manchester on 27 November.[23] The following month, a coalition of nonconformists and liberal intellectuals formed themselves into the Jamaica Committee, headed initially by Charles Buxton, son of the eminent anti-slavery campaigner Thomas Fowell Buxton. Other Members of Parliament soon joined the movement, notably the liberal economist John Bright, the lawyer Tom Hughes, author of *Tom Brown's Schooldays* and longtime associate of the Kingsleys, and the philosopher John Stuart Mill. It was Mill who was to assume the leadership of the movement to indict Eyre before the courts. Largely as a result of pressures brought by such men, the Commission of Inquiry was sent out to Jamaica the following January. After hearing the evidence of 730 witnesses, including Eyre himself, soldiers and victims of various outrages, it submitted an equivocal report, praising Eyre for his "skill, promptitude and valour", but criticising the severity of the punitive measures. In March, Eyre published a letter in *The Times* justifying his conduct, dictated, as he saw it, by a dire and widespread emergency.[24] Despite this appeal, the Commission relieved him of his responsibilities, and on 24 July he set sail for England. He arrived on 12 August to find the country divided into two camps: one vociferous in his favour, the other determined to prosecute him by every legal means.

Uncertain what to do next, Eyre hung around Southampton for several days, though the town was as divided as the rest of the country.[25] Soon a delegation from the Jamaica Committee arrived and started leafleting the populace. For his part the mayor met Eyre's ship as it docked and had soon organised an official banquet, at which the ex-Governor was praised in lavish terms by Lord Cardigan, another Crimean hero. In the newspaper reports that followed, however, Cardigan's speech was eclipsed by the rhetorical efforts of the orator who addressed the company next: the Revd Charles Kingsley.

Kingsley had attended the banquet by chance, since he had been spending the holiday period at the house of his friend Lord Hardwicke, who invited him along. The invitation placed him in an awkward position: Kingsley was well known as an activist and social reformer whose opinion on matters of current concern was likely to be quoted. Before going, Kingsley wrote to his wife Fanny promising discretion: "I quite agree with you about not speaking, and shall avoid it *if possible*, and if not, only compliment him on his *Australian* exploits."[26] In the event, he avoided making one of the main speeches for the evening, but was prevailed upon to propose the last of the formal toasts rounding off the proceedings: a toast to the two Houses of Parliament. Starting with a résumé of Henry's article in *Macmillan's*, he went on to laud the guest of honour as the epitome of that "English spirit of indomitable perseverance, courage and adventure" and "of good nature, or temper, of the understanding of human beings, of knowing how to manage men". He finished by converting his comments into a graceful tribute to the parliamentary institutions which were the subject of the toast. *The Times* paraphrased his concluding remarks thus:

> By what that noble man [Eyre] did in Australia, by his walk of 700 miles round The Cape of Carpentaria, he showed he possessed in a very high degree that spirit which carried the Anglo-Saxon tongue around the world, and which has made us the Fathers of the United States and the conquerors of India. Of his proceedings in Jamaica he would say nothing except that knowing what he did of the West Indies and Mr Eyre, he took him and his conduct upon trust. If we refused to take men upon trust, especially rulers and official men, there would be nothing except anarchy, which would be followed by despotism, and in due time by a big tyrant who would not take the people upon trust. If Mr Eyre should be blessed with health during the next 25 years, he should not be surprised to see him attain to a seat in the House of Lords, an assembly in which he would not be the least noble man among the peers of England.[27]

The correspondent from *The Times*, however, was not the only journalist in the hall. There was also a sprinkling of reporters from the liberal press, and from the highbrow fortnightlies and monthlies. Amongst this sector of opinion Kingsley held an ambiguous reputation. Radical and advocate of democratic causes Kingsley indubitably was; he was, for all that, an ordained representative of the Established Church, the natural political allies of which were Tories. The ardour of Kingsley's expostulation took these liberal-minded scribes aback. Some of them found his comments so gratuitous that, in reporting them, they went out of their way to exaggerate, almost to lampoon, the speaker's obsequiousness. A liberal monthly quoted by Bernard Semmel, for example, gave quite a different, and apparently verbatim, version of the climax to the speech, without mentioning that it had been delivered as a formal toast. As a result, Kingsley's eulogy to the House of Lords, a body which was already an object of suspicion in radical quarters, appeared not as the conventional flourish for which it was intended, but as the expression of deep-seated, reactionary principles:

> Mr Eyre is so noble, brave and chivalric a man, so undaunted a servant of the crown, so illustrious as an explorer in Australia and a saviour of society in the West Indies that Peers—actual Peers—my soul sinks with awe as I repeat Peers—members of the sacred order, which represents chivalry, which adopts into its ranks all genius, all talents, all virtue, and all learning, condescend, not indeed to give him dinner—that would be too much—but to dine in the same room with him.[28]

The liberal press had a field day with this version, which was all the more surprising considering the man who was supposed to have delivered it.[29] That Kingsley was a clergyman was not itself felt to be incongruous, since the Established Church had been quick to leap to the defence of the devoutly Anglican Eyre. But since the late 1840s the Revd Kingsley had identified himself with a series of humanitarian causes: conditions in the tailoring industry; sanitation in Bermondsey; the rights of farm labourers. He had been closely connected with the Christian Socialist Movement, in whose periodical he had published a column championing the cause of the oppressed. He had played a minor but much publicised role in the celebrated Chartist meeting on Kennington Common of April 1848, and his novels on behalf of such causes had done much to damage his ecclesiastical career. All of this he had borne willingly: why, his allies now wished to know, was he taking a stand in support of the butcher of Morant Bay? The general amazement was trenchantly expressed in verse by the historian and humourist George Otto Trevelyan, who asserted his astonishment

> That he, whose brave old English tales, set all our hearts aglow,
> Should teach that "modern chivalry" has forced its noblest egress
> By burning Baptist villages, and stringing up a negress.[30]

Kingsley also received short shrift from former associates in the Christian Socialist Movement such as Tom Hughes and the radical barrister J.M. Ludlow, who were soon refusing to speak to him.[31] Their indignation intensified when Kingsley gave his tacit support to the Eyre Defence Fund, set up under the chairmanship of Carlyle at a meeting on 29 August which Henry and Froude attended.[32] What especially worried these activists was Kingsley's alliance over this matter with Carlyle, the so-called sage of Chelsea, whose racialist views had been bluntly expressed in an earlier disquisition on the condition of Jamaica, "Occasional Discourse on the Negro Question", published in *Frazer's* in 1849. Carlyle had made no bones about his opinion of the black population of Jamaica, whom he had regarded as work shy and in need of a strong hand.[33]

Considering the biased reporting of the Southampton speech in certain periodicals, the reaction of Kingsley's socialist friends may at first sight seem extreme. It seems less so in the light of Kingsley's own subsequent statements. As the weeks passed by, he reacted as he so often did when placed in the wrong: he dug his heels in. That winter he received a letter from one of his working-class admirers congratulating him in veiled terms for his support for one "sorely tried". Kingsley wrote back:

> I *have* followed the sage of Chelsea's teaching about my noble friend, ex-Governor of Jamaica. I have been cursed for it, as if I had been a dog, who had never stood up for the working man when all the world was hounding him (the working man) down in 1848–9, and imperiled my own prospects in life on behalf of freedom and justice. Now, men insult me because I stand up for a man whom I believe ill-treated, calumniated, and hounded to death by fanatics. If you mean Mr Eyre in what you say, you will indeed give me pleasure, because I shall see that one more "Man of the people" has commonsense enough to appreciate a brave and good man, doing his best under terrible difficulties: but, if not, I know that I am right.[34]

KINGSLEY, CARLYLE, NEWMAN AND THE CULT OF THE HERO

Kingsley took no active role in the administration of the defence fund— "Charles hanging back afraid," Carlyle noted sardonically in a letter.[35] Eventually, the bureaucratic burden fell on the shoulders of Ruskin, who clearly though that Kingsley had become half-hearted because he feared calumny: "I never", he complained much later in life, "thought much of Muscular Christianity after that."[36] The relatively passive role that Kingsley took in the controversy, however, is far less interesting than the fact that someone with his views should have subscribed to the case for Eyre at all.

Certainly the Carlylean idea of the explorer as hero had swayed him, and he was not slow to place Eyre in that mould. Justifying his indiscretion to Fanny after the Southampton dinner, he explained: "Eyre is one of the most noble and interesting men I ever saw—I *had* to speak to propose Lds & commons, & in all my allusions to him I stuck to his Australian work."[37]

His protestations of impartiality, however, do not ring entirely true: what comes across instead is his rapt admiration for a particular kind of overseas or imperial swashbuckling. Kingsley had always cherished his own pantheon of adventurer-idols, such as Rajah Brooke of Sarawak, the renegade British administrator and trader who had set himself up as a chieftain in the wilds of Borneo, and whose rough-and-ready methods had also brought him into disrepute with the authorities. Kingsley had sprung to Brooke's defence, and had part dedicated his buccaneering novel *Westward Ho!* to him. He was also convinced that Eyre was a scapegoat, commenting, again to his wife, "I still believe...that the man has been sacrificed to a paltry and weak government." Moreover, together with Dickens, Ruskin and others who had taken a strong line on working-class rights, Kingsley almost certainly felt that a double standard was being applied by Eyre's detractors: demanding justice overseas when so many abuses persisted at home. His position in the controversy, however, only really makes sense if viewed against a general backdrop of political and philosophical principles. By November 1866, the Jamaica Committee had won the support of perhaps its most persuasive advocate: the biologist Thomas Henry Huxley, who wrote to Kingsley putting the matter in a nutshell:

> In point of fact, men take sides on this question, not so much by looking at the mere facts of the case but rather as their deepest political convictions lead them. And the great use of the prosecution and one of my reasons for joining it, is that it will help a great many people find out what their profound political beliefs are.[38]

Kingsley's mixed reaction to the Eyre dispute—his vocal advocacy, his reluctance to become practically embroiled—may partly be explained by the fact that he had recently been traumatised by a controversy almost as bitter, in which he had also found himself on the same side as Froude. The subject of this *contretemps* had been remote from West Indian affairs, yet it affords an interesting, sideways clue to the deep-seating attitudes of some of Eyre's supporters. In 1864 Froude had published the seventh and last volume of his *History of England from the Fall of Wolsey to the Death of Queen Elizabeth*, a study of the English Reformation on which he had been engaged for several years.[39] It had been candid in its distrust of Roman Catholicism, and especially of the casuistic tendencies of the Papacy and of a succession of Spanish ambassadors in London, whom it had implicitly accused of a deeply ingrained tendency to lie. The following month, Kingsley had reviewed the book for *Macmillan's Magazine* where he had gone to some length to emphasise and endorse his brother-in-law's anti-Papist stance. "Truth, for its own sake", Kingsley had declared in a soon notorious sentence, "had never been a virtue with the Roman clergy."[40] He had reckoned without Rome's most eminent English convert John Henry Newman who, stung to the quick by this aspersion cast at his adopted Church, had replied at exhaustive, and virtually unanswerable, length in his autobiographical justification *Apologia Pro Vita Sua*.

Kingsley was widely thought to have been worsted in this battle of words. As on the later occasion, he had seemed unrepentant, with Froude still faithful at his side. All this would be of purely personal or theological significance, were it not for the fact that in England in 1865 Catholicism was still a politically charged issue. Since the repeal of the Test and Corporation Acts in 1829, the influence of the Catholic Church had grown to an extent worrying to Broad Church Anglicans: the re-establishment of the Catholic hierarchy in 1850 had been a turning point, and even within the Church of England Catholic tendencies had not ceased to grow.

In Kingsley's mind, there seems to have been a strong psychological connection between Romanism and the West Indies. His most successful novel *Westward Ho!*, written in Devon in the early months of the Crimean War, describes the exploits of the Elizabethan worthy Amyas Leigh. Early in the book Leigh's fiancée, the symbolically named Rose, is seduced by a Spanish sea captain called Don Guzman, who elopes with her to the Caribbean, where Amyas hunts them down. Rose is taken to South America, where she perishes under the Inquisition. Meanwhile, Amyas returns to Europe, where he eventually commands a battle ship against the Armada. In the climactic scene he catches sight of his erstwhile rival driving his own boat up the west coast of England; Amyas intercepts the vessel, and is about to crush it and its captain against the rocks when storm and lightning sink the ship, depriving him of his moment of revenge, and blind him. The blinding, as many of Kingsley's readers will attest, is probably the most effective moment in his fiction, since it appears to reprove the protagonist and, by extension, the author for their own ethical purblindness, their deliberate and sustained pursuits of prejudice. The novel's commercial success, which, as John Sutherland reminds us,[41] more or less launched Macmillan as a general publisher, was the result of its pandering to the patriotic fervour during the early months of the war. In the novel, Spain and the Catholic Church are the enemies rather than

Russia; yet, if for the audience the xenophobia worked on the level of analogy, for the author the anti-Romanism was real enough, and its playground, seemingly free from the political embarrassments of Britain, was the West Indies.

Kingsley, Jamaica and Ireland

Roman Catholicism, in any case, was far from an isolated issue, since in English Protestant eyes at the time it could not be separated from the problem that was to dominate the political horizon more and more: the nagging, seemingly unsolvable conundrum of Ireland. The Eyre controversy coincided in time with a crisis in Irish affairs. Fenian outrages, which had been increasing over the previous few months, culminated in the murder of a police sergeant in Manchester. In 1868 several bystanders were killed when part of the wall of the Clerkenwell House of Detention was mined by Fenians attempting to release their comrades.[42] When the suspected bomber, Michael Barrett, came to court, the prosecuting council was the very lawyer employed to defend Eyre: the Tory barrister Hardinge Giffard, later Lord Halsbury. In both the Fenian and the Eyre trials, Giffard stressed the imperative need to impose order on volatile populations. The argument proved so persuasive when used in the Shropshire Magistrates' Court, before which Eyre was arraigned on a charge of murder, that the case was thrown out amidst loud rejoicing.

As the Eyre campaign proceeded, its relevance to the Irish problem became increasingly apparent. Baulked in their attempt to have the ex-Governor tried for murder, the Committee hauled two of the more bloodthirsty militiamen before a Middlesex Grand Jury. The charge was read by Lord Cockburn, Lord Chief Justice of England, whose opinion it was that the issue boiled down to the validity of martial law. After six hours, Cockburn gave his opinion that "the law of English knows no such thing as martial law". His opinion was rejected by the jury, but the subtext of the trial became apparent in the House of Commons the following day when an Irish member, M.W. O'Reilly, stood up and asked whether "this house would regard as utterly void and illegal any commission or proclamation purporting or pretending to proclaim Martial Law in any part of the Kingdom".[43] The intervention spelled out the wider implications of the Jamaica dispute, clarifying the unspoken considerations that had motivated the juries in both of the recent trials. Confronted by the implied application of the Cockburn opinion to law-keeping in Ireland, the Secretary for War Edward Cardwell, who, as Colonial Secretary, had appointed and then supported Eyre in Jamaica, urged O'Reilly to withdraw his remark.

The parallels between colonial affairs, Irish politics and religious division were not merely coincidental.[44] As both Kingsley and Froude's statements make clear in a number of contexts, the connections were deep-seated and structural. Indeed, Froude would later betray the existence of such conscious or unconscious links by referring to the Morant Bay rising in *The English in the West Indies* as "the Gordon riots", a phrase which could not but remind those aware of England's religious history, and readers of Dickens's *Barnaby Rudge*, of the anti-popery riots in London in 1780. Both Froude and Kingsley regarded the Irish as mendacious and ungovernable. Kingsley's mother's family had been planters in Barbados; he always revelled in a personal mythology of the Caribbean based on his childhood reading in which Elizabethan admirals such as Drake and Grenville—both of whom appear in *Westward Ho!*—lord it over dastardly Catholic sailors and unruly blacks.

These streams of prejudice were to continue to co-mingle long after Eyre's final acquittal in 1868, and Kingsley's death in 1875. The Morant Bay rebellion, and the case that followed it, had bitten deep into the psyche of Victorian England, from which they had a tendency to well up at times of surface tension. Such a moment, for example, was the political crisis of 1886/7 caused by Gladstone's conversion to the principle of Home Rule for Ireland. Though Gladstone's Home Rule Bill was defeated, bad feeling continued to seethe through the year of the Jubilee, and the Colonial Conference convened to mark it. Prominent amongst the lobby opposed to Home Rule were Froude, Tennyson, Kingsley's former pupil John Martineau, and a number of others who had once defended Eyre.[45]

Froude and Counter-Froude

Froude's response to that crisis was the book with which I began this chapter, *The English in the West Indies*. Running through it is a double theme: a lament for the author's cherished brother-in-law—priest, novelist and political ally—and a sustained consideration of democratic representation in the colonies. The text begins with a discussion of the extension of self-government mooted at the recent imperial conference. Such proposals have their merits when applied to the older dominions, Froude argues, but

When we think of India, when we think of Ireland, prudence tells us to hesitate. Steps once taken in this direction cannot be undone, even if found to lead to the wrong place...The danger now is that [self-government] will be tried in haste in...countries either as yet unripe for it or from the nature of things unfit for it. The liberties which we grant freely to those whom we trust and who do not require to be restrained, we bring into disrepute if we concede them as readily to perversity or disaffection or to those who, like most Asiatics, do not desire liberty, and prosper best when they are led and guided.[46]

The severity and bigotry of this judgement shed light in a number of areas: Froude's otherwise inexplicable decision to illustrate his divisive theme by writing about the West Indies, the importance of the Morant Bay rising in his account, and Thomas's anger at his froudacity. Manifestly Gordon, Bogle and their supporters had been amongst those who, in Froude's eyes, did "require to be constrained" if not "led and guided". And, inadvisable as Eyre's more draconian measures may have been, his abolition of the Assembly had been justified as forestalling any extension of representation amongst those "from the nature of things unripe for it". Froude's sinister conclusion, correctly inferred by Thomas, was that there existed two standards of political responsiveness, one applicable to Anglo-Saxon populations and another to Irish Catholics or Jamaican Baptists. This invidious distinction had been enunciated all too clearly in the parliamentary election of 1886 in which Lord Salisbury, the jingoistic leader of the Conservatives, had argued, in a reviled phrase combining exclusivity of religion and of race, that certain peoples, "Hindoos and Hottentots" amongst them, were incapable of self-government.[47] In the apologetics of burgeoning imperialism in the 1890s, this was precisely the lesson that Morant Bay was employed to drive home.

The Morant Bay rising continued to linger in the national consciousness as a kind of bogie event. Without doubt, it drew on deep-set fears which emerged elsewhere in rumour, in folklore and in popular culture. An interesting side-light may help to bring this fact out. At Rugby School in the 1840s a shadowy figure would appear in the dormitories at night. No pupil was ever known to have seen him. He was the shoe-black and, his job once done, he would disappear in the thin light of dawn. He was known to the boys as the "bogle".[48] The appearance of this fleeting, feared figure in Tom Hughes's enduringly popular *Tom Brown's Schooldays*, which went through dozens of editions in the mid to late Victorian period, is amply suggestive of the communal phobia on which such fictional episodes drew.

Indeed, the noun "bogle", common in Scotland since at least 1500, is cognate with the equivalent English term "bogie".[49] Like the despised, nocturnal shoe-black whose name he shared, Paul Bogle—leader if not instigator of the Morant Bay insurrection—soon became a bogie figure in the minds of respectable British folk. No doubt such neurotic transformations of personalities connected with the insurrection were rife in the minds of many a middle-class Englishman at the time, and doubtless too they underlay Froude's book, where their presence was sensed by Thomas. Thomas's gut reaction to such phobic over-reaction was topical and polemical, but, bearing in mind the history of the Morant Bay rising and its aftermath, a more lasting verdict is voiced by John Campbell, the octogenarian narrator of *New Day*, who, remembering the dreadful events of 1865 long after, exclaims, with a fine mixture of horror and incredulity, "But God O! Look what my eyes ha' lived to see!"[50]

NOTES

1. Edward Said, *Culture and Imperialism* (London: Random House, 1993).
2. Angus Calder, *Revolutionary Empire: The Rise of the English-Speaking Empires from the Fifteenth Century to the 1780s* (London: Jonathan Cape, 1981).
3. John Jacob Thomas, *Froudacity; West Indian Tales* (London: T. Fisher Unwin, 1889).
4. J.A. Froude, *The English in the West Indies: The Bow of Ulysses* (London: Longmans & Co., 1888).
5. Thomas, 5.
6. Froude, 256–63.
7. V.S. Reid, *New Day* (New York: Alfred A. Knoft, 1949; London: William Heinemann, 1950; London: Heinemann Educational Books, Caribbean Writers Series, 1973), 1.
8. Sydney Haldane, Baron Olivier, *The Myth of Governor Eyre* (London: Leonard and Virginia Woolf at the Hogarth Press, 1933).
9. For Mill's account of the Eyre controversy, and his views on the case, see John Stuart Mill, *Autobiography*, Third Edition (London: Longmans, Green, Reader and Dyer, 1874), 295–99.
10. Gad Heuman, *"'The Killing Time'": The Morant Bay Rebellion in Jamaica* (London and Basingstoke: Macmillan, 1994), 44.
11. For Gordon's background and career, see Ansell Hart, *The Life of George William Gordon* (Kingston, Jamaica: Institute of Jamaica, 1972).

12. The standard late Victorian account of Eyre's life and career is Alexander Hamilton Hume's *The Life of Edward John Eyre, Late Governor of Jamaica* (London: Richard Bentley, 1867), written in the immediate aftermath of the rising and of Eyre's official exoneration by the courts. Hume is ardently pro-Eyre. For a full, balanced and psychologically penetrating modern account, see Geoffrey Dutton, *The Hero as Murderer: The Life of Edward John Eyre, Australian Explorer and Governor of Jamaica (1815–1901)* (London: Collins; Sydney, Melbourne: Cheshire, 1967).
13. Edward John Eyre, *Journals of Expeditions of Discovery into Central Australia, and Overland from Adelaide to King George's Sand, in 1840–1, Including an Account of the Manners and Customs of the Aborigines, and the State of Their Relations with Europeans*, 2 vols. (London: T. & W. Boone, 1845), vol. ii, 158–59.
14. Edward Brathwaite, *The Development of Creole Society in Jamaica, 1770–1820* (Oxford: Clarendon, 1971), 259.
15. Heuman, 38, 64.
16. Reid, 8.
17. Henry Kingsley, "Eyre, the South-Australian Explorer" Part II, *Macmillan's Magazine*, November, 1865, 55.
18. In other ways, Carlyle substantially prepared the way for the public reaction to the Eyre controversy. It had been his anonymous article "Occasional Discourse on the Negro Question", printed in the December 1849 issue of *Frazer's Magazine*, pp. 670–9, that had first sewn in the public mind the idea that the relative poverty of the Jamaican populace was due less to inclement economic circumstances than to the people's endemic laziness. The following passage is typical: "The West Indies, it appears, are short of labour; as indeed is very conceivable in those circumstances: where a Black man by working about half an hour a-day (such is the calculation) can supply himself, by the aid of sun and soil, with as much pumpkin as will suffice, he is likely to be a little stiff to raise into hard work! Supply and demand, which, science says, should be brought to bear on him, have an uphill task of it with such a man" (672). This routine argument was trotted out several times during and after the rising, both by Eyre himself and by others in support of the Governor's hard line, especially in response to the demands of the Baptists. Suitably toned down, it appears both in Eyre's submissions to Cardwell at the Colonial Office and in the "Queen's Letter" posted as a result.
19. Heuman, 116.
20. The chain of command at the time of the rising had been complicated by the political evolution of the island in recent years. Technically all orders had to be issued, or at least confirmed, by General O'Connor, who held the rank of Commander-in-Chief of the British Troops in the West Indies.

Confusingly, however, Eyre, who had no military experience, was Captain General and Supreme Commander-in-Chief in Jamaica, in which capacity he acted, with the support of the council, to put down the rising in the draconian manner he saw fit. Moreover, because of reforms at the War Office, for which the Secretary of State Cardwell had been responsible, the large-scale British military force had recently been withdrawn, leaving a handful of officers and an impromptu militia. The lack of a substantial regular armed force had been a constant bone of contention between Eyre and the Colonial Office. Eyre cited this deficiency as a reason for his severity during the rising, continuing to do so for some time afterwards (see note 18). Despite Eyre's protestations, it is doubtful whether the insurgents made a distinction between the militia and regular troops.

21. Reid, 4. But see *New Day*, 151: "Deacon Bogle is a-hang from the yardarm o' the *Wolverine*." Bro' Davies's account of the method by which Bogle was executed conflicts with the official version. Nonetheless, it reflects a powerful image as handed down by folklore, according to which Bogle was "strung up from the arch of the very court house that he had gutted. Where, in the iconography of Caribbean nationalism, he remains: the hanged god of colonial Jamaica." Robert Fraser, *The Making of the Golden Bough: The Origins and Growth of an Argument* (Basingstoke: Macmillan; New York: The St Martin's Press, 1990), 137.

22. V.S. Naipaul, *The Loss of El Dorado: A History* (Harmondsworth: Penguin, 1973). See especially chap. 6, pp. 182–221.

23. For the response to the massacre in England, and the successive trials, see Bernard Semmel, *The Governor Eyre Controversy* (London: MacGibbon and Kee, 1962).

24. *The Times*, 6 March, 1866, 10 col.d. Written from Flamstead, Eyre's up-country residence on the island, and dated 7 February, the letter read: "It can hardly be denied that the emergency occasioned by the rebellion in Jamaica was a great one, when that rebellion spread 20 miles in one direction in two days and a half, and 40 miles in another direction in three and a half days; or that the peril threatening the entire island was imminent when disaffection, seditious feelings, and sympathy, with a readiness to join the rebels, were known to exist in almost every parish, while at the same time the local Executive had not a single soldier available to serve any locality whatever, should further outbreaks in other parishes have taken place. Under such conditions the most prompt, certain and severe punishment became unnecessary as a means of self-defence to insure the public safety. I do not doubt but that the Inquiry now being instituted will make all this, and much more, fully apparent to the public." Eyre's sanguine confidence that the Inquiry would find in his favour was only partially justified.

25. Eyre arrived in the West Indies on the mail steamer *Tasmania* on Sunday 12 August. According to *The Times*, reporting the following Monday, 20 August (page 7, col. c.), the late Governor who "has since remained in the town, has accepted to attend a banquet from some of the inhabitants who sympathize with him and his conduct during the rising last year".
26. Charles Kingsley to Fanny Kingsley, August 1866. BL Add. Ms. 62555. f. 123., written "before August 23, 1866."
27. *The Times* for August 23rd, 1866, page 7, columns a–c.
28. Quoted in Semmel, 94.
29. Charles Kingsley to Fanny Kingsley from Eversley Rectory, August 1866: "Look at *The Times* about Eyre. The speeches are very well reported. *The Times*, as you see, is against Eyre. But is civil enough to me…I still believe him in the right, and that the man has been sacrificed to a paltry & weak government." BL Add. Ms. 6255. fol. 127. Kingsley's suspicion that Eyre was being made a scapegoat by an inefficient administration doubtless continued to play a part in his reasons for carrying on defending him, even if thenceforth his support was mainly tacit. See also letter from Bishopstoke, August 1866, ff. 137–38: "*The Times* is evidently *hedging* for the change of feeling which must take place about Eyre when he comes to be known. Meanwhile I have the consciousness of having stood by a good man in all verity, and *not* having committed myself about the Jamaican details."
30. Quoted in Semmel, 100.
31. After Kingsley's death, Ludlow explained his attitude in a letter, quoted at length in Susan Chitty's biography of Kingsley: "I continued corresponding with him till the time of the Jamaica committee. Then, when the Jamaican massacres took place, and Tom Hughes and myself joined the Jamaica Committee, I was amazed to hear that, without saying a word to either of us, he had joined himself to the antagonistic organisation, the Eyre Defence Fund. I wrote to him to tell him that our paths ran so divergent that it was worthless to correspond any longer." Susan Chitty, *Charles Kingsley: The Beast and the Monk* (London: Hodder and Stoughton; New York: Mason/Charter, 1975), 242–43. Ludlow's interpretation of Kingsley's position seems slightly at odds with Carlyle's here, though of course the two men were approaching the issue from opposite vantage points. What seemed to Ludlow like bloody-minded obduracy might very well have seemed to Carlyle to be more like timorous holding back. In any case, Ludlow and Kingsley did not meet again until the funeral of their mutual friend F.D. Maurice in April 1872.
32. The meeting, held on 29 August 1866, is described at some length in J.A. Froude, *Thomas Carlyle. A History of his Life in London, 1834–1881*, 2 vols. (London: Longman and Green, 1884). Froude quotes a letter by Carlyle to Miss Davenport Bramley written the day after it, 30 August:

"Yesterday, in spite of the rain, I got up to the Eyre Committee, and I've let myself be voted into the chair, such being the post of danger on this occasion, and truly something of a forlorn hope and place for enfants perdus. We seemed, so far as I can measure, to be a most feeble committee: a military captain, a naval ditto, a young city merchant, Henry Kingsley, Charles still hanging back afraid..." Froude, *Carlyle*, ii, 329. Charles Kingsley's non-attendance would tend to suggest that he had been more wounded by criticisms of his Southampton speech than he had let on to Fanny. To be fair to Kingsley, however, his time was at a premium in 1866, since he was combining the responsibilities of Rector of Eversley (where, however, he had a curate), Regius Professor of Modern History at the University of Cambridge and Chaplain to the Queen. Moreover, if Carlyle's journal is anything to go by, even the sage of Cheyne Walk was in two minds. "Eyre Defence Committee", he notes on 26 September, "small letter of mine has been raging through all the newspapers of the empire, I am told; for I have carefully avoided everything pro or contra that fooling populace of scribblers in any form put forth upon it or me." Froude, *Carlyle*, ii, 364.
33. *Frazer's Magazine*, December, 1849, 670–79.
34. Frances Eliza Kingsley, *Charles Kingsley: His Letters and Memories of His Life* Edited by his wife, 2 vols. (London: H.S. King and Co., 1877), vol. ii, 235. The correspondent was a Mr T. Dixon, a "cork-cutter of Sunderland".
35. See note 25 above.
36. Quoted in Semmell, 113. Ruskin's further judgement, also quoted by Semmel—admittedly delivered late in life, some time after the Eyre controversy had died down—was that Kingsley "failed in the most cowardly way when we had the Eyre party to fight", and that on that occasion he proved himself to be a "flawed—partly rotten, partly distorted—person".
37. Charles Kingsley to Fanny Kingsley, Eversley Rectory, August 23, 1866. BL Add. Ms. 62555, ff. 125–26.
38. Quoted Semmel, 122–23. Huxley's further comments clarify the issues at stake as viewed by contemporaries: "The hero-worshippers, who believe that the world is governed by its great men, who are to lead the little ones justly if they can; but if not, unjustly drive or kick them the right way. Will sympathize with Mr. Eyre. The other set (to which I belong), who look upon hero-worship as no better than any other ideology, and upon the attitudes of mind of the hero-worshippers as essentially limited, who think it better for a man to go wrong in freedom than to go right in chains; who look upon the observance of inflexible justice as between man and man as of far greater importance than even the preservation of social order, who believe that Mr. Eyre has committed one of the greatest crimes of which a person in authority can be guilty, and will strain every muscle to obtain a declaration that the belief is in accordance with the law of England..."

39. J. A. Froude, *A History of England from the Fall of Wolsey to the Death of Elizabeth*, 8 vols. (London: Longman, Green, Longman, Roberts and Green, 1862–64). Kingsley's remarks in his review refer principally to Froude's account of the behaviour of the Spanish legation in London during the reign of Elizabeth I as related in vol. viii.
40. Reproduced in 'Mr Kingsley and Dr. Newman. A correspondence on the question 'whether Dr. Newman teaches that Truth is no virtue?', John Henry Newman, *Apologia Pro Vita Sua*, ed. Martin J. Svaglic (Oxford: The Clarendon Press, 1967), 341.
41. John Sutherland, '"Westward Ho!" 'A Popular Successful Book'" in *Victorian Novelists and Publishers* (London: The Athlone Press, 1976), 117–32.
42. R.F. Forster, *Modern Ireland, 1600–1972* (Harmondsworth: Penguin, 1989), 394, 608.
43. Quoted Semmel, 156.
44. For an astute discussion of these connections, especially as they featured in the minds of Kingsley and his associates, see David Alderson, *Mansex Fine: Religion, Manliness and Imperialism in Nineteenth-Century British Culture* (Manchester and New York: Manchester University Press, 1998), especially chap. 4, pp. 98–119, '"Hysteric Celts"'.
45. Philip Magnus, *Gladstone: A Biography* (London: John Murray, 1954), 346.
46. Froude, *West Indies*, 4.
47. Magnus, *Gladstone*, 358.
48. Tom Hughes, *Tom Brown's Schooldays By an Old Boy* (Cambridge: Macmillan, 1857), 150–51: "It was in this state that Master Tom lay at half past seven in the morning following the day of his arrival, and from his clean little white bed watched the movements of Bogle (the general name by which successive shoeblacks of the School-house were known) as he marched round from bed to bed, collecting dirty shoes and boots, and depositing clean ones in their places."
49. See *The Oxford English Dictionary*, 1989 edition, vol. ii, 360, where Bogle is defined as "a phantom causing fright…(Usually supposed to be black, and to have something of human attributes, though spoken of as *it*.) Also applied contemptuously to a human being who is 'a fright to behold'."
50. Reid, 2.

CHAPTER 9

Beyond the National Stereotype: Benedict Anderson and the Bengal Emergency of 1905–06

One fashionable theoretical paradigm of cultural and political history in the 1980s operated to this effect: the evolution from the seventeenth century onwards of print media, and more especially of newspapers and the novel, had the cumulative consequence of summoning up in the collective mind the image, or perhaps mirage, of the nation-state. A strong case may be made out for that claim, but an equally convincing one may be entered for the opposite: namely that, in certain contexts, far from cementing national consciousness, print technology has worked to weaken it. This counterclaim is especially relevant to the complicated case of India. The examination of certain dramatic events in Bengal in the first decade of the twentieth century offers some evidence of this fact. It further tends to suggest that, when arguing that newspapers have created nations, it is wise at the outset to establish how the nations concerned were defined, and in what languages the newspapers concerned were printed. It is especially prudent to work out how far the second coincided with the first, or whether any cases of overlap or of divergence occurred. If stories such as the one I am telling in this chapter are examined closely, it will be found that, under some circumstances, the organs of news and cultural dissemination fostered by print, rather than consolidating borders, have had a marked tendency to cross and to dissolve them. At the very least, the effect has sometimes worked both ways.

Anderson and Beyond

Over thirty years after its first publication, Benedict Anderson's *Imagined Communities* continues to stoke controversy, and to serve as the stimulus—or at least a strong point of reference—for studies located in a plethora of disciplines within the humanities. On the face of it, this is surprising. The book is quite loosely constructed around a cluster of themes, and it makes little attempt at what might be called a Grand Theory of any sort. The Preface disowns global ambitions, and the second edition of 1991—the one most often used nowadays by students—represents less of a revision that a modified re-printing, with two extra chapters tacked on to the end in a mood of amplification. Indeed, I think I would argue that from the very beginning the work was conceived in a spirit closer to Higher Journalism than academic scholarship. Eschewing the constraints of Area Studies, it launches a series of forays into the cultural unknown, exploring the highways and byways of historical analogy, dropping statistics here and there, taking on establishing positions, risking generalisations, laying old ghosts. It may in fact be this very risk factor that has seen it through the years. Written with grace, aplomb and a sort of delighted and humorous abandon, it offers us all the delights of unabashed comparative speculation. In more than one sense, this is a book written with its author's left hand.

It is apt that the word "imagined" is in the title, since this is a work of the scholarly imagination that appeals to the reader's own. It is also a book that takes the imagination seriously as an agent not just of personal, but also of social and political, change. No wonder it has caught on so well across the Humanities. Its opening and re-iterated allusions to print culture flatter the susceptibilities of all those who take writing and publishing seriously. One is used to Marxist-inspired studies claiming that literature reflects the world. Here is one that makes the much more arresting, and radically humanist, claim that the world reflects literature. We are what we dream or, at the very least, what we read.

The suggested vehicles of this collective self-positioning, let us remind ourselves, are two-fold: the novel and journalism. It is the second of these fields of activity with which I am particularly concerned in this chapter. When it comes to fiction, suffice it to note that the examples drawn on by Anderson are surprisingly parochial and, to some extent at least, vitiated either by mistranslation, or else by his own imperfect control of the relevant linguistic medium. In 1991 he conceded that eight years earlier he had launched a paradigm of fiction in the Philippines in partial ignorance of Spanish.[1] I will not dilate on this aspect of his work much further, except to stress that in 1983 Anderson's view of the novel as a *genre* was somewhat unusual, and that it has since proved extraordinarily influential. In the early 1980s the *locus classicus* for discussion of the inception of fiction cited in most literature departments was Ian Watt's *The Rise of the Novel*. Dating back to 1957, it carried an index listing twenty-five references to Individualism—several of them many pages long—twenty-seven to Realism, a number to Naturalism, but nothing whatsoever on the nation or Nationalism, however broadly conceived.[2] Nowadays, few critics would embark on a discussion of the novel's formidable historical power without glancing at this—to Watt invisible—strand. Its source in Anderson's thinking derives from his view of chronological time in the modern world, since the characters in any novel in his opinion inhabit a simultaneous but empty space, grasped by the reader alone, in which all of these separate bodies and minds act independently, yet as participators in some conceptual and "imagined" continuum. In this respect they act much like people in a newspaper who feature in different stories on adjacent pages or columns, yet illustrate severally and collectively that greater community to which the reader herself, or himself, is allied.

Anderson's model for social interaction leading to loyalty to a community—be it village, city or nation-state—is a variety of shared solipsism, or perhaps solipsistic sharing, stimulated by freely circulating media with a common point of view. For this process to work, however, there has to be genuine coincidence, and substantial collusion. The conditions for this, needless to say, are not always present. Not enough attention has been paid to the contradiction in Anderson's terms of reference between the plural of his principal title—*Imagined Communities*—and the singular abstraction—Nationalism—on which his subtitle ends. Communities, after all, come in all shapes and sizes, and the nation—let alone the nation-state—is only one of them. Throughout his account there accordingly runs a tussle between the author's desire to pay homage to the versatility of human imaginings, and the singular model—historically conditioned, arriving at a distinct period of time—on which he wants his readers to fasten. The first edition of his book makes his motives in this regard clearer than the second: Anderson wants us to concentrate on nations because he is trying to explain to himself and us the persistence into the later twentieth century of war: the destructive Angel of History with which the first edition of 1983 concludes. There is a remarkable congruence in this regard between the leftish Anderson and a more recent darling of the right, Niall Ferguson. Ferguson has taken to insisting that empires are justified because they keep the lid on inter-communal violence and, potentially, on friction between neighbouring states.[3] "Take but degree away, untune that string, and hark what discord follows".[4] Anderson would of course abominate that conclusion, but a sense of nationalism as a tide without which the bloodbath of the twentieth century is hard to understand is essential to his case.

Yet if we are to understand his argument, and its relevance to recent times, the question of its applicability inevitably arises. Those who have read the book are more than familiar with its historical logic: the way it insists, against much received opinion, that nationalism was a tide that arose in the New World, specifically in South America, and then washed across the Atlantic to Europe. That at least seems to be his drift if you follow his book chapter by chapter. But texts have lives beyond as well as within their covers, and in this case the ultimate source of the argument seems to lie thousands of miles away from its projected origin. To be specific it lies in South East Asia where Anderson grew up, and where his area of academic expertise was also situated. Professionally Anderson was an expert on Indonesia, about which he wrote a lot, and on the Philippines, about which he wrote less but with some trenchancy. Now both these locations and nation-state configurations have one thing in common: they consist of archipelagos of islands that have come together to form political wholes, partly as a result of colonial intervention, and partly as a result of the movement towards national independence. It is in vain I think that some traditionalist scholars insist that his paradigm is "most interesting" when applied to the Old World, that is to Western Europe. It may well be so, but the origin of the model is a Far Eastern one, and a postcolonial one, and its paradoxical application to, say, France, Germany and even Switzerland, fascinating and revealing as it may be, represents a transfer of scope, and is paradoxical to the core.

So I suggest that we take a harder look at its Eastern and postcolonial positioning, and ask ourselves the difficult question of how far it can be stretched, even within that arena. There is, to my mind—but not only to my mind—a very large hole in the middle of Anderson's exposition, a hole in the shape not of South East, but of South Asia. There are, for example, only eight references to India in the 1991 edition, most of them passing, many of them short, and all of them highly stereotypical and restricted to the English-speaking elite. Well might you respond that Anderson's study is principally concerned with elites. Pursuing the trail of its evidence, however, it seems also to concern itself with all who read novels, and all who read newspapers. It is certainly concerned with all who do both—or one—of these things, and furthermore busy themselves with the national struggle. The way the book fleshes out such a scenario in an Indian context can be illustrated by its reference in Chap. 6 to a passage in the writings of Bipin Chandra Pal. Pal was one the early leaders of the nationalist movement in Bengal, an active journalist and leading light in the Congress Party. In his recollections published shortly before his death he recalls the local Magistrates of his youth: "In those days the India-born....Civilian practically cut himself off from his parent society, and moved and lived and had his being in the atmosphere so beloved of his British colleagues. *In mind and in manners he was as much an Englishman as any Englishman.*"[5]

The italics are Anderson's, and he winds up the quote by saying "So far, so Macaulay." The comment is arch, but its frivolity superficial. Macaulay, as Anderson has earlier reminded us, is Thomas Babington Macaulay who, in a celebrated Minute submitted to the Committee of Public Instruction of the East India Company in 1835, swayed their vote in favour of investing in English-medium education at the expense of Orientalist scholarship.[6] Javed Majeed amongst others has argued that the impact of Macaulay's directives has been wildly exaggerated.[7] If Pal's local Magistrate, described by him almost a century after the Minute, is its remote product, we still have to ask ourselves how typical he was of those at the time working for nationalism, or of the newspaper- or novel-reading public. The year before the publication of Pal's memoir—that is, in 1931—literates in India, as Judith M. Brown reveals, represented 9.2% of the total population. Of this relatively small group, what is more, only 14.9% could read English with any fluency.[8] That puts men like Pal's magistrate (and even Pal himself) in a minority of just over 1%. In Bengal, the most Anglophone of all the Provinces, the educator Michael West, conducting a survey eight years later, discovered that 1 in 2407 citizens spoke English with any degree of confidence.[9] Yet, then as later, Bengal was a hotbed of nationalist agitation. Anderson's waxwork figure, with his English conversation, his English reading habits and cultural affinities, seems less and less typical of those working for political change the harder one looks at him. He was certainly typical of a class, but how crucial or extended was the class?

Certainly if one confines one's gaze to the Mimic Men such as Pal's Magistrate, the picture summoned up is highly flattering to Anderson's approach. It is early evening, both for the clock and for the Raj. All over

India lonely male figures sit in their government bungalows after work. They are leafing through back numbers of the *Illustrated London News* or that morning's *Times of India*, as the ceiling fan ruffles the pages before them, and a lower-caste flunkey serves tiffin in the gloaming. The servant bows and withdraws, the off-duty official yawns. He puts down his newspaper and, culling a notebook from an inner pocket, licks a pencil and plots his revenge. The bastards may have banned him from the European club, but his hour will come, he knows that. He and his 1% will inherit the land in the fullness of destiny. He takes a sip from his drink, he leans back, stretches his legs, and dreams fervently of India. And so on and so forth.

But this is a figure out of Kipling, and the argument that suggested him is also Kiplingesque. Hurree Babu, for example, is a wonderful comical creation in *Kim*—an equivalent figure from an earlier generation, a caricature of that Bengali *bhadralok* middle class whom the British at one time found so threatening, and whom Kipling in particular thought he knew so well. He and Pal's token Magistrate also exemplify just the kind of local personage who may well have constituted the readership of the English-language newspapers for which Kipling himself worked in North India between 1882 and 1889: as sub-editor on the *Civil and Military Gazette* in Lahore, and later as correspondent for the *Allahabad Pioneer*.

The question is, exactly how many people read newspapers such as these? How many of them were Indians? Of what caste and educational background were such subscribers, and what was their politics? And how many other newspapers were published daily, weekly or fortnightly in the same districts? In what languages were these periodicals couched, what were their circulation figures, and what ideological profiles did such rival publications espouse? Who, in other words, was reading what and when, in what numbers and tongues, and to what exact effect? Caricature is no substitute for the literary demographics on which a sociological argument such as Anderson's alone should surely have to depend.

Imagining the Fragments

Anderson's work, it has to be said, is quite well known in India, but it has not gone down well there. In 2006 I attended an international conference in Kolkata convened by a group of especially active book historians in the School of Cultural Texts and Records at Jadavpur University. Its declared theme was "New Word Order: Emerging Histories of the Book", and it was partly concerned with setting up that elusive and multi-layered project, a National Book History for India.[10] Given the intense cultural, religious and linguistic balkanisation of the subcontinent, the task seems a daunting one, but of one fact most of the intending participants seem certain: Anderson will not help.

And, of course, there is an umbilical cord between those two perceptions, since it is precisely the balkanisation of which I have just spoken that makes Anderson seem so problematic. Perhaps the most measured rejoinder to his views in the Indian context so far has been provided by Partha Chatterjee, doyen of Subaltern Studies and an author appropriately enough from Bengal, in his monograph of 1994, *The Nation and Its Fragments: Colonial and Postcolonial Histories*. Written eleven years after the first appearance of *Imagined Communities*, it takes Anderson's book for its starting point. "Whose Imagined Community?" runs the title of its first chapter[11] and, while Chatterjee pays proper tribute to the ways in which Anderson has advanced the terms of discussion—at least Nationalism is no longer a monolith, and a given one at that—he also enters a dignified plea that the peoples of the earth should be allowed to imagine the nation in their own distinctive ways. For Anderson, it sometimes seems, wants to do everybody's imagining for them. No doubt his was a generous gesture, but it has had the effect of exacerbating a dilemma common amongst political scientists in several former colonies. Admittedly the structure of the state was to some extent bestowed, or perhaps bequeathed, from outside. But that is far from being the end of the matter. Chatterjee for one has always acknowledged that the colossus of state power was transferred at a given moment in time (in fact, in the case of India and Pakistan, in the year of his birth), but that very fact leaves the imagination scurrying around its edges proposing, or more usually reflecting, alternatives.

To illustrate his point Chatterjee adroitly quotes Pal's memoirs back at Anderson, but it is a very different passage that he chooses. In it Pal is recalling the boarding houses of the Calcutta in his youth, around the year 1875.[12] These were places where students or young aspirant members of the professions stayed: would-be-lawyers or teachers (amongst them was the poet Jibanananda Das, whose posthumously published novels sometimes describe them). In such locations, as Pal remembers, decisions were taken in a rough-and-ready democratic fashion, but very much along the lines of courtroom procedure, or the agendas of committees. Now Anderson, had he dealt with this passage, might very well have chosen to view such communities and procedures as microcosms or prototypes of the emerging nation. For Chatterjee, however, they are alternative spaces where a kind of grass-roots popular consultation, very different from the rigidities of national consultation, once flowered.

Imagining the nation, in the South Asian context, Chatterjee insists, has never been an easy task. What the mind summons up most naturally is an array of competing communities—ethnic and linguistic groups; castes; competing spiritualities: Hindu, Muslim, Jain and what have you. Pressure groups and, of course, families. To say nothing of the disenfranchised tribals who feature, for example, in the novels of Mahasweta Devi. Despite the blandishments of the politicians and the projections of officialdom, the nation as an integral mental whole remains an exceptionally elusive phenomenon. No doubt this is true of many nations—there are many Scots who would say the same of the United Kingdom—and no doubt in a postcolonial environment this fragility is especially evident—look at the Congo, or Iraq—but there seem good grounds for thinking that in South Asia the resistance in several polyglot or multi-cultural societies to cohesion—or, in Chatterjee's own terms, to "hegemony" with its "modular" structures—remains particularly extreme.

Anderson seems not to have registered this particular local awkwardness, and one reason is the highly arbitrary nature of his evidence. In the context of the Philippines or South America, he is happy to look to the novel for its evocation of peopled and simultaneous spaces where the national consciousness is implicitly alive. For India, with which his intimacy seems minimal, he is quite content to rely on some highly selective quotation from autobiographies such as Pal's taken wildly out of context, and such facts and figures that have come his way in the course of casual reading. There is, for example, not a single reference to Indian fiction in *Imagined Communities*, a text first published the year after Salman Rushdie's *Midnight's Children* won the Booker Prize in Britain. Rushdie's ample novel, needless to say, takes the nation for its canvas. Indeed, if Anderson had wanted a vivid illustration of his theme of the novel-as-national-template, what better example could he have chosen than this saga of one thousand and one infants born on the stroke of independence and kept constantly in touch with one another through some mysterious but definitely symbolic form of radiophonic telepathy? Anderson should have leapt at the chance. But even in 1991, Rushdie's ever-so-helpful endorsement is ignored, I can only think because Anderson's bedside reading is conditioned largely by his specialism.

So I propose a paragraph or two on Rushdie as a minor addition to future editions, in full recognition of the assistance it offers to Anderson's case, the coach and horses it appears to drive through Chatterjee's argument, and the spirited counterbalance it supplies to the regionally based case study I am about to offer. If Chatterjee concentrates on the fragments, Rushdie gives us the sprawling whole, an instructive contrast since both men were born in the year of India's independence—1947—as, incidentally, was I.

It is, of course, entirely possible that both of these visions apply: that—as Chatterjee's title itself concedes—India is both a nation *and* its fragments. Indeed, if Anderson had wanted support for such an assertion, he need have looked no further than the English-language fiction published in the same decade as Pal's memoir. In 1935, three years after Pal's death, here is the opening of Mulk Raj Anand's early novel *Untouchable* (1935):

> The outcaste's colony was a group of mud-walled houses that clustered together in two rows, under the shadow both of the town and of the cantonment, but outside their boundaries and separate from them. There lived the scavengers, the leather-workers, the washermen, the barbers, the water-carriers, the grass-cutters and the outcastes from Indian society...The absence of a drainage system had, through the rains of several seasons, made of the quarter a marsh which gave out a most offensive smell. And, altogether the ramparts of human and animal refuse that lay on the outskirts of this little colony, and the ugliness, the squalor and the misery which lay within it, made it an 'uncongenial' place to live in. At least, so thought Bakha, a young man of eighteen, strong and able-bodied, the son of Lakha, the Jemadar of all the sweepers in the town...[13]

If Anderson had got round to quoting these one-and-a-bit paragraphs, I think he would have been obliged to concede a number of, to him, resistant points. As a rhetorical gesture this passage is hardly an invitation to inclusiveness, simultaneity or parity. Of course it enjoins sympathy, empathy even, preaches that we are all one, but the *we* in this context are the human race, and what we are confronted with here is a radical (and in 1935 Marxist) humanism in the face of social divisions and religiously endorsed discrimination. But to preach something and to evoke it are two very different procedures. Anand's famous opening depends in the first instance on an impulse of recoil, which it then undermines by letting us know that the touristic term "uncongenial" distils a reaction to deprivation that the inmates in the untouchable's community on the edge of everything have themselves internalised. Anand has no reputation as a wordsmith, but he pulls out a few plums here, especially the spelling of "outcast" as "outcaste". The general implication is that this nation-in-the-making should be unified, but isn't.

Or take the beginning of Raja Rao's *Kanthapura*, published two years later in 1937. It opens in a village in Kerala:

> Our village—I don't think you have ever heard about it—Kanthapura is its name, and it is in the province of Kara. High on the Ghats is it. High up on the steep mountains that face the cool Arabian seas, up the Malabar coast is it, up Mangalore and Puttar and many a centre of cardamom and coffee, rice and sugarcane.[14]

Like Anand, Rao wants us to take his locale seriously as a battle-ground for justice and equality—his story concerns the struggle of the villagers for decent living conditions against the callousness of the local tea plantation—but again he begins with a sense of separateness and even obscurity: "Our village—I don't think you have heard about it". The speaker is an elderly woman, illiterate I suspect, but in any case extemporising verbatim. True, her village comes eventually to be treated as a kind of microcosm for the Gandhian struggle. But Anderson's argument addresses itself not to messages, but to assumptions, and it is the exclusion, the separation, that is assumed by this elderly woman at the outset.

Again, the 1930s was the decade in which R.K. Narayan began his series of Malgudi novels, set in a small provincial town near Mysore. You would have to try very hard indeed to turn Malgudi into a microcosm of the nation and, even if it was, I am not sure that this is what interests Narayan. It is the eccentricity, the uniqueness, the slightly barmy individuality of his community that concerns him, and from which he derives his peculiar comic effects. Simultaneous empty spaces have little to do with it—less than they do, for example, in an eighteenth-century English novel (one of Defoe's, say). Malgudi time is its very own season.

So the "we're all in this together" effect that Anderson invokes as a dominant tone in fiction of an emerging nation-state seems, at least to my mind, quite inappropriate to the Indian novels in English written during the period in which he seems most interested. Whereas, according to his own argument, it is very much in the English-language fiction that one should expect to find it, English being for example the *lingua franca* of the India National Congress. The fact is: one does not find it by and large. One reason, I suspect, relates to the literacy figures for the period cited above. A language-based genre addressing itself to 1% of the population is likely to feel hard-pressed to sound inclusive. Another reason may have to do with faddishness, or else censorship, of reading amongst even this tiny group. In 1935 people for the most part were not reading Rao or even Narayan in India, even if they had the necessary English. And Anand's novels were not being read for the perfectly good reason that they were on the official banned list, and could be confiscated at any port of entry.[15] So, all in all, one begins to see why Anderson might have been wary of including Indian fiction in his account at all. To glean a more realistic idea of what the majority of the reading public were looking at during this period, it would be wiser to edge outwards towards the larger constituency of novels written in the vernacular. Even here there are problems, since Anderson in his exposition of early modern Europe tends to assume that vernacular usage is a sign of emergent national consciousness, and to ignore the very many instances—replete throughout the Third World, but present also elsewhere—in which vernacular usage does the very opposite, namely divide. Which brings me neatly back to the communication medium in relation to which Anderson's case generally seems to be strongest: that is, to the newspapers.

Soft and Hard Anderson

I want to present a fairly detailed case study based on archival research so as to test the strength of Anderson's ideas on the emergence of Nationalism against the realities of press activity in India. But before doing so, it might be wise to bring Anderson's ideas on the press into closer focus, so that we can tell what he is—and what he is not—saying. It is my contention that there are two spirits in which his words can be taken, what one might style a soft and a hard approach. I will start with the "soft" approach, as set out in the second of his chapters, "Cultural Roots". Here the citizens of a country are compared to news items, and the unhelpfully cosmopolitan example given is *The New York Times* as it covers a famine in Mali. (Not, one notices, the Malian *L'Essor* or *Les Echos* as they deal with a heat wave in New York.) "If", it proposes, "Mali disappears from the pages of *The New York Times* after two days of famine reportage, for months on end, readers do not for a moment imagine that Mali has disappeared or that famine has disappeared or that famine has wiped out all of its citizens."[16] In this way, Anderson maintains, Mali acts like a fellow citizen who is invisible to us most of the time, or like a character in a novel who appears and disappears and is supposed to be residing and acting elsewhere in between.

It is an ingenuous example, since few New Yorkers actually know where Mali is (some do not know where Scotland is), so the supposition that they somehow recognise and connect to this character on his or her second appearance seems a little far-fetched. Another source of confusion is that Anderson cannot seem to work out whether each and every issue of the newspaper acts like a work of fiction, or whether the whole run does. At one stage he talks of dailies as "one-day bestsellers". From the point of view of circulation that may be true enough, but his analogy does not extend to the plot. It would only do so if Mali appeared and disappeared within the covers of, say, the issue for 4 February 2006. What Anderson means is that Mali makes an appearance in January, disappears in March and then re-appears in June. But with that proviso I think we can accept that certain of the conventions connected with the newspaper industry possess a quasi-"fictive" air. And fiction, with its underlying assumption that we all occupy empty chronological time, acts a bit like our attitude to our fellow nationals. There is, then, a double analogy going on: between a newspaper and a novel, and a novel and the nation. As an analytical instrument for the discussion of particular case studies, however, it is too vague to be of very much use.

The argument grows tighter as Anderson shifts his gaze backwards in time to the creation of national consciousness in the New World. In the chapter "Creole Pioneers", he looks at the beginnings of newspaper production in America North and South (though he misses out the Caribbean).[17] Here the news items invoked are those that concern everybody in such circumstances, like the arrival and departure of ships. In reading about these events day by day, week by week, so the argument runs, colonials got used to the idea that they constituted a community with certain common routines. Over time this produced an imaginative response whereby they came to see themselves as fellow members of a community with vital interests, principally economic interests, in common.

Initially this approach looks like an extension of the first, but it is very different in emphasis. No longer is Anderson arguing simply from analogy, since he comes as close as dammit to saying that newspaper production actually produces the effects described. Print capitalism issues in the nation. The relationship posed is therefore a causal one. I do not think he ever goes quite so far as to posit the connection in terms of a necessary or sufficient condition: newspapers do not of themselves produce nations. What Anderson does seem very much to imply, however, is that, where print capitalism emerges and newspapers flourish, the combined total result will be that readers gradually come to see themselves as nationals. That is a lesser claim than attributing all forms of national consciousness to the impact of the popular press. But it is a dramatic claim nonetheless.

This what I call the "hard" approach to the question, and it is one that Chatterjee for example accepts with some reservation. Anderson, he says, is entirely right to claim that the advent of print capitalism in Bengal in the last two decades of the eighteenth century ushered in "the development of a modern 'national' language", by which he means English. One result of this shift was the creation of a bilingual Bengali elite. He goes on to insist, however, that "The crucial moment in the development of a modern Bengali language comes…in mid-century, when this bilingual elite makes it a cultural project to provide its mother tongue with the necessary linguistic equipment to enable it become an adequate language for "modern" culture. An entire institutional network of printing presses, publishing houses, newspapers, magazines, and literary societies is created about this time, *outside* the purview of the state and the European missionaries, though which the new language, modern and standardised, is given shape."[18]

Once again, I think, we are bumping up against Anderson's radically lopsided notion of languages, and what they achieve politically. It is perfectly true to say that in Latin America, a large land mass dominated at a certain point in time by two imported European languages—Spanish and Portuguese—the inception of newspapers and magazines in those languages inevitably if slowly made for a national consciousness. It is also true to say that in the European context, the vital communications shift (to use Elizabeth Eisenstein's term) occurred at the end of the fifteenth century when the presses, having exhausted the supply of material in Latin, turned to the vernacular tongues and, in so doing, created a reading public that thought in national terms. It might even be possible to claim that in widely spread island groups such as Indonesia, national cohesion eventually produced a distillation of national languages that caused speakers of a bewildering variety of local (and for the most part unwritten) tongues to express themselves through a common national medium. In all of these instances, the totalising tendency of print culture is comparatively clear: towards homogenisation within national frontiers. In the context of India, however, we are dealing with ancient, well-established vernaculars, each with many million speakers and possessing a script culture and a literature many centuries old. In the period prior to British intervention, the Mughals had imposed a certain uniformity of administration, and even caused Persian to be accepted as the language of government. They had, however, entirely failed to put down India's legacy of Indio-European and Dravidic languages, each of which served as a force of considerable regional cohesion; nor indeed had they tried. Against such a background, the chances of the new print technology *of itself* effecting a shift in people's linguistic and hence communal affinities were quite slight. The chances of the local languages absorbing and taking over the available resources of this revolution in communication technology, on the other hand, were very high.

Partition and Print

The consequences of this appropriation are very easy to observe in modern India. To appreciate its full impact it is simply necessary to walk around the 100-odd tents pitched across the spacious Maidan at the annual Kolkata Book Fair. At the thirty-first such event in 2006, a mere fraction of the 60,000 titles currently in print in West Bengal were on display, but the balance in favour of production in India's very many languages was well in evidence. From the historical point of view the essential task is to chart the stages by which this proliferation occurred, and what its consequences for nation formation may once have been (the Book Fair, needless to say, excludes newspapers and magazines). The problem here is that the study of print and publishing history is in its infancy in South Asia, and at the moment relatively few statistically trained book historians have emerged. Not that statistics themselves are lacking, at least for the colonial period. One of the fortunate by-products of the imperial paranoia bred by the Sepoy rising of 1857 was that the British became very particular about charting the spread of communications all over the subcontinent. After 1867, quarterly returns had to be made for each presidency of the productions of all registered presses. The details were then collated centrally in Calcutta (or in Simla if the exercise carried on until the dry season) and issued in an annual report.[19] From the 1870s an equivalent system of surveillance existed for newspapers, which were scrutinised fortnightly, their contents summarised and where necessary translated, and lengthy quotations of compromising passages supplied for official scrutiny. (All of this, of course, is well in line with Anderson's own remarks about information and tabulation in colonial cultures, as ventilated in Chap. 10 of the 1991 edition of *Imagined Communities*, called "Census, Map, Museum".) The result is a vast repository of data concerning material published under the

Raj, one far too extensive for the purview of any one scholar—or even team of scholars—a treasure trove of information which up to the present day, as Robert Darnton has memorably complained, remains almost untouched by historians of print or, indeed, by serious students of colonialism or nationalism.

Darnton's own contributions to this embryonic field are contained in two consecutive numbers of the journal *Book History* for 2001 and 2002.[20] In the article "Literary Surveillance in the British Raj: The Contradictions of Liberal Imperialism" (2002), he surveys the whole field of spying, scrutiny and control as they operated in post-Mutiny India, but elects in the end to concentrate on the impact of the one event which, he believes, was more instrumental than any other in laying bear the fault=lines running across the entire system: "The event that opened up the contradiction at the heart of the Raj," he proclaims, "took place in 1905: the partition of Bengal."[21] Darnton lays out the reasons for his choice of example well, setting it against the background of an imperialism in crisis: the election of a Liberal Government in Britain in 1905 with a non-jingoistic outlook and a mandate to reform, the rise of systemic nationalism in India, the influence of the India National Congress and so on and so forth. Darnton's concern, however, is with the embarrassment that the emergency in Bengal of that period caused to the colonial authorities. To pursue this inquiry, he fixes on drama and fiction, and on the mechanisms of censorship as they swung into action in one or two high-profile court cases. My own concern, however, is to test out Anderson's predictions about identity and nation formation, and in order to do so I would like to concentrate on the same sequence of events as viewed through the eyes of the local press.

I have my own reasons for closing in on this particular case study, reasons that are quite independent of those that Darnton gives for his. Partition remains a topic of energetic and agonised debate in early twenty-first-century South Asia. The primary focus for discussion, inevitably enough, is the act of Partition that gave rise to the separate nation-states of India and Pakistan in August 1947, an event contemporaneous with the birth of independent India itself. Memories still rankle here. Nor is a younger generation of Indian scholars, critics and commentators, raised well after the event itself, immune from its thrall. It would be no exaggeration to say that the whole vexed topic of nationalism in the South Asian context is inseparable from this tragic theme. It is seldom that one meets any sustained consideration of one matter without reference to the other. And, naturally enough, the obverse is true too.

Partition in any shape or form, however, is a subject that Anderson himself appears to avoid like the plague. Not only is there not a single reference to the Partition of India and Pakistan in his book, there is also no reference at all to the Partition of Ireland. In fact, references to Ireland are themselves fairly thin on the ground. I count five in the edition of 1991: two to the place of Early English in medieval Ireland; one to the intermediary role of the nineteenth-century Catholic priesthood; one to the existence of the Irish Sea as a barrier to integration; and one to the Young Ireland Movement. The open wound of Irish experience in the twentieth century is next to invisible. Of the Irish Free State, the Black and Tans, the Irish Civil War and, of course, the Troubles, there is never a word. Yet Anderson's Roman Catholic Irish background seems to be formative in his thinking, and it certainly features in his literary imagery. In a study of this scope, of course, lacunae are inevitable. But the scarcity of Irish evidence is not, I believe, on a par with the absence of, say, Venezuela. It is a shrieking gap.

I remain suspicious that the cursory treatment meted out to India and Ireland in *Imagined Communities* has the same essential cause. Both places witnessed the presence of vocal nationalistic groupings in the first half of the twentieth century, and in both cases the result was division. In both India and Ireland too the press played a formative role in fostering and expressing political alignments. Anderson is interested in the effect of print capitalism in bringing communities together. All the more reason, therefore, that we pay close, documented attention to those historical instances in which the ultimate result of press agitation and comment may have been to hold communities apart.

Darnton sketches the lead-up to the crisis, but to get the whole scene fully in perspective, I would like to extend his perspective by several months. The Partition of the existing Province of Bengal in 1905, purportedly for reasons of administrative convenience, was one of the last acts of the term of Lord Curzon as Viceroy. Despite reassurances from the British, many Bengalis were deeply suspicious of the government's motives in effecting this change. Then as now the people of Bengal, though united by language, were divided by religion, the eastern part of the region (corresponding roughly with modern Bangladesh) being predominantly Muslim, the western (coinciding approximately the present-day Indian state of West Bengal) being for the most part Hindu. A complicating factor was the proximity of Assam to the north east, Hindu in character by and large, but fairly distinct in language and even script. The new arrangements brought together Assam and East Bengal under one "Lieutenant Governor", while leaving the western sector of the country as a distinct Province. For very many years—and especially since the formation of the Indian National Congress in 1885—the whole area had been perceived as a hotbed of anti-Imperialist agitation (Pal, whom we have already mentioned twice, chaired the Congress's second convention). The suspicion in many minds, of both sides of the newly created divide, was that the British—in classic "Divide and Rule" fashion—were attempting to break the back of this resistance by splitting up those most vigorously engaged in it, and fomenting Muslim suspicion and resentment of their Hindu brethren to the west.

Press activity was hectic at every stage of this process, and the spectrum of expressed opinion was pretty wide. One of the first acts of the newly appointed Lieutenant Governor of East Bengal and Assam—a career civil servant flamboyantly named Joseph Bampfylde Fuller[22]—was to give a newspaper interview in which he casually remarked that he now had two wives, of whom the Mohammedan was his considered favourite. Needless to say, this remark did not go down well in Assam; it found even less favour in West Bengal, where the pro-Islamic bias of the Raj had long been noted. Already political opposition to Partition was well under way, giving rise to the Swadeshi—or "Our Country"—Movement, pledged to reverse the new dispensation by every means in its power. (Interestingly in the light of the parallel traced above, the instigation of this movement was almost contemporaneous in time with that of Sinn Fein in Ireland, also pledged to the creation of a united homeland.) The rallying call of its name, however, disguised considerable differences as to the methods to be employed. At successive conferences in Calcutta Town Hall in March 1904 and January 1905, a programme of petitions, lobbying and press agitation was launched. Advocates of more extreme measures were not, however, lacking, leading to more strident demands. As the limited usefulness of moderate means became apparent, alternatives were soon to be tried, including a boycott of British goods and from April 1907 a campaign of what, following a series of articles that month by Aurobindo Ghosh, came to be known as "Passive Resistance".

Every shade of opinion was represented in the press. Selective quotation will bring home this fact but, in order to appreciate the sweep of the canvas involved, one needs to get into one's mind a clear and full picture of the spectrum of newspapers on offer in early twentieth-century Bengal. This is a fair challenge, since the local field of periodical publication at the time represented a number of converging, and sometimes overlapping, interests. I have chosen to fasten on the busy newspaper industry in Calcutta, complex enough in itself since the city was both the metropolis of commercial, cultural and political life in the region and—until December 1911—the capital of British India. Though Bangla (that is, Bengali) was its distinctive language, the city—like several others throughout the length and breadth of the subcontinent—was host to many different religious and linguistic communities, several of whom were effectively polyglot, and all of whom had their own reasons for assuming individual and vocal postures of agreement, affiliation or dissent. The range is amply suggested by the weekly *Reports on Native Papers in Bengal* issued by the Bengali Translator's Office in Calcutta from 1876 through to 1916. Runs of these are available in both New Delhi and London, and selectively now on microfilm from the South Asian Microfilm Project.[23] From them I have complied the list in Table 9.1, adopting the Translator's office's own figures for distribution, and concentrating on daily and weekly titles.

The first remark to make is that, in the Indian context, especially at the period in question, "distribution" is a flexible term. Rather than thinking of solitary readers imbibing the contents of their favourite rag in office, bus or living room—a scenario derived from the twentieth-century West, but foisted by Anderson on a bewildering variety of contexts—one has, I think, to visualise a far more community-based mode of consumption. To find something equivalent in Britain one has, I believe, to go back a century or more—to, say, Fanny Price's father in the Portsmouth of the Napoleonic Wars, perusing a daily newspaper "the accustomed loan of a neighbour" by the unsteady light of a "solitary candle held between himself and the paper".[24] Newspapers in the Calcutta of 1905, as in the Portsmouth of 1805, were as often or not shared. And in both circumstances, illumination was limited. Electric light was non-existent, gas lighting a rarity and a privilege. Lord Curzon presumably read by gaslight; most of the readers in the statistics just given would have been dependent, in the long hours after nightfall, on a gas or oil lamp, or worse.

Even this parallel is inadequate to the scene, since it assumes a higher rate of individual literacy than applied in Bengal at the time (Judith Brown's figure for 1911 is 11.3%. Assuming a rise of 2% per decade—a rough indication of what her general survey suggests—this means that in 1905 only one in ten Bengali males read any language, even their mother tongue, and far fewer, of course, read English. For women the figures were a tenth of that again, or less than 1% literacy overall). But individual

Table 9.1 Newspapers published in the Province of West Bengal, 1905–06

Newspaper title	Language medium	Frequency of publication	Place of publication	Average circulation
Banga Vidya	Bengali	Daily	Calcutta	300
Prakashika	Bengali	Daily	Calcutta	300
Dainik-o-Samacher	Bengali	Daily	Calcutta	1000
Samvad Prabhakar	Bengali	Daily	Calcutta	1132
Samvad Punachandrodaya	Bengali	Daily	Calcutta	200
Sulabh Dainik	Bengali	Daily	Calcutta	3000
Hitavada	Bengali	Weekly	Calcutta	20,000
Bangavasi	Bengali	Weekly	Calcutta	20,000
Basumasi	Bengali	Weekly	Calcutta	10,000
Hitaishi	Bengali	Weekly	Calcutta	8000
Mikir-o-Sudhachir	Mikir	Weekly	Calcutta	2000
Sanjivani	Bengali	Weekly	Calcutta	1000
Som Prakash	Bengali	Weekly	Calcutta	1000
Sulabh Samacher	Bengali	Weekly	Calcutta	1000
Samay	Bengali	Weekly	Calcutta	500
Sahakir	Bengali	Weekly	Calcutta	400
Vikrampur	Bengali	Weekly	Calcutta	300
The Daily Hitavada	English/Bengali	Daily	Calcutta	2000
The Hindoo Patriot	English	Daily	Calcutta	5000
The Indian Daily News	English	Daily	Calcutta	10,000
The Statesman	English	Daily	Calcutta	1000
The Bengalee New Indian	English	Daily	Calcutta	1500
The Indian Mirror	English	Daily	Calcutta	1200
Suhrid	Bengali	Weekly	Noakhlali	150
Chatu Mikir	Mikir	Weekly	Howra	1000

Source: Indian National Archives, Delhi

consumption of news sheets was incalculably extended by reading aloud. In order to recreate an equivalent situation in Britain you probably have to go back to the Civil War period and envisage the small production figures, yet far larger patterns of active and passive consumption, applicable to the pioneering periodicals, broadsheets and pamphlets later collected in the Tomasin Tracts. And who knows exactly how many people read those? The scarcity of lighting in all but the most pucker of districts would, naturally enough, have increased the reliance, in both contexts, on performed reading. In families (where few women were literate), in neighbourhoods, in the boarding houses whose active cultural life Pal invokes, one has perforce to imagine huddles of attentive listeners—as many as twenty perhaps—huddled around the lone reader in his fitful pool of light.

In practice, however, I am suggesting that the technically correct circulation figures in Table 9.1 should be multiplied by a factor of at least five. I have taken a comparatively modest differential, since with vernacular newspapers the element of passive reading would certainly have been more significant than for English-language titles, the purchase of which would have been confined to the British and the, often bilingual, *bhadralok* class. But whatever way you have it, and wherever in India you look, Anderson's previous—and analytically pivotal—paradigm of a single reader in his comfortable personal space must go.

Against this background, it is perhaps not surprising to find that the most impressive circulation figures for any category of Calcutta newspapers given in Table 9.1 pertain to Bengali-medium weeklies, which could be sent round from hand to hand, or read out loud to eager off-duty workers, during the relatively relaxed hours of the weekend. My real point of inquiry, however, has less to do with who read what under what kind of circumstances—though those questions impinge on my theme—as what these various categories of newspapers were saying at the time, and specifically in 1905–06 how each reacted to the unfolding crisis. Especially revealing in these circumstances are the editorial comments of the city's few bilingual newspapers, aimed fairly and squarely at the educated constituency of the small *bhadralok* middle class—teachers, civil servants and the like—from whom the active participants in the ongoing debate on Bengali political destiny—including the Swadeshi Movement—were drawn. Here, some way into the crisis and writing on the officially fostered governmental view of the opinions aired in the local press, is the comment of *The Daily Hitavadi* for 29 June 1906:

> In the last *Bengal Administrative Report* the native press has been accused of disseminating sedition in this country. It is true that a study of the vernacular newspapers sometimes leads people to get dissatisfied with many officials. But there is no help for it, because the chief duties of a newspaper are to discuss the real conditions in this country, the acts of officials, the income and expenditure of the state. The Anglo-Saxon press has escaped the censure of the Lieutenant-General simply because it seldom discusses these matters in a spirit of fairness and independence. *The Statesman* is the only Anglo-Indian newspaper in Calcutta that does not consider it to be its duty

to support the Government in almost every case in which the natives are concerned...The prevalence of distress among a few thousand labourers in England has created a violent agitation. But if we speak of our starving millions, we are considered rebels by our rulers.

The Daily Hitavada, with its relatively small circulation and two-language format, was in an unusually good position to survey the panorama of press activity around it, since presumably its readership was derived from a mixture of Bengali speakers who wished to check their imperfect English literacy against an Indian-language original, English readers keen to try out their imperfect Bengali on a parallel text, and others who were simply curious about what this cross-language fraternity was thinking and feeling. In any case, its conclusion is a comparatively conventional one: that the medium dictates the message. English-language publications, it implies, have a strong motive for taking the government line; vernacular newspapers by contrast are freer to dissent. This had long been a common view on both sides of the rift. Chatterjee himself quotes a relevant statement made by Ashley Eden, the then Governor of Bengal, as far back as 1876. Eden had just passed one of those intermittent, and frequently rescinded, regulations muzzling the efforts of the newspaper industry in his Province. The measure had been criticised for demanding registration, deposits and warranties of good behaviour from the vernacular press alone. Defending the distinction, Eden had commented, "The papers published in this country in the English language are written by a class of writers for a class of readers whose education and interests would make them naturally intolerant of sedition; they are written under a sense of responsibility and under a restraint of public opinion which do not and cannot exist in the case of the ordinary Native newspapers. It is quite easy and practicable to draw a distinction between newspapers published in English and papers published in the vernacular...."[25]

Predictably enough, Eden's curbs were repealed by Lord Ripon in 1882. And when in the 1890s consideration was given to a fresh measure, the discriminatory factor in favour of the English press was felt no longer to be appropriate. Following the appearance of the India National Congress two years after Ripon's appeal, opinions of a robustly critical kind were now, it seemed, being published in all sectors of the press. In the light of this, the *Daily Hitavada*'s editorial is remarkable. Especially interesting is the fact that, though Eden and the editorial writer are a quarter of a century apart from one another in time, and approach the question of press coverage from opposite sides, a certain consistency of vocabulary is present. Notice in particular a phrase that they both use: "in this country", meaning quite unambiguously "in India".

In stark contrast, a week later, observe the summary given in the Bengali-medium weekly the *Hitavadi* (the two names should not be confused). The weekly *Hitavada* was widely recognised as an organ for the burgeoning Swadeshi Movement. It had this to say on 4 July 1906:

> The higher intelligence and capacity of the Bengalis has always made them an eyesore to the English…But it was Lord Curzon[26] who first clearly saw that so long as the unity of the Bengalis remained intact, nothing could arrest their progress. And the partition of Bengal was conceived and carried out with the object of destroying that unity. But the move on His Lordship's part produced quite the contrary effect. It revealed the true nature of the English as an oppressive and unjust people, and roused the sleeping energies of the Bengalis. The latter forgot their mutual quarrels and launched the *Swadeshi* movement as a measure necessary for self-preservation. The efforts of such advocates of force as Sir Bampfylde Fuller and Messrs Briscoe, Lyon, Emerson and Clarke to check the spread of the movement having proved unsuccessful, Government had recourse to another artifice. It placed all sorts of temptations before the Musulmans in order to induce them to break with the Hindoos. Sir Bampfylde accepted the Musulman as his favourite wife and began to shower favours on him. A few short-sighted Musulmans were won over by this means and joined the opponents of the Hindoos in order to bring ruin on their own kith and kin.

This is a lot more rhetorical and amusing (to me at least), and somewhat more demonising. It also relies quite heavily on a conspiracy theory of a much more convoluted (but not necessarily more paranoid) version than in the earlier extract. Curzon, Fuller and the rest are cartoon figures and duly lampooned: all of this adds to the rhetoric. What interests me, however, is the editor's self-alignment, and the way that he lines up his readership. There is a Muslim community and a Hindu community, both of whom are implicitly addressed. Calcutta, then as now, has a substantial Muslim community, and several times a day the muezzin's call to prayer echoes across the city, intermingling with church bells. But, again then as now, Calcutta newspapers were not confined to Calcutta, or even to West Bengal. Dhaka, on the other side of the newly imposed frontier, possessed its own very active newspaper industry (and acted, for much of this period, as a major supplier of Bengal's school textbooks). On the other hand,

Calcutta newspapers were greedily taken up in Dhaka, and vice versa, in much the same way as, in the modern world, Bangladeshi viewers and Western Bengal viewers enthusiastically watch one another's television channels.

The fact that these communities were linguistically continuous across their sectarian differences has, in this passage, a further all-consuming effect. Appealing over the head of Divide and Rule, the editor of these rabble-rousing paragraphs is able to angle his remarks at a greater community defined not by locality or religion, but by language and, in the inflammatory impulse of the hour, by race. "Kith and kin" is a term familiar to me as a nostrum cited by opponents of UDI (Unilateral Declaration of Independence) imposed by Ian Smith's Rhodesia in 1964. It signals less a national configuration than a transnational and ethnically self-determined one: "Though torn apart by circumstances, we whites (or we Bengalis) must stick together through thick and thin," thus the logic runs. No mention in the *Hitavada* of "this country" or of India. Its sights are set elsewhere.

Famine, Riot and Blame

But Partition in itself constituted only one element in the compound and continuing crisis of 1905–06. In the following year famine struck across large swathes of Bengal. Its effects were felt with peculiar ferocity in the east, but the knock-on reaction was experienced throughout the region and gave rise both to strenuous efforts at every level to address the practical problems involved, and to a vigorous debate across the press as to the causes of the situation. The Swadeshi Movement predictably enough blamed the government, whilst the government itself blamed Swadeshi extremists for disturbing supplies. Both views were reflected in the newspapers, where the main subjects of debate and sometimes acrimonious disagreement became the question of the reality of want, its actual as opposed to vaunted severity, and who—if it was indeed authentic and extreme—was responsible for letting it occur in the first place, and for putting the matter right now.

On one question there was agreement on almost every side: human agency had played a large part, if not in triggering the developing disaster, then for letting it get so badly out of hand. In this respect it has to be said there was an element of premonition, not so much of future disasters of this kind as of later theories as to their cause. In the early twentieth century famine was so common in colonial Bengal as to be almost considered endemic. The worst example ever was to occur at the height of the Second World War in 1943, when a combination of crop failure, poor administration and the need to feed troops, both British and Indian, involved in the war effort against the Japanese led to food shortages that were to kill well in excess of a million people; 1.5 million was the official estimate of the death toll, though it is now thought to have been twice as high. Again, explanations have been copious and varied. While, according to statistics collected by S.Y. Padmanabhan, it seems probable that blight in some areas led to a loss of up to 90% of the rice crop, human fallibility, the presence of large numbers of troops and the stress to normal patterns of distribution caused by the military conflict indubitably played a major role. The classic study is Amartya Sen's *Poverty and Famines: An Essay on Entitlement and Deprivation* of 1984, in which the Bengali Nobel Laureate economist argues that the initial causes of the problem were the temporary employment of many thousands of local men in the armed forces, the additional entitlement to food their pay packets allowed them, and a consequent hoarding by the few thus privileged.[27] But, as Sen himself stresses, poor consultation was also crucial. An interesting corollary of this fact, of much significance to Sen's thinking as a whole, is that although the population of the region has multiplied many times since 1947, there has not been a major instance of famine since independence. Colonies and other forms of despotic government, infers Sen, frequently permit famines to happen (look at Africa). In functioning, if imperfect, democracies such as modern India's they are inconceivable or, at least, very much less likely.

Whilst the shortages of 1906 were not quite on this scale, and have never been examined in such exhaustive detail, they were certainly examined on the spot and at the time by the local and national press. Few ignored the gravity of the state of affairs, though the *Indian Daily News*, an English-language paper widely read in the British community, played it down, and attributed the wilder reports then circulating to terrorist propaganda. Complacency of this kind, however, was rare. As an example of the middle ground of opinion, one can do little better than to quote *The Hindoo Patriot*, an English-language daily with a circulation of some 5000, in its issue of 18 July 1906:

> The *Indian Daily News* calls the distress now prevailing in East Bengal a "paper famine" and belittles or ignores the gravity of the situation...The action taken by the Government affords proof positive of the existence of

the famine, and the attack of the "Swadeshists" is founded on misrepresentation of the facts.

The bifurcation of opinion, the tendency of the press to cast aspersions in different and sometimes irreconcilable directions, was much exacerbated by the next, and practically inevitable, development: rioting across much of East Bengal. Whilst this proved especially serious in the city of Dhaka and Mymensingh (the district of East Bengal quite close to it), disturbances were fairly widespread in the east and even spread across to West Bengal, where on 19 July the ultra-loyalist *Bengalee New Indian*, which had earlier lambasted the authorities for commiserating with the starving, thundered: "The *New Indian* is surprised at the unusual leniency shown by the Government to the Mohammedan rioters in Mymensingh, as it was expressions of sympathy that really encouraged the outrage." Consider by contrast the mild rebuke handed out by English-language daily *The Indian Mirror* on the very same day. According to this government-friendly organ of opinion, the authorities on both side of the border were not doing quite enough: "The steps taken by the government to give relief to sufferers is deemed too inadequate, as they leave out of account those to whom it should be sent."

The government had a ready answer to such criticism. *The India Daily News* was wrong in denying the existence of want, but right in pointing the finger at the Swadeshi Movement, whose deleterious contribution to the evolving emergency, however, had not been to whip up panic in excess of the concern the situation demanded, so much as to disrupt the efforts being made to confront it. Two weeks later, stung to the quick by the accusation that his administration was doing too little, Sir Bampfylde Fuller, the beleaguered Lieutenant-General of East Bengal and Assam, made a statement to the Bengal National Chamber of Commerce to the effect that that the famine had been aggravated by "the methods pursued by those who desire to promote acceptance of Swadeshi principles". Reacting to this on 29 July the *Weekly Hitavadi*, whose ideological sympathies we have considered, countered by claiming that Swadeshi activists had been in the very forefront of efforts towards relief. "We do not know", mused this popular Bengali-medium periodical, "whether to praise the presumption of…Fuller or give him credit for his ignorance. Does not Sir Bampfylde know that in these days of distress the Swadeshi movement is enabling thousands of native artisans to earn their livelihood?"

The contrast between these opposing positions and interpretations could, of course, be put down to the respective scale and geographical coverage of the readerships to which these various newspapers appealed. This was not, however, a mere matter of differences between local and national interests. The *Weekly Hitavadi* enjoyed a large circulation throughout and beyond Bengal. Indeed, some of the newspapers most loyal to the government were the most parochial. *Suhrid*, for example, a Bengali-medium weekly whose readers were confined to a few hundred in the up-country district of Noakhali, charmingly congratulated the local Magistrate—evidently a Mrs Moore figure in the neighbourhood—for his personal magnanimity in the crisis. On 24 June 1906 it payed him this Dr Godbole-like compliment: "Mr Clayton, the Magistrate of Noakhali, is a kind and generous official. He is helping the distressed people within his jurisdiction even from his own pocket."

Two days later, in stark contrast, *Chatu Mikir*, a Bengali-medium weekly of a very different type, placed the whole scenario in a startlingly broad context by attributing the entire course of events to the obnoxious Partition of the year before. Though Curzon had now withdrawn from the scene, leaving Fuller to defend his policies in India and the newly appointed Secretary of State for India, John Morley, to defend them in London, partition, famine and riot seemed to this editor the inevitable working out of Curzon's warped priorities and logic. Although those priorities and that logic had been dictated by larger directives throughout the Raj, it was clear to this particular newspaper just who the principal victims of them had been, and on whose behalf it should therefore speak. Once more, kith and kin must have their say at last:

> Quiet will not be restored until a radical departure is made from the barbarism of Sir Bampfylde Fuller and the cunning statecraft of Lord Curzon...As it is the hideous aspect of His Honour's administrative policy has already come to be recognized in England by the Head of State. It may be prophesied that, sooner or later, the policy at present finding favour with the head of the Government of East Bengal and Assam is bound to receive a deathblow. But the same cannot be said about Lord Curzon's measures which, unless and until the evil that shrouds them is removed, will not be seen in their native meanness. Prestige is always a factor in favour of the ex-Viceroy. That is why Mr Morley[28] hesitates to undo the partition, a measure behind which is hidden a fatal poison that in time will poison the whole Bengali race.

Overlapping Circles

As Robert Darnton has noted, the British Raj in India does not come out well from the events of 1905–06. Fuller himself soon fled the scene, retiring to England in August with what dignity he could muster after his recommendation to the central government that two secondary schools be struck off for their involvement in the Swadeshi Movement was turned down. The Partition itself was rescinded in 1912, shortly after the capital of colonial India was moved to Delhi.

So what can we learn that bears on our theme from this short-lived though strategically important emergency? Certainly it was a turning point in the anti-imperialist movement, the juncture at which it decidedly moved centre stage and began to be recognised by the British as a political force to be reckoned with. My particular concern, however, is with the manner in which these events came to be viewed by different constituencies of Indians, and the ways in which the press at the time either provoked or reflected their attitudes. It is important not to over-simplify here. Personally I believe that Lord Eden in 1876 and *The Daily Hitavali* in 1906 were both wrong in discerning a necessary correlation between voiced opinion and language of expression. As we have already seen, there were, at least in 1905–06, several loyalist Bengali newspapers, and at least one English-language newspaper that adopted a strongly anti-government stance. What is true, however, is that the spectrum of available languages had the effect of enabling the newspapers to address different audiences and to conduct the ongoing debate in varying forums: some local, some regional, some national and some imperial. And, as each of these forums, so various in size, orientation, ideology and linguistic facility, came thus to be addressed, it constituted itself into an imagined community of sorts. The range is very marked and represents, I think, something far weightier than the conventional split between national and local dailies and weeklies as you might find it in Europe, America or anywhere else in the industrialised world. What we appear to be observing at this politically sensitive time in Indian history then are not so much the beginnings of a national consciousness, as Anderson would understand the term, as a matrix of different and alternative "imagined communities", each configuration lying across many others: a congeries of overlapping, intersecting circles.

So then, taking our bearings once more from *Imagined Communities*, which if either of the two interpretations of Anderson's theory of nationhood and the media sketched out earlier—the "soft" and the "hard" approaches—seems to be relevant in this quite formative period and setting for South Asia? It is my contention that neither works completely, and that the first, or soft, approach works hardly at all. There is no equivalent in the communications industry that we have been describing of *The New York Times*. Besides, the running references in the texts we have been examining are not to a remote famine in Africa, but to millions starving down the road. Compared to this pressing reality, remoter problems, even within the greater imperial complex, fade to almost nothing. In 1906, for example, it is known that many were starving elsewhere in India. The suffering was especially acute in the Punjab, and whilst figures for the whole subcontinent proved difficult to collect at the time, they have since been put as high as eleven million. The fact remains that it is not as a national emergency that this widespread tragedy was viewed in the sources at which we have been looking, but as an extension of—and an exacerbation to—stringent regional conditions.

For Anderson's "hard" or causative approach to be applicable, we would need under these admittedly somewhat special circumstances to discern a connection between the influence of print culture as a whole and the formation of national—that is, of Indian—consciousness. Transplanting Anderson's New World scenario to South Asia, thousands of men and women (principally men) all over India would need to be reading broadsheets with a global—and certainly a national—reach, couched in a national language, and edging towards an interpretation of events which placed the nation, and its problems, at its very centre.

Instead, what do we find? A multitude of different newspapers couched in various languages—or sometimes combinations of languages—each with a very different local orientation, perceived audience and court of public appeal. If, above and beyond this complicated mass of interests, a single unity is straining to be heard, it is one that Anderson would have had much difficulty fitting into his scheme. The clearly implied, though dimly present unity behind all these emanations is one inimical to, and certainly embarrassing to, Anderson's vision of things. It is an elusive entity freshly and cruelly torn asunder, one that would later be temporarily re-united before being rent apart yet again. A location defined less in political than in linguistic, in cultural, even—in some of the sources we have been looking at—in ethnic terms. A place which, however energetically imagined and articulated, was not, had not been and never would be a nation, a place that remains even now a palpable and passionate idea.

(Just as, for many people, Ireland remains a palpable and passionate idea.) I mean, course, not India, but Bengal.

Mind you, I am not claiming that, within my carefully chosen example, Anderson's instincts prove altogether unfounded. Evidently there existed even here *some* connection between print culture, specifically the newspapers, and the formation of communal consciousness. Evidently too, these communities were being "imagined" or projected, and the papers were to some extent stirring such imaginings. What does seem to be equally clear, however, is that whilst certain categories of readers were thinking in putatively national terms, others—the majority of the literate and aware—were thinking in regional, linguistic, cultural and "kith and kin" terms. And the factor determining this difference was not the impact of print culture in and of itself, but the languages that were being printed.

Print, Script, Language and Nation

An objection may well be lodged on the grounds that I have concentrated too hard and too long on quite a local example that represents if anything a mere blip in the performance of an overwhelmingly convincing paradigm. I want therefore in my closing paragraphs to broaden out again, and to consider the roots of Anderson's lopsidedness (I use this term advisedly in preference to "errors"). This is a salutary exercise in itself because, while it may look from the surface of the foregoing discussion that a simple misalignment has occurred between print and nation, in reality I think that the causes of Anderson's myopia intervene much earlier on in his argument: in his expressed views about language.

In Chap. 2 of *Imagined Communities*, Anderson deals with the relationship between religious communities in the pre-modern world and a number of what he calls "sacral languages". In fact his list contains four items: Latin, Pali, Arabic and Chinese, the first corresponding to medieval Christendom, the second to traditional Buddhism, the third to the world of Islam and the fourth to the universe of Confucianism.[29] It might be, though, that there is a distinct Eastern bias in this inventory. Sanskrit, however, is a notable absentee. In later chapters he illustrates the breakdown of these respective hegemonies and the ways in which print eventually encouraged the use of vernaculars and, through them, the rise of national awareness.

Nobody, I think, could entertain serious doubts over this argument insofar as it covers Europe, least of all Febvre and Martin on whose evidence in *L'Apparition du livre* Anderson largely relies, or Elizabeth Eisenstein whose *The Print Revolution in Early Modern Europe* provides powerful corroboration.[30] I do not know enough to comment on his three other zones of linguistic development, but were he to confront the example of India, I think he would find himself floundering in deep and muddy water. The neglect of Sanskrit would, in my view, of necessity prove fatal to his theories in this environment. Not only does Sanskrit possess a written script and literature many centuries old (some even argue for one as long as 3000 years), but its relationship with the scripts, languages and literatures of later India—both pre- and post-print—is remarkable, and quite different from, say, the relationship between Latin and Spanish. Nowadays Sanskrit, when it is written at all—and certainly when it is taught—is written out in the Devanagari script with which readers of Hindi are familiar. In fact, Sanskrit can be written in a great many scripts. There is even a school of thought amongst Indologists—Sheldon Pollock of Columbia springs to mind[31]—who would argue that the various regional scripts of the subcontinent—Bengali, Gujarat, Malayalam and what have you—originated in the first instance as ways of domesticating high-level Sanskrit for local use, and were later applied to the colloquial Prakrits—or everyday vernaculars—out of which the local languages of India familiar to us today arose.

This development has been christened "literisation". It amounted to a script revolution and, whatever form and however long it took, it occurred very many centuries before print in India was thought of. (For the record, wood-block printing or *xylography* had been employed in Tibet for almost as long as in China, and Korea developed a form of movable type in the twelfth century AD, but none of this spread to India, where the first printed books were produced in Goa by early Jesuit missionaries, some 200 years before the British introduced the printing press into Bengal.[32]) Doubts may be expressed about the exact chronology of the script revolution, but of one fact Pollock and others are now convinced: it had a far deeper and more lasting effect on cultural development across the subcontinent than print ever did, or could have.

When print arrived in full force at the end of the eighteenth century, standardisation of various sorts seemed a distinct possibility. The missionaries of the Baptist Missionary Society, who settled in Danish-administered Serampore to translate the Christian scriptures into a multitude of vernaculars at the very beginning of the nineteenth century, briefly flirted with the idea of setting aside the bewildering array of different scripts with which they were obliged to wrestle, in favour of a standardised Devanagari which it was hoped might eventually attain the universal currency that the Roman alphabet had so long enjoyed in the West.[33] Much later on, in the mid-twentieth century, the Progressive Artists' Movement (of whom Anand was one) espoused a similar design, for overtly nationalist reasons. Both groups in the end were forced to concede that the task was an impossible one and that therefore, where it came to the media of published expression, print would need to accommodate itself to the linguistic balkanisation of the subcontinent rather than the other way round.

The end result was that print entrenched ever further the linguistic multifariousness of India. The nationalist movement as it developed through the twentieth century thus stressed the significance of vernacular usage, while conceding that this would be a source of welcome variety rather than of desired unity. At independence a compromise was achieved. English was retained for some official and diplomatic purposes, but the first Constitution would enshrine fourteen national languages, a number that would rise with successive revisions. Though Hindi has often seemed to set its sights on universal acceptance, and is frequently employed as a *lingua franca*, especially in North India, there exists nowhere on the subcontinent a national vernacular in Anderson's strict sense of the term.

Against this background, one does rather wonder what the pertinence in this setting of Anderson's procession through print culture, national vernaculars and national consciousness could conceivably be. There are a variety of possible responses to this quibble. The first is Chatterjee's surprisingly modest proposal that print culture, though a definitive event in the evolution of communications in India, finally led in two different directions: towards a pan-Indian identity expressed through English, and towards a regional renaissance based on, in his case, Bengali. A far more radical response, however, is to assert with Pollock and his school that the "printing revolution" of which Eisenstein has written so well in the European context either did not take place in India (at least in the transforming way in which she described it in the West), or did indeed occur, but was not all that revolutionary. The second of these views is a comparatively new one, whose implications have yet to be worked out. I shall soon be exploring them in a comparative monograph but, before I do so, I would like to close here by turning back briefly to the effect that all of this has on the ways in which we think about the novel.

Increasingly, it seems to me, the subject of "Indian Literature" is splitting down the middle. Forty years ago, when I first started teaching this subject at the University of Leeds, I had to do so via a textbook written by my old professor. This had a chapter which began with what seemed to me at the time to be an egregiously blinkered sentence: "Indians have been writing in English since Macaulay's minute and before Lord William Bentinck in 1835 endorsed it as government policy."[34] I had no objection to this as a historical statement; indeed, it is literally true. My only qualm was that it headed a chapter called "Indian Literature" in which there was no reference to anything apart from the tradition represented by Anand, Narayan and Raja Rao. (This was some ten years before the emergence of Rushdie.) One of the writers the chapter did deal with was Nirad C. Chaudhuri, who died in the closing months of the last millennium, and Chaudhuri had quite a different view: that authors from India who wrote in English belonged to the Great Tradition of English Literature (Chaudhuri liked saying that sort of thing). It is a maybe paradoxical view—that an author's literary as opposed to bureaucratic nationality is defined by the language in which he chooses to write. But it is one that we apply quite happily to Joseph Conrad, a Polish recruit into F.R. Leavis's regimental Great Tradition. Recently it has been re-iterated by the poet William Radice, a Bengali scholar of distinction and Rabindranath Tagore's most successful English translator. Amongst his other achievements, Radice has taught a course in "South Asian Literature in English" (SALE) in the South Asia Department (SAD) at London University's School of Oriental and African Studies (SOAS). He has survived all of these acronyms to assert that "I increasingly tend towards Nirad C. Chaudhuri's view that writers should be defined by the language they write in."[35]

Perhaps, though, both of these positions are too extreme. Critically both possess a certain logic, but a book historian—such as Bengal's irrepressible Rimi Chatterjee[36]—is more likely to say that she is looking at two different traditions within one subcontinental literature, both of which are beneficiaries of the fact of print. Where does that leave our debate over Anderson? The repercussions for his model of nationalism are, I believe, quite marked, since it is just about possible that each of these two traditions projects a different sort of national consciousness. Richard Cronin (in *Imagining India*, 1989) and Rumina Sethi (in *Myths of the Nation: National Identity and Representation*, 1999) have both come out with the very clear statement that India can only be described and evoked imaginatively as a whole—that is, as a nation—via the English language.[37] This is a bold assertion, the full implications of which, if traced through, might lend Anderson some support. It represents, however, only one aspect of a bivalent picture, both sides of which were observed in the year of Nirad Chaudhuri's death by another Chaudhuri—the novel and short story writer Amit Chaudhuri—in a searching article in the *Times Literary Supplement*.[38]

Amit Chaudhuri addresses himself to the "large" English-language novel from India, such as pre-eminently Rushdie's, a high-profile, fashionable and, let it be said, comparatively recent outgrowth of Indian letters. It is a tradition (if you can apply that word to something only a few decades old) of which, as a writer of slender books, he is somewhat wary, and maybe somewhat jealous. His view is that there is something about these doorstopper works that mimics India itself: something vast, sprawling, variegated but inclusive. He contrasts it with the tradition of Indian short story writing imported by Tagore into Bengal from France at the end of the nineteenth century. Tagore employed it as medium for fiction in Bengali and several have followed him, including Chaudhuri himself, whose own delicate miniatures of Calcutta life are nevertheless couched in English. The difference between these stories and Rushdie's, says Chaudhuri, is that they tend to mimic local rather than national reality. It strikes me now that Chaudhuri's view of the Rushdian novel as mimetic of the nation represents a fictive-critical application of Anderson's "soft" or analytical approach to print capitalism, except that in it, it is not the newspaper that is mimetic of the nation, but the novel. Yet it also strikes me that Chaudhuri's argument, though it relates principally to the scale of given works of fiction, could also be extended to include the language medium. Just as newspapers in India, as we have seen in one very limited example, supply different terms of communal reference depending on what language they are printed in, so novels have an equivalent effect depending on which they are written in English or, say, Bengali, Urdu, Gujarati or whatever.

All of which is perhaps to confirm that Anderson's view of culture applies to India only in subtle and much qualified ways. Of one last fact, however, I remain convinced: that none of us can reasonably conduct this sort of discussion without him, or without viewing the case he puts in the widest possible international context.

Notes

1. Benedict Anderson, *Imagined Communities: Reflections on the Origin and Spread of Nationalism*, Second Edition (London and New York: Verso, 1991), xii.

2. Ian Watt, *The Rise of the Novel: Studies in Defoe, Richardson and Fielding* (London: Chatto and Windus, 1957).
3. See especially his *War of the World: History's Age of Hatred, 1914–1989* (London: Allen Lane, 2006) and *Empire: The Rise and Demise of the British World Order* (London: Basic Books, 2003).
4. Shakespeare, *Troilus and Cressida*, 1, iii, 109–10.
5. *Imagined Communities*, 92, quoting Bipi Chandra Pal, *Memories of My Life and Times* in the 1973 reprint by the Bipin Chandra Institute in Calcutta, 223–3. The vagueness of Anderson's grasp of Indian chronology here is re-emphasised in his only other reference to Pal on page 119, where he speaks of the "*first* generation in any significant numbers to have received a European education (cf. B.B. Pal)". Pal, however, was writing some hundred years after Macaulay's Minute.
6. Quoted in full in George Otto Trevelyan, *The Life and Letters of Lord Macaulay* (London: Longman, Green and Co., 1889), 290–92. I am citing my maternal grandfather's copy of the "Popular" edition. The book first appeared in 1876, and went through very many reprints.
7. Javed Majeed, *Ungoverned Imaginings: James Mill's The History of British India and Orientalism* (Oxford: Clarendon, 1992), 69, 85, 179, 192–93.
8. Judith M. Brown, *Modern India: The Origins of Asian Democracy* (New York, Delhi and Oxford: Oxford University Press, 1985), 250.
9. Michael West, *Bilingualism—With Special Reference to Bengal* (Calcutta: Bureau of Education of the Government of India, 1926), 4. A copy is kept in the Oriental and India Office Collections of the British Library at I.S.336.
10. "New Word Order: Emerging Histories of the Book": Asia-Pacific Conference of the Society for the History of Authorship, Reading and Publishing. Centre of Advanced Studies, Department of English and School of Cultural Texts and Records, Jadavpur University, Kolkata, 30 January to 1 February 2006. See Chap. 10 of this book for one output of this meeting relevant to our theme.
11. Partha Chatterjee, *The Nation and Its Fragments; Colonial and Postcolonial Histories* (New Jersey: Princeton University Press, 1994), 3–13.
12. Lal (1973 reprint), 156–57. Quoted in Chatterjee, 11–12. The messes, though Chatterjee does not call attention to this fact, were organized on a regional basis. Lal himself, from the Sylet area of eastern Bengal, put up at the Sylet mess, which was situated at 14 College Street.
13. Mulk Raj Anand, *Untouchable* (1935: London: The Bodley Head, 1970), 13.
14. Raja Rao, *Kanthapura* (1937; New Delhi: OUP, 2000), 1.
15. Norman Gerald Barrier, *Banned: Controversial Literature and Political Control in India, 1907–1947* (Columbia: University of Missouri Press,

1974), 135. Authors like Anand were often placed on the relevant Index, less because of their contents or subject matter than because they had been brought out by notoriously left-wing publishing houses, in Anand's case by Wishart, whose then Editor-in-Chief, Edgell Rickword, presided over a decidedly Marxist-inspired list. According to Barrier, "Between 1935 and 1938 Customs seized 450 titles, most of which were Communist-linked. John Strachey, Mulk Raj Anand, Agnes Smedley and P.R. Dutt fell snare either to Customs or postal inspectors around India."
16. *Imagined Communities*, 33.
17. *Imagined Communities*, 61–65.
18. Chatterjee, 7.
19. An incomplete though still extensive collection of the quarterly returns is kept in the British Library (OIOC catalogue number SV 412); the annual reports are available on microfiche at V/23.
20. Robert Darnton, "Literary Surveillance and the British Raj: The Contradictions of Liberal Imperialism", *Book History* 4 (2001), 133–76; "Book Production in British India, 1850–1900", *Book History* 5 (2002), 239–63.
21. Darnton, "Literary Surveillance", 150.
22. Fuller, Sir Joseph Bampfylde (1854–1935) was also author of *Studies of Indian Life and Sentiment* (1910), *The Empire of India* (1913) and *Etheric Energies* (1928).
23. The National Archives on Janpath in New Delhi have a complete set for the whole of India, which fill one large side room. The SAMP microfilms cover Bengal alone and are on MF 10279 (reels 18–44).
24. Jane Austen, *Mansfield Park*, ed. Claudia L. Johnson (London: W.W. Norton, 1998), 259.
25. Quoted in Chatterjee, 25.
26. Curzon, George Nathaniel (1859–1925), Viceroy of India, restorer of the Taj Mahal and architect of the first Partition of Bengal (July 1905, revoked 1912). Of him it was said:

> My name is George Nathaniel Curzon,
> I am a most superior person.
> My cheeks are pale, my hair is sleek,
> And I dine at Blenheim once a week.

27. Amartya Sen, *Poverty and Famine: An Essay on Entitlement and Deprivation* (Oxford: Oxford University Press, 1981).
28. Morley, John first Viscount Morley of Blackburn, editor of *The Fortnightly Review* (1867–82) and *The Pall Mall Gazette* (1881–83), founder of the English Men of Letters Series and Secretary of State for India (1905–10).

29. *Imagined Communities*, 14.
30. Lucien Lefevre and Henri-Jean Martin, *L'Apparition du livre* (Paris, 1958); Elizabeth L. Eisenstein, *The Printing Press as Agent of Change; Contradictions and Cultural Transformations in Early-Modern Europe* (Cambridge, 1979) and *The Printing Revolution in Early Modern Europe* (Cambridge, 1983).
31. See especially Sheldon Pollock, "Literary Culture and Manuscript Culture in Pre-colonial India", *The History of the Book and Literary Cultures*, eds. Simon Eliot, Andrew Nash and Ian Willison (London: The British Library, 2007).
32. See David Diriger, *The Book Before Printing: Ancient, Medieval, Oriental* (New York: Dover Publications, 417–20 and 354–72.
33. See *Memoir Relative to the Progress of the Translations of the Sacred Scriptures in the Year 1816, Addressed to the Society at Serampore* (Serampore: The Mission Press, 1816), esp. p. 15:

> the Deva-nagree is familiar to most who can read, and as the alphabet is perfectly complete. While some of the local alphabets are greatly deficient, it seems desirable to extend the Deva-nagree as widely as possible. It would greatly facilitate the progress of knowledge, if it could have that extension given to it in India, which the Roman alphabet has attained in Europe.

34. William Walsh, *Commonwealth Literature* (Oxford University Press, 1973), 1.
35. William Radice, *A Hundred Letters from England*, foreword by Martin Kampchen (New Delhi: Indialog Publications, 2003). Letter 28, 140.
36. Novelist and author of the indispensable *Empires of the Mind: The History of the Oxford University Press in India under the Raj* (New Delhi: Oxford University Press, 2005).
37. Richard Cronin, *Imagining India* (London: Macmillan, 1989) and Rumina Sethi, *Myths of the Nation: National Identities and Literary Representation* (Oxford: The Clarendon Press, 1999).
38. Amit Chaudhuri, "Lure of the Hybrid: What the Post-Colonial Novel Means to the West", *The Times Literary Supplement*, 3 September 1999, 5–6.

CHAPTER 10

Migrating Stories: How Textbooks Fired a Canon

Whether we are speaking of demographic or of cultural migration—phenomena that inevitably proceed hand in hand—the processes involved seldom flow in one direction alone. As men and women cross boundaries and seas, they carry ideas, customs, images, words and whole stories with them, changing as they do so both themselves and their hosts. Sometimes the customs and stories precede the people. (The penetration of Britain by Indian and African forms of English during the nineteenth century, well before the mass immigration of the mid-twentieth, is an obvious case in point.) On other occasions they follow them. Within the imperial and immediate post-imperial nexus, a tide of immigration has very often been eased or even instigated by a prior period of acculturation whereby words, images and even forms of memory were ingested well before the moment of departure. (In many British territories in sub-Saharan Africa, a commonplace denomination for England—affectionately or derisively phrased—was "Home".) In such instances the implanting of metropolitan images or narratives in the minds of the colonised, laced with aspiration and desire, was frequently a major contributory factor in the decision to embark. Those who crossed the seas to Europe, or more specifically Britain, in the immediate post–Second World War period were never coming to an environment that was completely new and strange. This was especially true when the spoken languages of migrant and host were contiguous: English, for example, had been used by Paul Bogle's countrymen for well over two centuries before the docking of the former troopship

MV *Empire Windrush*, bringing 492 Jamaican passengers and one stowaway to London, in 1948. The language brought in its train a school system, and with it the whole apparatus of syllabi, textbooks and the like. The most pervasive influences on the individual colonial imagination were therefore the earliest to be absorbed. It is a complicated history, full of unsuspected corners. In this chapter I hope to demonstrate how the activities of one particular Scottish publisher during the earlier part of the twentieth century helped to unloose not simply a tide of hopeful migration but, as one result of it, a dynamic tide of innovative writing.

* * *

I begin with an image so familiar it hardly needs showing: John Constable's painting of 1823, "Salisbury Cathedral from the Bishop's Grounds" (Fig. 10.1). To children everywhere it is known in the shape of a jigsaw

Fig. 10.1 John Constable, "Salisbury Cathedral from the Bishop's Grounds", 1823 (Victoria and Albert Museum, London)

puzzle, but for many who passed through the elementary school system in the British West Indies between 1926 and the early 1960s it possesses an additional resonance, reproduced as it then was on page 199 of volume five of Nelson's much-used *West Indian Readers*.

Many would have encountered it aged eleven in Standard Five, and read with greater or lesser fluency the accompanying commentary by the editor Captain James Oliver Cutteridge, Director of Education for Trinidad and Tobago and a keen amateur artist. Cutteridge treats the picture as an exercise in perspective. He calls attention to the framing of the South Front by trees, and illustrates on the following page how the sightlines meet at a vanishing point at the base of the famous steeple. Then he issues a curt invitation: "Write a paragraph describing, *in your own words*, what you can see in Constable's picture."[1]

During the early 1940s in wartime Port-of-Spain, this invitation was addressed to an elementary schoolboy of Indian ancestry shortly before he proceeded to Queen's Royal College. Three decades later, from his cottage near Salisbury, he responded in literal terms to Cutteridge's challenge by conveying in his own words—and in exactly one paragraph—the image's original and continuing effects. The passage occurs towards the beginning of his novel of displacement *The Enigma of Arrival* on which we touched in Chap. 2, the narrator of which has newly arrived in Wiltshire:

> I saw what I saw very clearly. But I didn't know what I was looking at. I had nothing to fit it into. I was still in a kind of limbo. There were certain things I knew, though. I knew the name of the town I had come to by the train. It was Salisbury. It was almost the first English town I had got to know, the first I had been given some idea of, from the reproduction of the Constable painting of Salisbury Cathedral in my third-standard reader. Far away in my tropical island, before I was ten. A four-colour reproduction which I had thought the most beautiful picture I had even seen.[2]

The passage is all the more revealing because disingenuous in certain respects. If this narrator really did meet that Constable landscape in school before his tenth birthday, then his reading age—and the author V.S. Naipaul's—was two years in advance of his contemporaries. I suspect also that his consciousness of the process by which the plate was reproduced—four-colour printing—owes something to an article in Arthur Mee's ten-volume *Children's Encyclopaedia*, where that technique is explained via successive impressions of a self-portrait by Van Gogh. The middle-aged Naipaul complains of a lack of context, though his paragraph places the experience firmly against a backdrop of colonial desire. Perhaps the best-known judgement on Constable is given in Ernst Gombrich's *The Story of Art*. Constable, remarks Gombrich, aimed "to paint what he saw with his own eyes".[3] To this definition of realism Naipaul responds by the disclaimer that, as a colonial child—or even initially adult—viewer, he had little idea what he was seeing. The truth surely is that he saw what he wanted, and what he wanted was England. In a modern British setting, recognition of Constable's naturalism is impeded by intervening nostalgia. In the imperial environment it was obstructed by longing. The difference between these conditions is one of the themes of Naipaul's novel, which as well as addressing migration conducts a master class in interpreting landscape and, through it, alternative histories: of the land, of architecture and of the conditioned, observing self.

Indubitably school readers of that period instilled an anxiety of influence in writers who once studied them. West Indian literature is peppered with acknowledgements to these modest books, and the detail of the references, specifying the volume and in some case even the page numbers, suggests not only the avidity with which they were absorbed, but the frequency with which pupils failed to hand them in. Why did this standard school fare—and Nelson's readers in particular—retain that sort of a hold? Thomas Nelson and Sons had been providing school readers for domestic and imperial use since the late nineteenth century, but the proliferation of branches and offices in far-flung dependencies had gradually entailed a localisation of provision. Until about 1907 the pattern was for uniform Crown or Royal Readers that served the needs of pupils throughout the Empire, including as it happens Naipaul's Mr Biswas. But in that year Nelson's Toronto office, which was expanding its educational provision, decided to issue a "Special Canadian Series", drawing on indigenous oral and literary sources where it could find them and organised imaginatively, as their Prefaces carefully explained, around the successive seasons of the Canadian year.[4] Popular and successful, these locally orientated books were systematically updated. From the Nelson archives in Edinburgh it is clear just how anxious the firm became at the time of the Great Depression to ensure that its readers were officially sanctioned as set books throughout the Dominion. From the 1920s, with growing competition from other companies, the priority was to work in close collaboration with directors of education in the various Canadian provinces, several of whom were appointed as consultants. The model of regionalisation and fraternisation with government was then exported. Since 1909, moreover, a preferential trading agreement had existed between Canada and the West Indies, extended in 1920 and again in 1925, as a result of which the Toronto branch gradually assumed responsibility for sales in the Caribbean.

The turning point for business there—and the origin of the West Indian Readers—lies in the appointment in December 1922 of S.P. Jones as a travelling representative in the region. After a six-month tour through Bermuda, St Kitts, Antigua, Monserrat, Dominique, St Lucia, Barbados, St Vincent, Trinidad, Grenada, British Guiana and British Honduras, he reported that the rapid evolution of elementary education among the black and Asian population entailed a need for purpose-made textbooks. As his boss in Toronto, S.B. Watson, then wrote back to Edinburgh on 31 July 1923, enclosing Jones's recommendations: "You will notice that on folio five he makes a definite suggestion for a West Indian Reader, or set of Readers. I am going more fully with him into this idea, and will write you a separate letter in a few days."[5]

The following winter, Watson himself toured the Caribbean, and while in Port-of-Spain he met Cutteridge. It was the beginning of a long and fruitful association, not untouched by controversy. Four years earlier, Cutteridge had arrived in Trinidad to take over as Principal of Tranquillity Boy's Model School, perhaps the best elementary school on the island. He came equipped not with a university degree, but with a First World War field commission, a fellowship of the Royal Geographical Society, a zeal for educational reform and an eye for a telling picture. By the time Watson turned up, he had been elevated to Chief Inspector of Schools and Assistant Director of Education. Taking a maple leaf out of Nelson's Canadian book, he volunteered not simply as consultant for the projected textbooks, but as author. He proved unstoppable. In twenty years he was to be responsible for several volumes of elementary school arithmetic, successive editions of these readers and—his all-time commercial success—*Nelson's Geography of the West Indies and Adjacent Islands*.[6] The maths was sometimes questioned, the geography scorned. The books sold mightily.

Captain Cutteridge's versatility, or hackwork if you like, was his strength, though in some it seemed a weakness. By temperament he was a geographer and artist, and his inclination to allow these interests to shape his writing was consonant with Nelson's own editorial policy. After all, the books were to be illustrated and, following the Canadian model, they were to reflect the natural environment and the social setting of their young readership. Cutteridge's revolutionary idea—though to some at the time it seemed a misdemeanour—was to situate literature in the Caribbean itself. In their distinctive red covers, his readers—six in number including an introductory book—covered all sorts of subjects, from folklore and customs to fauna and flora and history, but the organising theme was that of travel, and inter-connections between different places. It was a tendency enhanced by his pedagogical tactic of re-enforcing each subject by repeating it in successive volumes at different linguistic levels. Consciously or not, through graded exercises and extracts Cutteridge conveyed a vision of Caribbean culture as a continual inflow and outflow, movement and coalescence. He was less exercised by hierarchy than by variety, exploration, diversity, gravitation and change. The upwardly mobile, Garvey-inspired, middle-class Asian and Afro-Trinidadian did not forgive him. And nor did Mr Biswas.

The introductory volume got off to a promising start by introducing Creole tales, including Brer Rabbit, the Caribbean manifestation of the Ashanti trickster figure Ananse, and as such a migrant from West African folklore.[7] "Nancy" stories, the critics dubbed them, and accused the editor of dumbing down. His inventory of livestock, including beef, was no more popular. "In a mincing voice" Biswas reads aloud from the chapter in Volume One on "Our Animal Friends": "The cow and the goat give us milk and we eat their flesh when they are killed. You hear the savage?"[8] Book Two introduces the salient topic of travel with Lesson 21, entitled "A Voyage to London".[9] It takes the form of an imaginary two-week journal by a passenger on a steamship ploughing across the Atlantic, through the "Sea of Weed" (the Sargasso Sea), eventually sighting the Dover shoreline and Tilbury beyond. There is a four-colour print of a steamer with attendant tug and the funnels of leading shipping lines, then black-and-white photographs of various sea- and landmarks, including the Azores and the legendary White Cliffs. It seems conventional enough until you realise that it was the generation of seven-year-olds entertained by this lesson in the 1930s who in 1948, eighteen years after the primer's publication, set sail on the *Windrush*. Is there another a school reader anywhere which, through describing a metropolis to groups of schoolchildren who have yet to visit it, helped change that destination forever? And there is more. Volume Three, set in the next standard up, re-enforces this travelogue by dwelling on the Sargasso Sea itself, wild and forbidding, introducing a motif recurrent in West Indian literature, and not just in Jean Rhys.[10] And Volume Four takes its young readers into the heart of the Empire itself with a chapter on "London", evoking the Tower of

London, Trafalgar Square and Oxford Street.[11] Sam Selvon would have been ten when he read these descriptions in Standard Four in 1933. Twenty-two years later, in *Lonely Londoners*, his character Moses exults over these self-same sights and congratulates himself, unlike Moses of old, for setting foot in the Promised Land.[12]

But the gaze is not always trained overseas. Cutteridge was also interested in the demography of the Caribbean, and to that end inserts a running sequence of essays about its various communities, starting in Volume Two with a lesson entitled "India". There it was that seven-year-old Naipaul, author-to-be of *An Area of Darkness*, must have perused the opening sentence: "MANY boys and girls who will read this book are East Indians. Their parents or their grandparents came from India." Son of aspiring author and one-time journalist, he would have continued reading with the words "In India most boys do not choose the kind of work that they do, but they follow their father's trade."[13] When in the next book the infant Naipaul learned about "East Indian in the West Indies",[14] impressions were laid down that would be of use when depicting the Tulsis, impressions re-enforced for a third time in Book Four with its linguistically more demanding account of "A Hindu Wedding".[15]

Cutteridge did not compose all the lessons from scratch. Many are synopses of classics, selected with a view to local relevance, and culled from existing Nelson compilations like *Robinson Crusoe* and *Tales from the Iliad* from the "Told to Children" series. The motif of exile, for example, appears in an early volume with a paraphrase of Defoe's *Crusoe*, including J.C. Dollman's sketch of a castaway staring gloomily out to sea.[16] As the poet Derek Walcott later put it: "The starved eye devours the seascape for the morsel/ Of a sail./ The horizon threads it infinitely", in the title poem to his volume *The Castaway* published in 1965, twenty-eight years after he saw that illustration in St Lucia in Standard Two.[17] By the time he read Cutteridge's synopsis of the Homeric duel between Hector and Achilles in Book Three, the future author of the postcolonial epic *Omeros* was eight.[18] And if the contest between his Homerically named fishermen in that eventual mock-epic possesses a bathetic, Heath Robinson–like air compared with the Greek original, it may well be because the accompanying illustrations in the primer, taken straight from *Tales from the Iliad*, are indeed by the English cartoonist William Heath Robinson.[19]

History, geography and source come together in the editor's continual recounting of seafarers' tales: Columbus, and most suggestively Sir Walter Raleigh. The account of the latter is drawn in the first instance from *Sir*

Walter Raleigh in Nelson's "Teaching of English" series, which itself relies largely on Raleigh's own *The Discoverie of Guiana* of 1596.[20] Thus Cutteridge is able to echo the Elizabethan's descriptions of the Asphalt lakes of Trinidad and Venezuela, and to reproduce his approximate map of the South American coastline. Prompted no doubt by this, Naipaul, who had noted these details in Standard Four, sat in the British Museum Library in the 1960s poring over Raleigh's rare volume, which in turn became a major source for the early chapters of his history of Trinidad, *The Loss of El Dorado*, conveying its own impression of Raleigh's career, as Naipaul's Preface explains, largely in Raleigh's words.[21]

Raleigh had encountered the aboriginal Caribs, subject of an exercise in Book Three in the generic readers published from 1928.[22] Ten years later, however, distinct regional requirements led Cutteridge to collaborate with Frank Ogle on a parallel Jamaica edition. Distinguished by its orange covers, but with identical pagination to the original version, this substituted individual chapters more in line with local needs. The lesson on the Caribs, for example, went to make way for one on the Arawaks, of particular pertinence when this run of readers was placed on the syllabus in British Guiana.[23] It was therefore this version of Exercise 34 that an infant Wilson Harris studied in the Georgetown of the 1940s, kindling an imagination that would later populate a whole hinterland with the Arawak archetypes of his *Guyana Quartet* and many subsequent novels. Nothing is more celebrated in the Quartet than the encounter at the close of *Palace of the Peacock* (1960) with a giant waterfall, up the face of which Donne and his hard-pressed companions toil.[24] It had been long in the making, since Lesson 25 of Book 5 in the Jamaica edition is devoted to A Visit to the Kaieteur Falls "in the far-away interior of British Guiana", abridged with one tumultuous illustration from Sir Edward Davidson's survey *The British West Indies* of 1903.[25] "Although it was discovered in 1870," runs the text, "very few people beyond the aboriginal Indians who inhabit the neighbourhood have seen this great natural wonder owing to the difficulty and expense of the long journey from the coast-lands. Where most of the people in the colony reside." Hence, one suspects, the astonishment experienced by Harris's explorers, and the transforming effect of that memorable final scene.

The successive exercises of both editions not only supplied images and references that fed works of the postcolonial imagination, they also supplied future writers with metaphors for the colonial condition itself: enslavement, indentured labour and its aftermath. In *The Polished Hoe*,

Austin Clarke's prize-winning novel of 2003 set in the Barbados of the 1940s, a policeman named Sargeant is led through an underground dungeon beneath the Great House of a sugar plantation by a woman who has just confessed to murdering the manager. The dungeon is a site of constriction, punishment and terror, profoundly symbolic of enslavement in many senses. He thinks of the "reading exercises in *Nelson's West Indian Reader*, Book Three, about a spider who bores a hole in the ground and covers it with a lid made of pieces of straw and mud, as a protection and as a guillotine. As a weapon."[26] Sargeant's memory, like the author's, is uncannily precise. What both are recalling is the "Trap-door spider" as described on page 119 of Lesson 29 of that book, with a drawing of the arachnid's hide-away or nest, the tiny cap laid open and resembling a slice of coconut shell. "The trap-door spider is a very interesting one," Cutteridge records. "It makes a hole in the ground for its dwelling, and covers the top with a little door made of its threads and earth. This hole forms its hiding-place until it sets out on a hunting expedition."[27]

In the section from Naipaul's *The Enigma of Arrival* entitled "The Journey", the narrator speaks of the early months of his sojourn in Wiltshire, and recounts how a lifetime of wandering has left him feeling impaled, spread-eagled, feminised, washed up. He had been working on a historical saga, evidently meant to be taken for *The Loss of El Dorado*, when "I had the waking fantasy of myself as a corpse tossing lightly among the reeds at the bottom of a river (a river like the one in the Pre-Raphaelite painting of the drowned Ophelia, reproduced in the *Nelson's West Indian Reader* I had used in my elementary school in Trinidad, a river that turned out to be like the river in Wiltshire at the back of my cottage)."[28] That local stream, of course, is the Avon, and the literary and pictorial one is the "weeping brook" depicted in John Everett Millais's painting of Ophelia after her suicide, reproduced in Cutteridge's paraphrase of *Hamlet* in Book Five of his famous readers, where Naipaul the elementary pupil would have seen it at the age of ten.[29]

In effect, these well-thumbed textbooks proved a quarry from which are hewn the plots of several of the more remarkable Caribbean novels of the second half of the twentieth century, together with the something of the region's poetic sensibility, its sense of history, culture and place. From public reaction in the early years one would scarcely have expected this result. Far from receiving credit for his re-positioning of literature in a late colonial setting, the editor was reviled by the parents whose children's eyes he was attempting to open. The assault was initiated in the late 1920s by

Howard Bishop, a one-time teacher, a disciple of Marcus Garvey and editor of the *Trinidad Workingmen's Journal*, who drew attention to the Director of Education's lack of a degree. The same criticism was levelled by Eric Williams, a former pupil of the Captain's at Tranquillity, an Oxford history first and Prime Minister of Trinidad and Tobago. "Cutteridge was not a university graduate," Williams snobbishly pointed out. In 1942 the much-maligned Captain, who had done quite nicely out of his many publications, withdrew weeping to the tax haven of the Isle of Man. Six years later *The Clarion*, instrument of the Trinidad Labour Party, invited its readers to envisage the geriatric former Director of Education in an old folk's home, "spending his last days in a wheel chair and wearing a bib".[30] But his books continued to sell, in edition after revised edition, up to and beyond his death in August 1952, as the weekly printing and monthly sales figures preserved in archives rescued from Nelson's Park Side works abundantly confirm.[31] They continued in use until a drastic revision of the early 1960s, a local imprint of which is available to this day.

It was not for his alluring visions of Salisbury or London that Cutteridge received such opprobrium, nor for his recasting of the classics, his summaries of Defoe or Dean Swift, but for side-tracking local aspirations to universal excellence through the siren call of relevance. That conflict of interest is now a matter of history. To recognise its onetime existence, however, is to question one well-received theory that may be styled the "reactive model" of postcolonial writing. According to this view, school authorities throughout the Empire force-fed Wordsworth's "Daffodils" poem to their tender charges 'til, sick of this foreign diet, they revolted by producing writing of their own. The example of the Caribbean tends to suggest on the contrary that—in this context at least, and over one protracted period—publishers and teachers sought valiantly to localise literary appreciation, in the teeth of parochial *petit bourgeois* resistance. But what the conscious mind of one generation rejected, the unconscious mind of the next permanently absorbed, yielding in the long run a literature.

Notes

1. J.O. Cutteridge, ed. *Nelson's West Indian Readers*, v (Edinburgh: Nelson, 1928), 200.
2. V.S. Naipaul, *The Enigma of Arrival: A Novel in Five Sections* (London: Penguin, 1987), 12. Naipaul settled in England in 1950.

3. Ernst H. Gombrich, *The Story of Art* (London: Phaidon, 1961), 374.
4. *The Royal Readers* Special Canadian Series. Third Book of Reading Lessons (Edinburgh and Toronto: Thomas Nelson and Sons and James Campbell, 1883), iii–iv.
5. S.B. Watson to G.C. Graham, 31 July 1923. Nelson Archive Gen. 1728.37,471 (Toronto House Letters).
6. J.O. Cutteridge, ed. *Nelson's Geography of the West Indies and Adjacent Islands* (Edinburgh: Nelson, 1931).
7. J.O. Cutteridge, ed. *Nelson's West Indian Readers* (Edinburgh: Nelson, 1928), 130.
8. V.S. Naipaul, *A House for Mr. Biswas* (London: Penguin,1969), 339–40, citing *West Indian Readers* 1, 65. For further allusions in this novel to Nelson's Readers, see *Biswas*, 196–97, 231, 233–34, 310 and 485.
9. J.O. Cutteridge, ed. *Nelsons West Indian Readers*, ii (Edinburgh: Nelson, 1928), 77–86.
10. J.O. Cutteridge, ed. *Nelson's West Indian Readers*, iii (Edinburgh: Nelson, 1928), 135–38.
11. J.O. Cutteridge, ed. *Nelson's West Indian Readers*, iv (Edinburgh: Nelson, 1928), 77–86.
12. Sam Selvon, *Lonely Londoners* (London: Allan Wingate, 1956).
13. Cutteridge, *Readers*, ii, 34–37.
14. Cutteridge, *Readers*, ii, 17–21.
15. Cutteridge, *Readers*, iii, 78–81.
16. Cutteridge, *Readers*, ii, 105–13.
17. Derek Walcott, *Collected Poems 1948–1984* (New York: Noonday, 1986), 57.
18. Cutteridge, *Readers*, iii, 102–05.
19. Derek Walcott, *Omeros* (London: Faber, 1990), especially 14, 93, 97, 117–18, 125.
20. Cutteridge, *Readers*, iv, 150–57.
21. V.S. Naipaul, *The Loss of El Dorado* (London: Penguin, 1973), 21.
22. Cutteridge, *Readers*, iii, 139–43.
23. J.O. Cutteridge and Frank Ogle, eds. *West Indian Readers*, Jamaica Edition, iii (Edinburgh: Nelson, 1936), 139–43.
24. Wilson Harris, *Palace of the Peacock* (London: Faber, 1960), 144–52.
25. Cutteridge and Ogle, eds. *Nelson's West Indian Readers*, Jamaica Edition, v, (Edinburgh: Nelson, 1936), 157–63.
26. Austin Clark, *The Polished Hoe* (Kingston, Jamaica), 343.
27. Cutteridge, *Readers*, iii, 119.
28. Naipaul, *The Enigma of Arrival*, 156.
29. Cutteridge, *Readers*, v, 145.

30. For Cutteridge's contribution to the Trinidadian educational system, and the reactions of the local bourgeoisie to it, see Car C. Campbell's *Colony an Nation: A Short History of Education in Trinidad, 1834–1986* (Kingston: Ian Randle, 1992) and also his *Endless Education: Main Currents in the Edcational System of Modern Trinidad and Tobago 1936–1986* (Barbados: University Press of the West Indies, 2000).
31. Nelsons Archive, University of Edinburgh 1/W/MB.

CHAPTER 11

Towards a New World Order: Literacy, Democracy and Literature in India and Africa, 1930–1965

Ironically enough, as the mantle of the British Empire retreated, the English language—that supreme conduit of cultural migration—spread around the world in ways, to places and by routes hitherto undreamed of. In a sense it became a new international *lingua franca* that replaced the Latin of Milton and Purcell's day. This linguistic migration, with its strong cultural undertow, was a thoroughgoing affair. The primary movement, and about the most effective migratory route, had been to America, later on to Canada, Australia and New Zealand. The "English-Speaking Peoples", as Churchill styled them, arose. Thus it was that the ultimate source of all this verbal peregrination—England itself—was very often overlooked as a point of origin at all. One summer in the 1990s I was striding down Fifth Avenue in New York when I was accosted by a news vendor—that soon to be eclipsed figure—who asked me "Where you from, buddie?" "England," I truthfully answered. "Gee," he responded in some astonishment, "your English is pretty good."

In this chapter I would like to examine just one phase and aspect of this process of diffusion, and by means of it to suggest that this form of cultural "transference" was not as casual and accidental as might otherwise be supposed. In some instances it was not merely deliberate, but a matter of official policy. Its driving force was political idealism: nothing less than the establishment of what I have called a "New World Order".

* * *

On Armistice Day 1918, as bugles sounded the peace over Europe, two individuals met in a Cambridge common room. One was a psychologist interested in cognition, the other a philosopher absorbed by the operation of words. Inevitably their thoughts turned towards the causes of the late conflict and equally unsurprisingly, given their common interests, both saw the question in the light of the uses and misuses of language. For several years the psychologist, C.K. Ogden, had been working on so-called Word-Magic, by which he meant the tendency of language to draw attention to itself, to assume powers of communication over and above any ascertainable and useful meaning. He had detected this tendency in much recent political propaganda, and in the discourse of the great religions. With the philosopher, I.A. Richards—later eminent as a university teacher of literature—he was soon at work on a project to discriminate in language between authentic statement and mystification of the kind both men had come, ideologically as well as intellectually, to suspect.

The book that resulted, *The Meaning of Meaning* of 1923, was a sustained exposition of semantics, and it began with a double assault: on Ferdinand de Saussure, whose *Cours de linguistique générale* had recently come to prominence, and on India, where Word-Magic seemed to the authors to be pervasive.[1] In Saussure the target was his theory of *langue* with its implication that, however arbitrarily disposed, every sign possesses a signified; in India it was the Vedas and related Brahminical literature, replete apparently with signifiers referring to nothing. The implication drawn was that language, in India as in Europe, should be cleansed from such ubiquitous and misleading locutions, should in Ogden's phrase be "debabelized". As in Wittgenstein's *Tractatus Logico-Philosophicus*, which Ogden himself had translated into English the previous year, the implication was this: if language could be rid of such excesses and stripped to the semantic bone, delusions of a dangerous tendency might eventually disappear.[2] Linguistics, even of the most technical sort, thus possessed a revolutionary potential. A new word order might usher in a new world order. In the international sphere, common sense might even prevail.

The view, a classically Utilitarian one, possessed a long antecedent history, in which coincidentally the battle-ground had frequently been India. Ogden himself cited Jeremy Bentham as his precursor, but an equally potent one was James Mill, who in his influential *History of British India* (1816) had questioned the praise lavished by the orientalist William Jones on the prolixity of Sanskrit. "The perfection of language", Mills's rejoinder had run, "would consist in having one name for everything which required a name, and no more than one. Redundancy is a defect of language".[3] Accordingly in the late 1920s Ogden embarked on a pared-down version of English, intended for general consumption. Christened Basic—an acronym culled by Richards from British American Scientific Industrial Commercial—it consisted of 850 words: 600 nouns, 150 qualities or adjectives, and 100 so-called operations, verbs or prepositions. Advertised as an "auxiliary" language to distinguish it from "artificial" tongues such as Esperanto, its advantages were heralded as ease of acquisition—reputedly in two months—and accessibility to wide swathes of the world's population. As Ogden put it in his book *Basic English* of 1930, English was the administrative medium of the East and, in the wider sphere, "nearly a quarter of the human race already knows English".[4]

Already, however, related developments were underway in the classrooms of Bengal. In 1923 Michael Philip West, psychologist and educator, had begun a series of experiments to see how fast he could teach middle school children in Calcutta to read English. The starting point for this project was a set of statistics that had recently come to his attention concerning the disparity between the reading and speaking abilities in English of the average educated Bengali. On the one hand, so it appeared, only one in 2407 citizens of Bengal spoke English with any degree of confidence. On the other hand, published works of non-fiction such as a member of any serious profession might rely on for instruction were overwhelmingly in English. In science the ratio was 434 English-medium texts to 9, in technology 686 to 3, in agriculture 228 to 4. The conclusion a latter-day educator might have reached is that Calcutta school children should be treated to a crash course in spoken English to bring their oral skills up to scratch. The conclusion that West had drawn was that, as a short-term academic objective, spoken communication in English should be shelved and—at least for students who were not to proceed beyond the school stage—teaching in reading and writing should proceed in isolation, leaving the student to converse day by day in his or her mother tongue.

The experiments took two years to conduct, and were written up in a government report entitled *Bilingualism*.[5] They went through three phases, as West and his colleagues felt their way. West was anxious to bring his students as rapidly as possible to the point at which they proceeded from what he called "observational"—that is, word-by-word—reading to "searching", or as we would call it skip-reading. The former yielded he thought 400, the latter 1200 words per minute. His first experiment came to a halt when he realised that the prescribed reading books were holding progress up, since lexical items were introduced haphazardly, sometimes too slowly, sometimes too fast, and in no logical order. He therefore set these aside whilst he and his team collated textbooks of their own, ten in number, in which new words were introduced incrementally at a rate of one new to every fifty known words, with frequent reinforcement of fresh items. That done, he repeated the experiment. This time most of the students made rapid progress, whilst a small but significant minority stalled at the starting block. He then tested these non-starters to find that they were incapable of reading Bangla either. The important inference he drew was that reading was a transferable ability between languages and scripts; what his no-hopers lacked was absolute reading ability. West then weeded out these unfortunates and, the third time round, discovered that all of his students sped ahead quite satisfactorily. Most made a gain of two years in their English reading age in 94 working days; even the indifferently gifted managed this in 141.

The results of this well-documented series of experiments formed the foundation of what came to be known as the New Method. In the long term it gave rise to a massive publishing initiative and large international profits for West's publishers, Longman, as textbook after textbook, reader after reader, was mass-produced to suit his fresh approach. Classics of world literature were scaled down to fit in with the new teaching methods, mostly by West himself. Bit by bit he informed the world in general as to the progress of his various schemes in his personal newsletter *The Bulletin*, with frequent skirmishes at the desk-bound Ogden.

Within a very few years West and his collaborator James Gareth Endicott set to work to produce an English-learner's dictionary incorporating their findings. Published as *The New Method Dictionary* in 1935, it undertook the ambitious task of defining 24,000 English words from a base vocabulary of 1490.[6] It proved immensely successful and would go into many editions, but far away in Cambridge the obdurate Ogden was seething. By now he had set himself up as the Orthographical Institute with offices at 10 King's Parade with a fine view of the chapel. From this address he issued his own broadside, *Psyche*, which in its turn was not well disposed towards West. How dare this upstart schoolmaster in India upstage him, and with real pupils too? Ogden waited until the publication in 1935 of *The New Method Dictionary*, then he dipped his pen in gall. In "How Not to Make a Dictionary", he gleefully pointed to West's errors, his inconsistencies, his omissions and coyness of phrase.[7] In music, a crotchet had been defined as a very short note and a quaver as a short one, which made a quaver longer than a crotchet. West did not know the difference between tonic and tonal. His ignorance of midwifery was shocking. Ogden's own crotchets added up to a semi-breve of disdain. Mindful of his reputation, however, he withheld his name from his review, preferring to adopt an alias. Fortunately one lay to hand, since Ogden had behind him a buried career as a campaigner for family planning. In that capacity in 1916 he had published a Marie Stopes–like tome, attributing the evils of the war not yet to lexical confusion, but—in the spirit of Malthus—to overpopulation.[8] He had published this now-forgotten indiscretion under a female pseudonym, which he conveniently resurrected, berating West, the Dictionary and the New Method in the likeness of "Adelyne More".

It is time to introduce my next principal actor in the formidable shape of an American Congregationalist minister, Frank Laubach, who in 1929 in the Philippines, prior to translating the scriptures into the local vernacular Moro, set himself the task of rendering the speakers of it literate in their mother tongue. Laubach was a successful teacher, and he soon found himself invited to India and Africa to share his expertise. Arriving in India late in 1936, he felt dismayed by the abundance of India's scripts, and the complexity of some of its alphabets. No wonder, he thought, that whilst literary campaigning in Hindi with its comparatively manageable Devanagari script had been quite fruitful, results in Tamil or Telegu had been relatively poor. Could universal Telegu literacy be a success? One problem Laubach identified was that much classical Indian literature was written in a style and register far removed from that of the street. To bridge the gap between such traditional literary fare and the average learner was, he thought, a daunting challenge. Nor did Laubach think much of the offerings of the popular press: "The literature on the railroad book stalls", he intemperately reported to his mission in New York, "is not worth wasting one's life to teach people to read…I began to realize that half of our literacy problem was the creation of a new literature."[9]

Seeking support for his ideas, Laubach took the train up to Santiniketan, where he sat for an hour listening to Rabindranath Tagore expound his plans for a demotic Bangla literature. "We need Tagore to lead the way in this reform," he enthused back to base. "His poetry and prose have done much for the Bengali language by using beautiful and simple language."[10] Laubach was never short of self-insurance. By September he had announced that the inherent vowel should be dropped; he had plans afoot for the introduction of Roman script for all Indian languages, and he had made the to him illuminating discovery that Marathi was written in circles because otherwise the pen would slice through the palm-leaf. Having as he thought sorted things out in India, in May 1937 he sailed to East Africa. Applying himself there to the teaching of Kiswahili, he happened across the pictorial method by which syllables could be illustrated by simple images, then combined to make up key words, and finally sentences. He then returned to India on 12 June and applied the method to Marathi. Satisfied by the preliminary results, he took ship to America on 28 June, applying himself when there to the orchestration of an international literacy campaign and the writing up of its manifesto, the defiantly titled—and in its time fairly influential—*India Shall Be Literate*.[11]

Sorting out the world's problems through linguistic intervention was clearly a major operation in the 1930s. I have outlined three different approaches, all of which were flourishing by the outbreak of the Second World War that they had severally failed to prevent. The first, Basic, aspired via a scaled-down vocabulary to universal but elementary literacy in a surrogate language intended in the international sphere to supplement or even take the place of both vernaculars and full-blown English. The second, West's New Method, intended through the introduction of incremental vocabulary to enable considerable sections of the world population to read some English, whilst leaving the vernacular full colloquial play. The third, Laubach's keyword method, aimed to render all peoples literate in their own mother tongue by gradual and easy-to-grasp stages. Pedagogically distinct, these approaches were however united by a common ideology, even if their proponents were reluctant to recognise the fact. Ogden's opposition to war is well authenticated, but in his book *Learning to Read a Foreign Language* West is equally clear about his political objectives. "National literacy", he affirms, "facilitates national propaganda and national feeling—the fruit of war. International literacy promotes international understanding and goodwill...International understanding can best be promoted by teaching the children of the world to read each other's languages."[12] By which, of course, West meant that Bengali children should be helped to read English literature—a high plateau towards which in his view they should aspire—rather than English children offered a helping hand with Bengali. Ambitious as Laubach's schemes were, he was perhaps more abreast of the time when he wrote in *Teaching the World to Read* of 1948 that "Illiteracy has an enormous bearing on world peace and security. If only a small part of our world remains on a fairly high economic plane, while the majority are in poverty and degradation, the areas containing the underprivileged peoples will be centres of resentment, unrest and revolt."[13] In Laubach's eyes universal literacy, especially in the local languages of the people, would form a bulwark against totalitarian tendencies in government, demagoguery and revolution, wherever they occurred and whatever form they took. By 1948, of course, the principal adversary had already emerged as Communism.

Bearing this in mind, it is hardly surprising that, in the closing stages of the Second World War and the period of reconstruction that followed it, literacy campaigners found powerful public allies. In fact, all three approaches found friends. Basic, for example, which had been made the subject of a White Paper, won short-lived support from the British government, reaching its apogee on 9 March 1944 when Churchill rose unsteadily to his feet to make a Commons statement in its favour. The White Paper unhappily entrusted responsibility for the scheme to the British Council, with a result summarised in Ogden's *Who's Who* entry as "bedevilled by officials 1944–6". West meanwhile benefitted from the widespread perception amongst publishers of the inexorable rise of English, resulting in a lucrative running contract to simplify and abridge classic after British literary classic in accordance with his New Method: *Robinson Crusoe*, *Gulliver's Travels*, *The Mill on the Floss*. His General Service Vocabulary, based on the dictionary, also enjoyed some short-lived success.

But it was Laubach with his universal literacy schemes who really came into his own with the creation in 1946 of UNESCO, the United Nations Educational, Scientific and Cultural Organization, explicitly wedded to his aims. Laubach was appointed as a consultant and was also widely adopted as a mentor by several Protestant missionary societies that broadened their scope of activity in Africa after the war. With the dawn of Indian independence, it was to Africa in any case that for the next twenty or so years the field of international action tended to turn.

Africa posed a very different challenge to India, in several important respects. First, though oral traditions of textual transmission abounded right across the continent, literary traditions were confined to a very few localities. Second, many of the region's hundreds of languages still lacked a script, and therefore orthography. Third, the percentage of adults who had at one time or another attended an elementary school was low. Fourth, and again in marked contrast to India, sub-Saharan Africa had no publishing industry to speak of, beyond a few modest missionary presses with limited scope and capacity. There was even, at the time of the Second

World War, only a handful of libraries. To mount local literacy campaigns against such a background necessitated a broad and multivalent approach, since the campaigners had in several instances to inscribe the language before teaching it, and then to supply reading matter to keep their new literates in trim. Right from the beginning Laubach had insisted that the ultimate difficulty was not the creation of newly literate groups, but their retention. This was feasible in India since, although the existing published works in the subcontinent's many languages may not all have been ideally suited to new readers, they at least existed, in impressive quantities and quality. To sustain literary rates throughout much of the African continent, however, reading matter would have to be brought into being. And the work would have to be done fast, since although independence for Europe's African colonies was still some way away, it was patently on the horizon. Laubach's stated objective of 1935 of creating "a new literature"—overbearing, even ignorant in the Indian context—suddenly made impressive sense.

What emerged in response to this situation were integrated programmes of literacy instruction and literary creation best illustrated by a now forgotten, but at the time strategically significant, project in rural Sierra Leone. The Bunumbu experiment, as it came to be known, was staged in Mende country in 1943 a hundred miles from any major town: its purpose was to discover how many of the adults in one village might be rendered literate in the local language within six months.[14] There were only eighteen published works in Mende at the time, none of them suitable for this purpose: not even the Bible had been fully translated. Bunumbu itself contained some 390 adults, of whom twelve males were one-time literates, eleven of them lapsed. However, the Methodist mission had a printing press capable of turning out charts and primers, and it was these that were used when the campaign got under way in February of that year, with 210 adults attending the classes. The method employed was a modification of Laubach's keyword technique. Using picture charts, individual words were taught, then split into syllables and re-combined. In the evenings returning school children were pressed into service as teachers, instructing their elders in small groups huddled around hurricane lamps. By these makeshift means 120 of the mature students were brought up to a level where they could tackle a primer within a very few weeks; by March the 3000 copies printed in advance were exhausted and orders were coming in from the surrounding country for two or three hundred at a time.

The demand had a transforming effect on the publishing capacity of the press. By the following year fifteen booklets had already been produced, thirteen manuscripts were ready for printing, and eight others were in preparation. By April 1945 operations had moved to the larger town of Bo, turning out material for the whole of the Protectorate—that is, the hinterland of Sierra Leone beyond the Colony enclave of Freetown— mostly booklets on health and citizenship, the mainstays of a future democracy. "There is", reported the Director, R.R. Young, "no reason why the majority of the people in this country should not be literate by 1955, and the Mende people could be literate by 1950."[15] Within a year, the press at Bo had been re-christened the Protectorate—later to become the Sierra Leone—Literature Bureau, and was turning out self-help booklets in ever-increasing numbers. These national literary bureaux became quite a feature of the pre- and immediate post-independence scene. They caught on especially in East Africa, where they played a major role in the nurturing of new literatures, both in the vernacular and in English, not merely serving new writing but in many cases actively soliciting and guiding it, as with the East African Bureau's publication of 1957, *Helps and Explanations for African Authors: Some Forms of Writing*. The suggested topics concentrated on the very skills required by citizens of a future democracy—voting, self-education and the like—but also made provision for imaginative writing, both in English and in African languages. Indeed, some of Africa's leading authors of the post-independence period, such as Uganda's Okot p'Bitek, began their careers in response to such invitations, by means of which the bureaux maintained their function as generators of new writing right up to the mid-1960s, and in some instances beyond.

It is worthwhile stressing this point, because the emergence of modern African literature has too often been portrayed as the result of the intervention of large and well-funded metropolitan firms and patronage. At grass-roots level, however, it was largely an achievement local in inspiration, staffing and scope, the unforeseen end product of a process that stared modestly with local literacy drives. Ultimately such literature of local manufacture remains the most satisfactory practical upshot of the theoretical idealism of the pre-war period. By the 1960s Basic, which had enjoyed a certain limited success in China, was dying a lingering death, caught in the trammels of its own prescriptiveness. Meanwhile the New Method had been set aside in India, where it was ultimately to be overtaken by the direct oral teaching methods of the 1970s. In Africa it survived largely in the form of graded readers that were imported in respectable numbers for the secondary school market. These were never, however, to fulfil West's declared goal of converting thousands of tropical school children into devoted admirers of the English canon. Indeed, their legacy can more truthfully be traced through a satirical passage in Chinua Achebe's novel *A Man of the People* of 1966, in which Chief the Honorable Nanga MP, a vulgar and corrupt minister in a venal government, boasts of having mastered at school a classic by his favourite English author, Mr Michael West.[16] The allusion is met by polite guffaws among his audience, expressions of a properly postcolonial mirth.

I consider it worthy of note that of the three approaches outlined above, the most theoretically cogent proved at the end of the day to be the least portable. In 2018, 10 King's Parade, onetime headquarters of Ogden's Orthographical Institute, houses Primavera, a gallery specialising in bespoke silver jewellery, and the only books in print to be couched in a version of Basic are the technical manuals of the Caterpillar Corporation. In his book *Basic English* of 1934, R.K. Ogden had explained the grammatical device by which the sentences of his auxiliary language held together on the analogy of a set of concentric rings that could be turned like the lock on a safe to compose infinite combinations. He proposed to call this gadget the Panopticon and, if the term is familiar, it is because it was the name given by Jeremy Bentham to the new-fangled prison buildings he wished to erect in British cities, where a warder positioned in a central tower could observe the behaviour of the inmates in the surrounding wings. Much the same sort of thinking, a hundred years before Ogden, had inspired the workhouses that Dickens so deplored and, like them, Basic English often came to be regarded as an instrument neither of emancipation nor of efficiency, but of control. For Utilitarianism is not always useful. Unglamorous fieldwork, on the other hand, sometimes is.

Notes

1. C.K. Ogden and I.A. Richards, *The Meaning of Meaning: A Study of the Influence of Language an of the Science of Symbolism* (London: Kegan Paul, Trench, and Trubner, 1923). On de Saussure, see especially pp. 5–8, 367.
2. Ludwig Wittgenstein, *Logisch-Philosophische*, ed. Wilhlem Ostwald, *Annalen der Naturphilosophie*, 14 (1921), translated as Ludwig Wittgenstein, *Tractatus Logico-Philosophicus*, trans. C.K. Ogden (London: Routledge and Kegan Paul, 1922)

3. James Mill, *A History of British India* (London: Baldwin, Cradock and Joy, 1817), vol. 2, 391.
4. C.K. Ogden, *Basic English: A General Introduction with Rules and Grammar* (London: Kegan Paul, 1930), 17.
5. Michael Philip West, *Bilingualism—With Special Reference to Bengal* (Government of India, Bureau of India, 1926).
6. Michael Philip West and James Gareth Endicott, *The New Method Dictionary* (London: Longman, 1935).
7. Adelyne More, "How Not to Make a Dictionary", *Psyche* (Cambridge: The Orthological Institute, 1935), 205–30.
8. Adelyne More, *Fecundity Versus Civilization: A Contribution to the Study of Overpopulation as the Cause of War and the Chief Obstacle to the Emancipation of Women*, intro. Arnold Bennett (London: George Allen and Unwin, 1916).
9. Frank C. Laubach, *Adventures in the Campaign for Literacy in India and Africa 1936–37* (U.S.A. The World Literary Committee, n.d. Typescript BL Wq1/1324 DSC), 3.
10. Ibid., 9.
11. Frank C. Laubach, *India Shall Be Literate* (Jubbulpore: The Mission Press, 1940).
12. Michael Philip West, *Learning to Read a Foreign Language: An Experimental Study* (London: Longman, 1926), 14–15.
13. Frank C. Laubach, *Teaching the World to Read: A Handbook for Literary Campaigns* (New York: Friendship Press, for the Committee on World Literacy and Christian Literature of the Foreign Missions of North America, 1947), 1.
14. The papers relating to the Bunumbu Literacy Campaign are held in the department of manuscripts in the library of the School of Oriental and African Studies (SOAS) in the University of London at CBMS/ICCLA Box 23 (256). A complicating factor, not dealt with here, is the pre-existence of an indigenous script called *ki-ka-ku*. For this, and a fuller treatment of the cultural impact of the campaign, see my *Book History Through Postcolonial Eyes: Rewriting the Script* (Abingdon: Routledge, 2008), 92–99.
15. R.C. Young, *Bulletin No. 1* (Sierra Leone Protectorate Literature Bureau, August, 1945), 1.
16. Chinua Achebe, *A Man of the People* (London: Heinemann, 1966), 61–65.

CHAPTER 12

World Music: Listening to Steve Reich Listening to Africa; Listening to György Ligeti Listening to Reich

My final example of cultural migration brings together two composers—one American, the other Hungarian—an English clergyman, two groups of drummers—one in West Africa, the other in New York—a village carpenter in Ghana, a British critic, some dancers and a recording machine. It also crosses boundaries, not simply between different countries and continents but between languages and art forms, ways of life and traditions of performing and of hearing. I offer it as a hopeful paradigm of cultural transmission in our postmodern and post-industrial world, and a token of things to come. That it possesses a slight autobiographical dimension renders it all the more poignant, and, dare I say so, more persuasive.

* * *

It was a solitary August for me: the dead vast and middle of the long vocation at the end of the first term of my first job, lecturing at a small, recently founded university college by the seaside in Ghana. So one afternoon I climbed into my second-hand Volkswagen Beetle and drove the hundred-odd miles down the coast to the swankier national university. That evening I entered its staff club, empty save for a lone figure, an American in his thirties wearing a baseball cap reversed, and hunched over his beer by the bar. I approached and asked how he was. Rather queasy, he told me. I asked him what he did, and he told me he was a musician of sorts. Then he asked me how I was spending the vacation. I told him that I had formed a drama group of young people in the housing estate where I lived to perform *Vulture, Vulture*, a "Rhythm Play" by the local playwright Efua Sutherland,[1] for which purpose I had acquired a goat skin from the village butcher, and had had it shaved and stretched on a wooden rectangle by the neighbourhood carpenter to create a frame drum that, forty-five years later, I still possess. That's interesting, he said, because he was in Africa to study drumming, so for two hours we drank and ranged in conversation over his specialism, music, and mine, poetry. He seemed very interested in the rhythms of both. After six or seven beers, I rose to my feet and said, "It has been a great pleasure, but I must go now. My name is Robert Fraser." "Mine", he replied extending his hand, "is Steve Reich."

I had no idea that I was talking to a world-famous composer, for the perfectly good reason that he wasn't. In 1970 few music lovers had heard of Reich beyond a tiny Manhattan avant-garde. This situation didn't last for long. His queasiness was malaria, and a couple of weeks later he returned to New York, where the following year he created *Drumming*, a work that by his own admission draws on his listening and studying in Ghana. It is the connection between the listening and the studying, and the subsequent composition and performance, that I am concerned with here.

The first step is to recognise that all of these relate to a very particular local tradition. The Ewe people, about six million strong, straddle the border between Eastern Ghana and the neighbouring territory of Togo. It was at feet of a Ewe master drummer, Gideon Alorwoyie, that Reich had come to study. No wonder he seemed interested in affinities between poetry and music, since the Ewe hardly distinguish between them: one single word, *heno*, serving for both their singers and their poets. The most distinguished cantor of the period was Vinoko Akpalu (1889–1980), then ninety-two, of whom several of my own students were keen admirers, and who always performed with a drumming ensemble. Two decades previously, his art and those of his fellow recitalists had been studied by the British missionary and ethnomusicologist Arthur Morris Jones (1889–1980), who had brought out a two-volume report entitled *Studies in African Music* in 1959, "addressed in the first place to musicians".[2] Eleven years later, ethnomusicology had yet to enter the American conservatoire to any significant extent. There were important exceptions since, as Philip Glass remarks in his 2015 memoir *Words Without Music*, Jones's book had been in the library of the Julliard School in New York in the mid-1960s, when both he and Reich had studied there.[3]

Jones is obviously a pivotal figure in the story, so it is as well to spend a while thinking about his ideas on African music. In 1959, the same year as the publication of his book, he had recorded a series of programmes for the BBC Transcription Service in which he had set out, perhaps for the first time, an all-embracing African musicology.[4] In melody he had noted the prevalence of fourths, and in harmony the habit of organum (singing in parallel fifths). Rhythm, though, was the core of the tradition. To account for it, he had coined the term "cross-rhythm", now a stock in trade of musical analysis but then quite new,[5] which he had carefully distinguished from mere syncopation. African music, he asserted, possessed an "intoxicating rhythmic harmony" demanding to hear and very hard to transcribe. Its salient quality was that, in African rhythmic polyphony, the downbeats of the various parts did not coincide. Instead they played against one another, obliging the listener's mind to work on several levels simultaneously. Such effects were the rule; percussive coincidence, when and where it occurred, was an incidental effect of no structural significance. "With Western music", he generalised in his book, "deliberate synchrony is the norm from which our music develops...If our suggestion has any truth, then the African also uses synchrony of pattern, but in a much more subtle way. His norm is the cross-rhythm, and the synchrony is derivative."[6] The result, he concludes, "is a principle which our western musicians are yet to exploit". Was this an invitation?

Jones's book abounds in transcriptions of Ewe music set out in full score. In 1971 he was eighty-two, and had long retired from teaching at the School of Oriental and African Studies (SOAS) in London where, in the year of the composition of *Drumming*, Reich visited him. It seems fairly likely that on this occasion Jones played some of his field recordings back to Reich; they are now kept in the National Sound Archive in the British Library. If we want to understand the way Reich heard African music, we have to bear in mind the transcriptions in Jones's book, his original recordings, and Reich's own exposure during those brief weeks when I met him. Here is a page from Jones's transcription of the Ewe "Nyayito" funeral dance from his *Studies in African Music*, reproduced from my own book *West African Poetry* of 1986 (Fig. 12.1).[7]

And here for comparison is Reich's own transcription of the Ewe Agbaza dance published in 1972 (Fig. 12.2).[8]

It is quite evident, even at a glance, that the line-up of percussion is very similar, and that neither has uniform bar-lines because, as Reich himself remarks, Ewe music has no unitary downbeats, consisting as it does of the superimposition of self-generated, individual drum patterns.

Fig. 12.1 Ewe Nyayito Dance. Robert Fraser, *West African Poetry: A Critical History* (Cambridge University Press, 1986), 11, reproducing Jones (1959), Volume Two, 32–33

At first hearing both Jones and Reich manifestly experienced some difficulty making sense of these elaborate superimpositions. Instead of recording the whole ensemble in the first place, Jones had started by asking each of the drummers to perform his motifs as a single line, working from simple repetitive to more complex patterns, and gradually combining several strands together so as to re-create an integrated composition. The way in which he did this was to get each performer to record the individual pattern allotted to his part onto a moving roll of paper that was electronically marked each time the musician tapped one of his metal pencils onto a sensitised plate. In an essay of 1972, Reich is very clear about the method involved: "As Dr. Jones tapped out the bell pattern, an Ewe master drummer would tap out one of the drum parts, and both patterns would be recorded in accurate graph form on the moving paper. This was

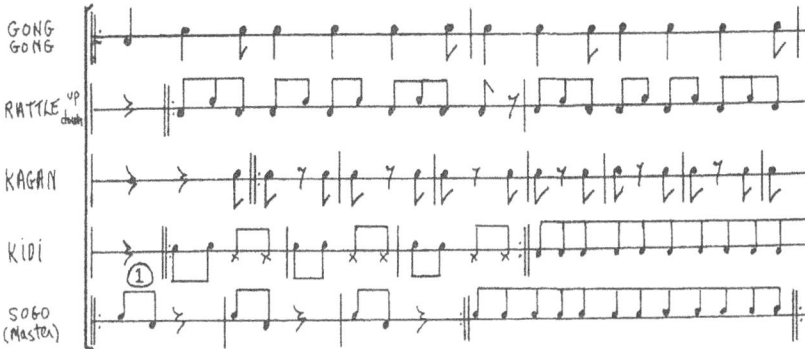

Fig. 12.2 Ewe Agbaza Dance, Steve Reich, *Writings on Music 1965–2000*. Edited with an introduction by Paul Hillier (Oxford University Press, 2002), 62

then transferred to conventional notation."[9] The superimposition of the notated parts produced the full score. Jones's method had been additive and analytical, building up the total sound picture from its barest elements.[10]

In the ensemble that results from the combination of several such lines, all of the sonorities—drumming, clapping and singing—are superimposed. An important difference between Reich's work and this African paradigm is that in the first three movements of Reich's *Drumming*, the sonorities are separated out.[11] The instruments featured in the first movement are tuned bongos; in the second movement these give way to marimbas, whose repeated patterns and tuning are imitated by monosyllables intoned by two sopranos; in the third these give way to glockenspiels, which in turn are imitated by the players whistling. In the fourth and final movement, all of these resources come together. In each movement, simple reiterated patterns are rendered more complex as additional players join in at short intervals from the basic pulse. If you listen to the excerpts from Reich with Jones's field recordings in mind, it is clear that in one respect Reich is adopting an equivalent approach. *Drumming* is a dramatic work, but it is also a cleanly analytical one which takes its bearings from Jones's research methods, or something very much like them. A player enters and sets up a fairly basic pulse on which he elaborates, before being joined by a second percussionist, who in turn is joined by a third. There is an intellectual fascination in the way in which the complex of sound gradually builds up from these basic cells to form a whole rhythmic soundscape. Like Jones, Reich clearly wants us to experience each component element in isolation before we tackle the combined effect, to attend to the rhythms before we confront their combination. He is studying the rhythms as well as listening to them, with the result that parts of the work have the air of being a sort of demonstration of how sophisticated effects derive from simpler ones.

Yet this analytical approach, in line with ethnomusicological theory and pedagogical practice, sets up a very different set of expectations from those underlying actual African performance. As Ali Momeni has observed, "There is a disparity between the complexity of the rhythmic material in traditional African music and the single rhythmic cell present in Reich."[12] Just as other forms of minimalist music endeavour to build and recreate traditional harmonic and melodic effects from the ground up, educating the human ear to hear again and more appreciatively what over the centuries it has learned to take for granted, whether in melody or harmony, so *Drumming* strips down and re-articulates the basic materials out of which the tapestry of rhythmic polyphony is woven, in order to show us what goes into the mix. It is a sort of defamiliarisation technique which places strict demands on the audience, precisely by depriving them of the props and clichés that support lazy listening.

Listening in our turn, we may be reminded of the fact that, prior to concentrating on music, Reich had been a philosophy student at Columbia, where he wrote a dissertation on Wittgenstein. Just as Wittgenstein had been interested in the procedures involved in various language games, so Reich had become fascinated by the workings of what you might call percussive sound games. Remember the opening paragraphs of *Philosophical Investigations*: "That philosophical notion of meaning is at home in a primitive idea of the way language functions. But one might instead say that it is the idea of a language more primitive than ours."[13] Just as Wittgenstein had endeavoured to dig down to the deepest roots of meaning, so Reich is attempting to uncover the most essential roots of rhythm. The problem is that, in Africa, the roots are far from being simple.

So what did Reich learn from Africa? In two respects, his debt is clear. Firstly, he convinced himself that a large-scale work made of mostly percussive means can be built up from quite elementary structures. Secondly, he seems to have copied the idea of a cueing technique according to which one performer starts a new set of riffs, and invites the others to follow. According to Jones, this is an important element in Ewe ensembles, where the Master Drummer initiates each new stage of the proceedings. Reich was soon to discover a similar approach in Balinese gamelan music, about which he was to write, and which Jones had been convinced had infiltrated African music at some point in the fairly distant past. (Because of this, Jones had concluded—and had spent a large part of his later years attempting to prove—that the xylophone had migrated from the South Seas to Africa.)[14]

The sound world of *Drumming* can be elicited by examining the score.[15] When he first prepared the work between the fall of 1970 and the following autumn, Reich jotted down his ideas in a series of notebooks before teaching the piece to his fellow performers. Only after the premiere did he reduce the music to a pen-and-ink score, which circulated in manuscript for forty years before he requested the Chicago-based composer Marc Mellits to rationalise the transcription.[16] The result is a seventy-nine-page score set out in a two-stave system, with a uniform time signature of 3/2 or 6/4 and a key signature of five sharps. The apparent regularity serves as a guide or clue to what, in other respects, is a quite flexible mode of delivery. Since each pattern may be delivered between two and eight times (with the permissible parameters being indicated in each case above the upper stave), the piece lasts between fifty-five and seventy-five minutes. Despite this, by Reich's own admission, "there is one basic rhythmic pattern for all of *Drumming* which governs pitch, phase position and timbre". The audible variations are caused by a scripted instruction that successive performers should delay slightly the beginning of each phrase. The phasing that results is quite in line with Reich's practice in earlier works such as *It's Gonna Rain*, in which two tapes are allowed to drift out of sync with one another and then to merge again, the difference being that in the new work these conditions are met by telling the percussionists gradually to fall out of step with its footnoted instruction that, in the first movement for example, the second drummer to enter should gradually accelerate his strokes so that, by the end of bar twenty, he is a full crotchet ahead. After gradually parting company, in all movements the parts are designed eventually to realign and coincide. In Jones's words, therefore, "synchrony is still the norm", since the rhythmic interest of the whole piece consists in listening to the parts as they sever company and then join up again. Reich was to adopt an exaggerated form of the same procedure in *Clapping Music* where, as he explains, one performer remains fixed "repeating the same basic pattern throughout, while the second moves abruptly, after a number of repeats, from unison to one beat ahead, and so on, until he is back in unison with the first performer. The basic difference between these sudden changes and the gradual changes of phase in other pieces is that, when phasing, one can hear the same pattern moving away from itself with the downbeats of both parts separating further and further apart, while the sudden changes create the sensation of a series of variations of two different patterns with their downbeats coinciding." Thus expounded, it is clear that what Reich achieves in all of these early works is a compromise between the synchronicity Jones had thought characteristic of the Western tradition and the rhythmic polyphony and density he had discovered amongst the Ewe and other sub-Saharan African peoples.

The very year in which *Clapping Music* was first performed, the Hungarian composer György Ligeti (1923–2006) was in residence at Stanford, where he discovered an early recording of the work and an LP of *It's Gonna Rain* in the college library. The following year, he returned to Berlin where he met Reich and heard a performance of *Drumming*. At the time he was writing *Clocks and Clouds* for twelve female voices and orchestra, featuring a wispy ostinato pattern akin to the humming of bees passed on from high cellos to flutes and thence to clarinets, Holst-like female voices and bells.[17] It was a work avowedly "heavily influenced by Reich". Soon he had embarked on an African adventure of his own as the echoing, hollaing polyphonic choral music of the Aka pygmies furnished him with a slightly schizophrenic listening experience caused by the repetition of its rhythmic cells and the asymmetry of the cells themselves. In his own words: "Gradually through repeated listening I became aware of this music's paradoxical nature: the patterns performed by the individual musicians are quite different from those which result from their combination. In fact, the ensemble's super-pattern is in itself not played and exists only as an illusory outline. I also began to sense a strong inner tension between the relentlessness of the constant, never-changing pulse with the absolute symmetry of the formal architecture on the one hand and the asymmetrical internal divisions of the patterns on the other. What we can witness in this music is a wonderful combination of order and disorder which in turn merges together to form a sense of order on a higher level."[18] Ligeti also suspected that these tendencies reflected some of the guiding principles of the Balkan folk music he had grown up listening to during his youth in Romania. This in turn is not as surprising as it may seem. Hungarian composers, as we saw in Chap. 3, have been preoccupied with folk music, and the question of the cultural roots of all music, since the time of Liszt.

There had thus been a sort of procession of influence: Ligeti listening to Reich listening to Africa, then listening to a different region of the continent with ears in turn trained by Reich. The response of both composers was partly dictated by their respective backgrounds: Reich by his earlier experiments with recorded tape, Ligeti by modernist practice overlying his own regional folkloric inheritance. If we pan out, I would suggest what we are observing is a kind of partition within modernism, stemming in Ligeti's case from the two schools to which he had previously been exposed: the experimental Darmstadt school taking its cue from Schoenberg, and the folkloric, regionally based approach of his countrymen Bartók and Kodály. It is no coincidence that by the 1980s Western music gave the strong impression of looking forwards and backwards at the same time, so that by the century's end the contemporary scene was dominated by this Janus-like stylistic face.

A further question arises as to how far the regional African musical traditions on which Reich and Ligeti drew were characteristic of the continent as a whole. Certainly the thinking of both composers does seem to have been in step with Jones's ideas as to a holistic African musical aesthetic, with rhythm as its bedrock. What is undeniable is that in 1970 I had accidentally witnessed the stirring of a development that was to pay rich dividends in the musical history of the following half-century, a period during which "world music" came to be accepted as a field of inquiry and endeavour, and barriers between national musical traditions gradually broke down. The consequences of this mutually informed mode of listening, and the opening up of perspectives that ensued, have proved rewarding for everyone. After all, as our countrymen the Greeks are wont to remark, Η μουσική δεν γνωρίζει σύνορα: "Music knows no borders."

NOTES

1. Efua Sutherland, *Vulture, Vulture and Tahinta: Two Rhythm Plays* (Tema: Ghana Publishing House, 1968).
2. A.M. Jones, *Studies in African Music*, 2 vols. (Oxford University Press, 1959), vol. 1, vii.
3. Philip Glass, *Words Without Music* (London: Faber, 2015), 130.
4. Catalogued as "Theory of African Music". A.M. Jones speaker, British Library Sound Archive, ICD0094802 and ICL002612-ICL002623.
5. In fact, Jones had almost certainly coined the term, first employing it in his articles "African Drumming: A Study on the Combination of African Music", *Bantu Studies*, viii/1 (1934) 1–16 and "The Study of African Rhythm", *Bantu Studies* xi/4 (1937), 295–321.

6. Jones (1959), vol. 1, 193.
7. Robert Fraser, *West African Poetry: A Critical History* (Cambridge University Press, 1986, 11, reproducing Jones (1959), vol. 2, 32–33.
8. Steve Reich, *Writings on Music, 1965–2000*. Edited with an introduction by Paul Hillier (Oxford University Press, 2002), 62.
9. Reich, *Writings on Music*, 56.
10. The British Library's sound archive, accessible through the internet, contains Jones's recording of one line from the Agbaza dance later transcribed by Reich. The opening, for gong gong then sogo drum, is reminiscent of Reich's *Drumming*; the rest is vividly reminiscent of his work *Clapping Music* of the following year. It may be heard at http://sounds.bl.uk/World-and-traditional-music/Arthur-Morris-Jones/025M-C0424X0104XX-0100V0
11. A filmed performance by the Portland Percussion Group may be watched at https://www.google.co.uk/webhp?sourceid=chrome-instant&ion=1&espv=2&ie=UTF-8#q=reich+drumming
12. "Analysis of Steve Reich's Drumming and His Use of African Polyrhythms", http://alimomeni.net/project/analysis-of-steve-reichs-drumming-and-his-use-of-african-polyrhythms/
13. Ludwig Wittgenstein, *Philosophical Investigations* The German text with an English translation by G.E.S. Anscombe, P.M.S. Hacker and Joachim Schulte. Revised Fourth Edition by H.M.S. Hacker and Joachim Schulte (Chichesteddr: Wiley-Blackwell, 2009), 6e.
14. See especially Reich, "Postscript to a Brief Study of Balinese and African Music", in Reich (2002), 69–71, and A.M. Jones, *Africa and Indonesia: The Evidence of the Xylophone and Other Musical and Cultural Factors* (Leiden: Brill, 1964).
15. In the first movement of *Drumming*, the phasing technique is easy to detect.
16. Steve Reich, *Drumming: For Percussion Ensemble* (New York: Hendon Music; London: Boosey and Hawkes, 2010).
17. A haunting recording by Cappella Amsterdam under chorus master Daniel Russ can be heard at https://www.youtube.com/watch?v=SyO7c6U5dEw
18. Quoted in booklet accompanying the CD *African Rhythms* Ligeti, Reich and Pierre-Laurent Aimard, Aka pygmies (Teldec Classics, 2003) 8573-86584-2. I am grateful to my old friend Dr Rachel Darnley-Smith of Roehampton University for pointing this out.

CHAPTER 13

A Cultural Cosmopolis

In my introductory chapter I referred briefly to the work of the philosopher Kwame Anthony Appiah in relation to migration and cosmopolitanism. I want in conclusion to return to—and to extend—his arguments, but before I do so, I would like to glance at Appiah's own background, on which he expatiated at further length in his 2016 Reith Lectures entitled "Mistaken Identities".[1]

In the same year in which I met Steve Reich in Accra, I attended a political rally at Osu Castle, the former Danish and British trading and slaving fort in that city, and onetime seat of the colonial government. The climax of the event was a rousing speech by Joe Appiah, former Gold Coast lawyer, leader of the West African students organisation in London, then Ghanaian nationalist politician, ally and subsequently opponent of Ghana's first president Kwame Nkrumah, by whom he was twice imprisoned for his resistance to a one-party state. In London Joe had met Peggy Cripps, daughter of Sir Stafford Cripps, former Socialist Chancellor of the Exchequer in the immediate post-war government of Clement Attlee. They married in June 1954, and Peggy joined her husband in the Ashanti capital Kumasi, where she was to spend the remaining half-century of her life. Kwame, thus named because born on a Saturday, was their first child.

So the backdrop to the philosopher's work is this rich and interwoven tapestry. The weavers of Kumasi specialise in the scintillating cloth known as *kente*, composed of many variegated strands. Filkins, the Cotswold town where Peggy grew up, boasts a fine woollen mill (I am wearing one of its Fair Isle sweaters now). A motley background of this sort is almost guaranteed to concentrate attention on the issue of identity. In his Reith Lectures, Appiah picks out four classic indicators of identity for scrutiny: creed, country, colour and culture. His general argument is that each of these narratives contains an element of self-delusion we would be wise to resist. His fourth lecture, delivered at the Law School of New York University on 12 November, focused on the theme of cultural identity, and it began by contrasting the two constructs of that difficult term expounded by Arnold in 1869 and Tylor in 1871. These, you will recall, are the two principal and contrasted senses of the term that I picked out in my historical treatment at the beginning of Chap. 1, and so it seems wise in conclusion to return to them.

Arnold's view, to remind ourselves, was that culture consisted of the "pursuit of our total perfection by means of getting to know, on all the matters which most concern us, the best which has been thought and said in the world", whilst Tylor, who was to some extent writing in reaction against Arnold's view, thought that "Culture, or civilization, taken in its broad, ethnographic sense, is that complex whole which includes knowledge, belief, art, morals, law, custom, and any other capabilities and habits acquired by man as a member of society." By which he meant *any* society. For Arnold, then, a person without culture is one who is imperfectly educated, whilst for Tylor a person without a culture is a contradiction in terms. We might call these the qualitative and comparativist paradigms.

Both Arnold and Tylor regarded culture as something universal, though in two quite different senses. For Arnold, it was universal because it represented an ideal towards which all might aspire. For Tylor, it was universal because all societies manifest a form of it and, though the forms differed, the human needs served were much the same. In one respect, however, they were agreed. Though they conceded that culture changes over time, they preferred to examine it *in situ*, as grounded in particular circumstances and in a given place. In his book *Cosmopolitanism: Ethics in a World of Strangers*, from which I quoted earlier, Appiah challenges this perspective by portraying all human culture as distinguished what he controversially calls "contamination". The phenomenon is far from new:

> It didn't take modern mass migration to create this great possibility... Alexander's empire moulded both the states and the sculpture of modern Egypt and North India; first the Mongols and then the Mughals shaped great swathes of Asia. Jews and people whose ancestors came from many

parts of China have long lived in great diasporas. The traders of the Silk Road changed the style of elite dress in Italy; someone brought Chinese pottery for burial in fifteenth-century Swahili graves. I have heard that bagpipes started out in Egypt and came to Scotland with the Roman infantry. None of this is modern.[2]

Appiah's own focus in on the field of ethics: he is concerned to find out how, granted the diversity of human customs and conventions, communication across the borders of belief and tradition is possible. His contention is that there exist certain terms and ideas that are "open-textured" and that enable us all to understand the decisions taken by others, even though we may not agree with them, and may ourselves have acted quite differently. His examples are "courage" and "cruelty". We all applaud bravery, though we might differ as to the actions that we esteem as brave. We all deplore cruelty, though what one society finds cruel, another may find acceptable and inoffensive.

Despite this, there are certain conditions which, at least at an official level, most societies have come to castigate as abhorrent. Appiah's own example is slavery, which is banned by international law, and which virtually all societies proscribe, although they may disagree as to precisely what it means to be a slave. One or two of the case histories in the present book may be taken as endorsing this point. The horror with which the violent suppression of the Morant Bay rising was received in several quarters across the world suggests that, in the aftermath of the abolition of slavery in the British Empire in 1833, this was already the case, even if some found Governor Eyre courageous, whilst others found him callous or cruel. The example cited in Chap. 11 of the spread of democratic ideals across the crumbling British Empire in the early twentieth century again suggests that there are ideals and aspirations to which all can respond, and which travel with them.

In his Reith Lectures, Appiah is insistent that there is nothing particularly Western about such ideals. In his fourth talk he employs the analogy of football. The game may or may not have been invented in England, but everybody now recognises the rules, and plays by them. In that sense, the Olympic Games, arguably originating in Greece but now proudly embraced, witnessed and participated in by every nation on earth, are a paradigm of the sort of behavioural cosmopolitanism that Appiah is talking about.

For Appiah, therefore, there exist basic ethical constants, our recognition of which defines us as human. Are there, we might legitimately ask, equivalent cultural constants that perform the same office? Can culture be considered as "open-textured" in a manner analogous to ethics? Is there even something we might style a "Cultural Cosmopolis"? To debate this possibility is by no means to commit ourselves to the sort of unthinking universalism traditionally associated with the imposition of the ideals of one culture (sometimes called, inaccurately in Appiah's view, "Western") on other, subservient, ones, as a result of colonialism or neo-colonialism. Communication and movement between cultures would, however, be impossible without a common currency by means of which the modes of expression of any given culture can be translated in terms comprehensible, and amenable, to others.

The recognition of such constants may offer one key to the facts of cultural migration. When Steve Reich journeyed to Ghana in the summer of 1970, he was not going in search of something exotically different from that with which he was familiar in America. He was seeking affinity in the shape of rhythmic pulse, arguably the most definitive and omnipresent element in all music-making. The object of his journey was to discover something that African and American musics have in common, to unlock resources embedded in traditions indigenous to human expression, and to the art of music itself. Reich had already found elements of these in Afro-American music and oratory, and was to use them to release certain facets of his own Jewish American heritage. Triple or quadruple rhythms are recognisable as such wherever they are heard, however overlaid with complex cross-beats and syncopation. Indeed, syncopation itself is a recurrent feature of most musical traditions.

If this is most obviously the case with the rhythmic element in music, it is arguably just as applicable to melody and to pitch. Pitch values have shifted over time (the A used in music of the European Renaissance is not quite what we have grown used to more recently. When tuning forks were introduced around 1711, the value of A was around 422.5 vibrations per second. This was the value that Handel knew; but modern concert pitch is closer to 440). Such "pitch inflation" has not, however, affected basic musical intervals. An interval of a fifth between notes is the same in Tokyo as it is in Vienna. When A.M. Jones investigated the aesthetics of African music in the 1930s, he found out that a melodic jump of a fourth is a recurrent feature of local music-making practically across the continent. An octave is an octave anywhere, as Pythagoras knew; to produce it, you simply halve the length of a string. There is also some parity in the use of scales: the pentatonic scale that can be reproduced by running one finger across the black keys on a piano is a recurrent feature in folk traditions from Asia to South America. In the first decade of the twentieth century there were simultaneous movements in several European countries to recover moribund folk traditions. Béla Bartók and Zoltán Kodály collected folk tunes in Hungary. They discovered a bumbling source of inspiration that in the previous century Franz Liszt had attributed to the Roma, but that is because the Roma have travelled so ubiquitously and have proved so culturally absorbent that Magyar and Romany idioms have inter-fused to a sometimes indistinguishable extent. In the same period, Cecil Sharp and Ralph Vaughan Williams were investigating rural English folk music. This was in some senses a musicological equivalent of the ethnographic field work on which Tylor and J.G. Frazer and, following them, several generations of social anthropologists drew, and to some extent what was revealed was the same: a constancy and a recurrence between traditions, partly as a result of features endemic to human expression itself, and partly because traditions had spread. In 1915 Sharp was in America where he was soon told that "the inhabitants of the Southern Appalachians were still singing the traditional songs which their English and Scottish ancestors had brought with them at the time of their emigration". He then spent several months drawing on this previous and transplanted resource. What he discovered over and over again was something as basic as the pentatonic scale.

The permeability of music as an art form makes it exceptionally portable. Literature is possibly a harder case, since it is inevitably grounded in language which, equally obviously, is an expression of place. There are, however, powerful mitigating factors which have worked against the centripetal pull of local and national traditions. The first is the emergence at several moments in human history of *linguae francae* that have assisted literary diffusion. Such were Greek across the Mediterranean basin in the Hellenistic period, and Latin during the time of the Roman Empire and the Middle Ages. As late as the seventeenth century, learned works in all European countries were written in the scholarly vernacular of this far from dead tongue; Newton wrote in Latin, which was the common coin of science. Religious literature par excellence availed itself of these facilities: Judaism spread through Hebrew; Christianity through Greek and later Latin; Islam through Arabic; Hinduism through Sanskrit; and Buddhism through Pali.

And such too in the post-Enlightenment world have been English, French, Spanish and, once more, Arabic. Modern literature in Arabic stretches far and wide. What Wole Soyinka, Rushdie and Achebe have been to global Anglophone literature, and Aimé Césaire, Léopold Sédar Senghor and Yambo Ouologuem to the ramifying banyan tree of *la francophonie*, so Fadia Faqir, Fatma Alboudy and Shahia Ujayi are in the Arabic literary firmament, and can be read from Riyadh to Jordan to Cairo. The twentieth-century literary fad Magical Realism was largely disseminated through the medium of Spanish. From Alejo Carpentier's Cuba, to Jorge Luis Borges's Argentinia to Laura Esquivel's Mexico the beneficent virus spread out, and then embedded itself in English with a little help from Rushdie and Ben Okri.

But reference to Magical Realism serves to remind us of an infinitely more fundamental factor enabling literary migration, one that echoes and reinforces the earlier points about music. What pitches and scales are to the acoustic realm, stories are to the literary. Many stories have been, and are, so constant in their generation and their appeal as to compel appreciation and assimilation. This is most obviously true of that oral form of narrative that we call myth, as the Comparative Method in anthropology soon discerned. In the 1870s, Tylor found deep veins of legend running across the world from Mexico to Africa to India; J.G. Frazer's vast anthropological thriller *The Golden Bough* is largely held together by its recital of fertility myths, myths of the death of kings and of sacred marriage.[3] Once again, the geographical net spread wide, and the locations from which the evidence is culled are frequently separated by considerable tracts of space and of time. So evident are the parallels between these widely diffused narrative traditions that they sometimes scarcely need pointing out. And yet of course they have been. Vladimir Propp's 1928 work *The Morphology of the Folktale* reduced all stories to thirty-one stock situations and four stock character types. These were the notes, or the rhythmic tropes, of all narrative. Claude Lévi-Strauss expanded the fruits of his Brazilian fieldwork in the 1930s to encompass a map of the human mind before he died, much honoured, at the age of 101.

There are two paradigms here that may seem to be in conflict with one another. According to one, parallel art forms emerge in separate locations as a result of forces inherent to the human mind, and essential to the forms of expression concerned. According to the other, art forms spread from one place to another as a result of demographic movement, of what Appiah paradoxically calls "contamination". The tension between these two views, however, is very superficial. In point of fact, it is because art forms are recognised by strangers, and interpreted in the light of something already present, that dissemination has been comparatively fluent. Appreciation aids digestion. In an increasingly inter-connected world, it is also practically inevitable. It is still possible to speak of French or Arabic literature, even though we respond to something that we have learned to call "world literature". The same may be said of "world music".

There is nothing deterministic about this process and, though much of it might be affected by chance, the results are usually the gradual result of shifting taste, and of choice. In support of his theories of cultural "contamination", as we have already seen, Appiah cites the presence of china ware in early Swahili tombs. There are numerous related examples. In Blenheim Palace in Oxfordshire, seat of the Churchills, there is a cabinet filled with priceless Chinese porcelain. It is exquisitely wrought, and kept under lock and key. Its presence there, however, had initially little to do with its beauty. When, in the early eighteenth century, the fashion for tea drinking caught on in England, ships were hired to ferry the valuable leaves from China. Though costly, the cargo was comparatively light, and ballast was required for the boats to assist their physical stability en route. The porcelain was therefore acquired at the port of embarkation and loaded into the hold. Its aesthetic appeal was hardly considered, and it was priced at a fraction of the tea. It was only after the beverage had been offloaded, sold and consumed that the porcelain found its way into British homes and came to be admired for its own sake. As they say, it "caught on". "China" was born.

Deterministic accounts of human migration get us nowhere. It might be said, for example, that the sort of migration of which Appiah, like so many others, has been the beneficiary is one accidental result of empire, or more precisely of the post–Second World War liberal reaction against empire, of which empire in its cruder and more oppressive forms was the *sine qua non*, the sometimes intolerable pre-condition. On that view, to borrow another Latin phrase from that North African scholar Saint Augustine of Hippo, empire has sometimes acted as the *felix culpa* or original sin from which we have been redeemed by human movement and cultural assimilation and/or rejection. Appiah is the heir to the cultures of Ashanti (in, successively, the Gold Coast and Ghana) and of Britain. Migration between these two parts of the globe has been constant, and mutually nourishing. But so has migration between Britain and India.

Yet Appiah now lives in the United States, to which for personal and professional reasons he has decided to move. America, it could be argued, is also the product of empire and migration, but there were no overwhelming historical forces that drove him there. Put bluntly, there is a vital theoretical distinction to be made between *identity*, however mixed, and *identification*. Identification is an elective affinity in which we all partake, even if we disagree as to the direction we would prefer it to take. Were this not so, the phenomenon would scarcely be elective. Migration is an expression of choice, and so is settlement. Despite the half-buried metaphor, we are none of us like migrating birds, driven on a regular cycle by need or unrelenting instinct. We are much more like snails who carry their houses with them. Culture is our house.

Nor is genetics of much help when it comes to understanding human culture. One of the opportunities opened up by the researches of Professor Sir Shankar Balasubramanian and his team in Cambridge into rapid DNA sequencing is that it is now possible to send away a sample of your spittle to a laboratory and, for a fee, to have it tested for ingredients associated with genetic groups. Some of the organisations offering this service have even started talking about "genetic communities" (otherwise styled, worryingly, as ethnic sub-groups), and interpreting individual human lives in the light of them. Such beguiling applications of an irrefutable science stimulate the imagination, and may even cause some of us to construct myths of origin, personality and habit supposedly encoded in our objectively discernible biology. The construction of such private histories, however, is the product of partiality, not of the underlying science.

Is there such a thing as cultural DNA? Almost certainly not. Still less can genetic DNA shed light on that peculiar mixture of language, taste, education, sexuality and private history that comprises each one of us. Nor would a composite or average of the DNA readings of any nation shed any light on its "national character", always supposing there was such a thing.

The dissemination of cultural norms, however, is a universal adventure in which we are all of us caught up. It is not the argument of this book that some culture is migrant culture and some not, but rather that all human culture has been implicated in complicated paths of migration, historical or contemporary. That is most obviously the case with some of the examples with which we have been concerned: with the music of the Roma, with most American literature, North or South, with Caribbean literature from all over the archipelago, with the literature of Canada, Australia and New Zealand. And it is also true of all works, such as Rushdie's novels, that almost announce themselves as lying between places. But the closer you look, the more it seems as if the generalisation holds true of all cultural artefacts, even seemingly the most insular, or regarded as the most narrowly patriotic. Take one famous example that few at first hearing would associate with hybridity or migration of any sort. It is a work well within the comfort zone of even the most conservative of us: a setting of texts by a diasporic people originally couched in Hebrew or Greek, but rendered into English at the orders of a Scottish monarch, set to music by a German impresario trained in Italy but resident in Bond Street, London, where he now shares his museum with an Afro-American rock star of part-Cherokee descent.

First performed in Dublin, but now all over the world, especially at an annual winter festival originating in the Roman Saturnalia, by musicians of every colour, race and creed, it has at its climax an ecstatic repetition of an onomatopoeic salute derived via Old English, the Greek Septuagint and medieval Latin from ancient Hebrew. When the Hanoverian-born British monarch George II attended the first London performance, he reputedly rose to his feet, as many have done since, convinced that they are responding to something quintessentially English, but yes, heard in the light of its cross-cultural history, Handel's *Messiah* is a migrant and hybrid work that can almost hold a candle to *Midnight's Children*. Stand up for it.

There is nothing distinctively modern about migration, whether of the cultural or indeed the demographic sort. It is our birth right, one of the things that make us fully human. It is a defining feature of our Cultural Cosmopolis, above every route leading out from which there hangs a road sign reading "No Exit".

Notes

1. Kwame Anthony Appiah, *Mistaken Identities*: The BBC Reith Lectures for 2016, http://www.bbc.co.uk/programmes/b081lkkj
2. Appiah (2006), 118.
3. For which, see Robert Fraser, *The Making of the Golden Bough: The Origins and Growth of an Argument* (Basingstoke: Macmillan, 1990).

Acknowledgements

Over several years during which I have been meditating on the themes expounded in this book, I have received help and advice from a number of individuals across more than one discipline. I would especially like to thank the following: from the literary-critical community, Professor Susheila Nasta MBE and Dr Shaf Towheed; from the musical community, Professor Colin Lawson, Dr Ingrid Pearson and Ivan Hewett of the Royal College of Music, Professor Bruce Wood of the Purcell Society and Professor David Rowland of the Open University. My warm gratitude also goes to my son Dr Benjo Fraser and to my companion Dr Brigid Allen, for their practical and moral support.

I have also benefitted from certain earlier publications of my own, for kind permission to draw on which acknowledgement is made as follows:

To the journal *Moving Worlds* (University of Leeds) edited by Shirley Chew, in Volume Two of which ("Reflections") Chap. 2 first appeared; to the journal *Wasafiri*, edited by Susheila Nasta, in Issue 39 of which a different version of Chap. 3 was first issued; to Dr Jacqueline Bannerjee and *The Victorian Web*, where an earlier incarnation of Chap. 8 was first published; to Merchiston Publications (Napier University, Edinburgh), for Chap. 9, an early form of which was published in *The Influence of Benedict Anderson* eds. Alistair McCleery and Benjamin A. Brabon; to Worldview Publications of New Delhi for Chap. 11, a draft of which appeared in *New World Order: Transnational Themes in Book History* eds. Swapan Chakrovarty and Abhijeet Gupta; and to the Open University's

Listening Experience Database, for aspects of Chap. 12 that draw on material used in my chapter in *Listening to Music: People, Practices and Experiences* eds Helen Barlow and David Rowland http://ledbooks.org/proceedings2017/.

The Purcell holograph in Chap. 7 (Fig. 7.1) is reproduced by courtesy of the British Library Board, and the Constable painting in Chap. 10 (Fig. 10.1) by permission of the Victoria and Albert Museum.

Index[1]

A
Akpalu, Vinoko, 186
Allegri, Gregorio, 71, 73, 74
Alorwoyie, Gideon, 186
Anand, Mulk Raj, 133–135, 155, 156, 158n13, 159n15
Anderson, Benedict, 125–157
Arabic, 153, 199–201
Arnold, Matthew, 1–5, 12, 15n1, 15n2, 62, 72, 196
Ashanti, 5, 166, 195, 201
Assam, 140, 141, 149, 150
Atkins, Ivor, 73, 74, 77n16

B
Bach, Johann Sebastian, 85
Bangla language, 142, 176, 177
Barbarino, Bartholomeo, 67
Bartók, Béla, 32, 47n3, 193, 199
Bateson, F.W., 25
Bengal, 10, 125–157, 175
Bentham, Jeremy, 174, 182
Bernal, Martin, 60–62, 64n19

Beza, Theodore, 92
Bizet, Georges, 33, 40
Blenheim palace, 201
Blow, John, 86–88
Bogle, Paul, 104–107, 117, 118, 120n21, 123n48, 161
Bohemia, 33, 35, 36, 38, 42, 44, 45
Bohemians, 42
Borgez, Jorge Luis, 200
Brahms, Johann, 33
Brathwaite, Edward, 104, 119n14
Brexit, 11
Bronte, Emily, 40, 41, 49n26, 49n28
Brooke, Rajah of Sarawak, 71, 113
Burgess, Anthony, 24–26, 30n7
Burkhardt, Jacob, 3
Burney, Charles, 69–76, 77n11, 77n17, 77n18

C
Calder, Angus, 97, 118n2
Caldwell, John, 91, 95n7

[1] Note: Page numbers followed by "n" refer to notes

© The Author(s) 2018
R. Fraser, *Literature, Music and Cosmopolitanism*,
https://doi.org/10.1007/978-3-319-68480-2

Carlyle, Thomas, 98, 106, 111–115, 119n18, 121n31, 121–122n32
Carpentier, Alejo, 200
Catherine, St of Alexandria, 53, 56, 58, 59, 63n8, 86, 88, 93
Catholicism, Roman, 56, 62, 64n20, 76n2, 92, 113–115
Césaire, Aimé, 25, 200
Chapel Royal, London, 86
Charef, Mehdi, 45, 50n38
Charles II, King of England, 86, 100
Chatterjee, Partha, 131–133, 137, 145, 155, 156, 158n11, 158n12, 159n25
Chatwin, Bruce, 8
Chaudhuri, Amit, 157, 160n38
Chaudhuri, Nirad, 156, 157
Chettle, Henry, 10
Chinua, Achebe, 182, 183n16
Churchill, Winston, 18, 173, 179, 201
Cimarosa, Domenico, 70
Clarke, Austin, 146, 169
Constable, John, 162–164
Contini, Caterina, 52, 59, 62n3, 64n17
Cooke, Captain Henry, 86
Coryate, Thomas, 66–69, 73, 74, 76n6, 77n7, 77n8
Cosmopolitanism, definitions of, 5–7, 195
Crawford, Robert, 22
Curzon, Lord George, First Marquiss of Kedleston, 140, 142, 146, 150, 159n26
Cutteridge, James Oliver, 163, 165–170, 170n1, 171n6, 171n7, 171n9, 171n10, 171n11, 171n13, 171n14, 171n15, 171n16, 171n18, 171n20, 171n22, 171n23, 171n25, 171n27, 171n29, 172n30
Cyril, St of Alexandria, 52–61, 63n11

D
Darnton, Robert, 139, 140, 151, 159n20, 159n21
Das, Jibanananda, 131
Defoe, Daniel, 11, 28, 134, 167, 170
Desani, G.V., 24–26, 30n7
Desceliers, Pierre, 33
Dickens, Charles, 28, 100, 113, 116, 182
Djenne, 6
DNA testing, 202
Donne, John, 66, 76n3, 168
Draghi, Giovanni Battista, 87, 88
Dryden, John, 94
Duff Gordon, Lina, 72
Duffy, Eamonn, 65, 76n1, 79, 83n1
Duffy, Maureen, 87, 95n2
Dzielska, Maria, 51, 52, 60, 62n2

E
Eagleton, Terry, 22
Eden, Ashley, 145
Eden, Sir Anthony, 21
Eisenstein, Elizabeth, 137, 154, 155, 160n30
Elgar, Sir Edward, 6
Elgin marbles, 6
Eliot, George (Mary Anne Evans), 71, 77n13
Eliot, T. S., 80
Ewe people, 186

F
Farinelli (Caro Maria Michelangelo Nicola Broschi), 13, 68–70, 72
Fenerri, Andrée, 57, 64n15
Fisher, Michael H., 8, 9, 15n8, 15n10
Florence, 69, 71, 72
Frazer, J.G, 112, 199, 200
Froude, 98, 99

INDEX 209

Froude, James Anthony, 63n14, 98–100, 106, 111, 113, 114, 116–118
Fuller, Joseph Bampfylde, 141, 146, 149–151, 159n22

G
Gabrieli, Adriana, 69
Gabrieli, Giovanni, 67
Gardiner, John Elliott, 75, 85, 95n1
Gibbon, Edward, 17–29, 51–62
Gipsies, *see* Roma people
Glass, Philip, 186, 193n3
Gombrich, Ernst, 164, 171n3
Gordon, George William, 99
Grant, Linda, 29n1

H
Handel, George Frideric, 7, 68, 74, 198, 203
Hare, Julius, 18
Harrison, Tony, 51, 62n1
Harvey, William, 35
Haydn, Joseph, 6
Herodotus, 26, 27, 29
Hicks, Antony, 95n8
Homer, 23
Hugo, Victor, 38–42, 49n21
Humfrey, Pelham, 86
Hutchin, John, 11
Huxley, John Henry, 113, 122n38
Hypatia, 13, 51–62

J
Jamaica, 28, 72, 99–101, 103–106, 108–110, 112, 113, 115, 116, 120n20, 120n21, 120n24, 121n31, 168
James V, King of Scotland, 36

James VI of Scotland, (I of England), 48n16, 66
John, Augustus, 44, 50n34
Jones, Arthur Morris, 186, 193n2, 193n4, 198
Julian the Apostate, 55

K
Kelly, Michael, 70, 77n10
Koser, Khalid, 12, 15n6
Kingsley, Charles, 22, 30n5, 52, 60–62, 62n5, 97–118
Kingsley, Fanny, 121n26, 121n29, 122n37
Kingsley, Henry, 106, 107, 119n17, 122n32
Kipling, Rudyard, 26, 130
Koch, Robert, 42, 43, 49n30
Kodály, Zoltán, 32, 193, 199

L
Laubach, Frank, 177
Leavis, F. R., 25, 80, 84n3, 156
Lee, Vernon (Viola Paget), 14, 72, 73, 77n15
Levinson, Paul, 61
Ligeti, Gyorgy, 185–193
Liszt, Franz, 13, 31, 32, 47, 47n1, 47n2, 192, 199
Literacy
 In Africa, 179, 181, 186
 In India, 129, 173–182
Locke, Matthew, 87

M
Macaulay, Thomas Babington, 129
MacDonald, Helen, 14, 16n16
Mahjoub, Jamal, 20
Mann, Thomas, 44

Mappa Mundi, 33
Maquay, John Leland, 71
Marcel, Jean, 58, 64n16
Merimée, Prosper, 40, 41, 49n25
Mill, James, 174, 183n3
Mill, John Stuart, 99, 109, 118n9
Milton, John, 23, 66, 79–83, 87, 92, 173
Momeni, Ali, 190
Monmouth, Duke of, 94
Monteverdi, Claudio, 74
Morici, Italia, 59, 64n18
Morris, Desmond, 8, 15n6
Mozart, Wolfgang Amadeus, 70, 71
Munday, Anthony, 10
Munster, Sebastian, 34–37, 39, 47n8, 48n19
Murger, Henry, 41, 42, 44

N
Naipaul, V. S., 28, 30n10, 108, 120n22, 163, 164, 167–169, 170n2, 171n8, 171n21, 171n28
Narayan, R. K., 134, 135, 156
Nelson, Thomas and Sons, 163–165, 167, 168, 170, 171n4, 171n5, 171n6, 171n8, 171n23, 172n31
Neumann, Iver, 41, 44, 49n27
Newman, Cardinal John Henry, 57, 112–115, 123n40
Newton, Isaac, 87, 199
Ngugi wa Thiong'o, 22, 30n6
Nomadism, 8, 13

O
Oates, Titus, 88
Ogden, C. K., 174–179, 182, 182n1, 182n2, 183n4
Okigbo, Christopher, 29
Okri, Ben, 28, 29, 30n9, 200

Ondaatje, Michael, 26, 27, 29, 30n8
Orestes, Governor of Alexandria, 52, 54, 59
Ouologuem, Yambo, 200

P
Pal, Bipi Chandra, 129, 131, 141, 144, 158n5
Palestrina, Giovanni Pierluigi, 71, 93
Palladas, 49n24, 51, 52, 58, 59, 62n1
Partition of Bengal, 139, 146
Pergolesi, Giovannni, 69
Pincherle, Marc, 75
Pitch, musical, 191, 198, 200
Popish Plot, 85–91
Powell, John Enoch, 23–26
Propp, Vladimir, 200
Purcell, Henry, 85–91, 173

R
Radice, William, 156, 160n35
Ramanujan, Srinivasa, 7
Rao, Raja, 156, 158n14
Raphael, Samuel, 46, 50n41
Raspail, Francois Vincent, 39
Reformation, English, 11, 65, 79, 113
Reich, Steve, 185–193, 195, 198
Reid, V. S., 99, 102, 105, 107, 118n7, 119n16, 120n21, 123n50
Robinson, George, First Marquess of Ripon, 167
Roma, 13, 31–47, 199, 202
Royal, 86
Rushdie, Salman, 15n5, 25, 26, 132, 133, 156, 157, 200, 202
Ruskin, John, 66, 79–83, 100, 112, 113, 122n36

S

Said, Edward, 97, 118n1
Saluzzo, Diodata Roero di, 55, 56, 63n12
Saussure, Ferdinand de, 174, 182n1
Scaliger, Joseph, 37
Selvon, Samuel, 27, 167, 171n12
Sen, Amartya, 148, 159n27
Sethi, Rumani, 156, 160n37
Shakespeare, William, 10, 15n6, 23, 29, 35, 47n6, 65, 76n2, 158n4
Sharp, Cecil, 23, 199
Sierra Leone, 180, 181, 183n15
Sinn Fein, 141
Slavery
  in the Caribbean, 62, 97, 165, 166
  legal and moral status of, 100
Smith, Zadie, 15n1, 15n2, 28, 147, 194n18
Soyinka, Wole, 62, 200
Sutherland, Efua, 186, 193n1
Swadeshi movement, 144, 146, 147, 149, 151
Synesius, Bishop of Cyrene, 52, 58

T

Tallis, Thomas, 87
Tennyson, Lord Alfred, 100, 116
Thomas, John Jacob, 98, 118n3
Tolland, John, 61, 63n9
Tremellius, Immanuel, 13, 91, 92, 95n9, 95n10

Tylor, Edward Burnett, 4, 5, 15n3, 196, 199, 200

V

Vali, Istvan, 37
Vaughan-Williams, Ralph, 6, 23, 199
Venice, 44, 66, 67, 69, 70, 75, 76, 82
Virchow, Rudolf, 39, 40, 42, 43, 48n19, 49n22, 49n23, 49n31
Virgil (Publius Vergilius Maro), 23, 24, 29
Vivaldi, Antonio, 73–76

W

Walsh, William, 160n34
Watt, Ian, 127, 158n2
West, Michael Philip, 182
Willcocks, David, 74
Wilson, Colin, 25, 50n37, 168, 171n24
Windrush, MV Empire, 17, 162
Wittgenstein, Ludwig, 174, 182n2, 190, 194n13
Wolseley, Garnet, 1st Viscount Wolseley, 6

Z

Ziedan, Youssef, 61
Zigmund, King of Bohemia., 36

The manufacturer's authorised representative in the EU is Springer Nature Customer Service Centre GmbH, Europaplatz 3, 69115 Heidelberg, Germany. If you have any concerns regarding our products, please contact ProductSafety@springernature.com

Printed and bound by CPI Group (UK) Ltd, Croydon, CR0 4YY

23/03/2026

02076735-0005